D0722635

Museum Matters

MUSEUM MATTERS

Making and Unmaking Mexico's National Collections

EDITED BY
Miruna Achim, Susan Deans-Smith, and Sandra Rozental

TUCSON

The University of Arizona Press
www.uapress.arizona.edu

ISBN-13: 978-0-8165-3957-4 (hardcover)

Cover design by Leigh McDonald
Cover art: *The stronger the light your shadow cuts deeper*, 2010 Paper cut, ⌀ 300 cm
© Mariana Castillo Deball
Interior designed and typeset by Sara Thaxton
in 10/14 Warnock Pro (text) and Regulator Nova (display)

Publication of this book is made possible in part by support from the Universidad Autónoma Metropolitana-Cuajimalpa, and by the proceeds of a permanent endowment created with the assistance of a Challenge Grant from the National Endowment for the Humanities, a federal agency.

Library of Congress Cataloging-in-Publication Data
Names: Achim, Miruna, editor. | Deans-Smith, Susan, 1953– editor. | Rozental, Sandra, editor.
Title: Museum matters : making and unmaking Mexico's national collections / edited by Miruna Achim, Susan Deans-Smith, and Sandra Rozental.
Description: Tucson : The University of Arizona Press, 2021. | Includes bibliographical references and index.
Identifiers: LCCN 2021004392 | ISBN 9780816539574 (hardcover)
Subjects: LCSH: National museums—Mexico—History. | Museums—Acquisitions—Mexico—History. | Material culture—Mexico.
Classification: LCC AM23.A2 M87 2021 | DDC 069/.510972—dc23
LC record available at https://lccn.loc.gov/2021004392

Printed in the United States of America
♾ This paper meets the requirements of ANSI/NISO Z39.48-1992 (Permanence of Paper).

To the people who care for these objects,
past, present, and future

Contents

Acknowledgments

This book came out of an interdisciplinary panel, "Matters of State, Matters of Dispute," organized by Miruna Achim for the 2018 annual conference of the American Historical Association, hoping to generate a conversation among historians, philosophers of science, archaeologists, and anthropologists who work on the convoluted histories of Mexico's national collections at different moments in time. The panel caught the attention of the then editor at large in Mexican history and indigenous studies at the University of Arizona Press Natasha Varner, who met with Miruna and Susan Deans-Smith to discuss the possibility of turning the panel into an edited volume. Sandra Rozental was unable to participate in the panel (she had just had a baby!) but joined the editorial team for the book given her expertise on the museum's more recent histories.

Some of the leading scholars on Mexico's national museum complex and its various iterations, as well as its collections, based in both the Mexican and U.S. academies, were invited to contribute to the volume. Discussions of individual chapters in an intensive two-day workshop, organized in March 2019 in Mexico City and attended by most of the contributors, not only confirmed how incredibly generative such an interdisciplinary dialogue was, but also clarified how each of our disciplinary and temporal focuses had to some extent obscured interesting connections and similarities, as well as differences. We also realized that a critical history of how these collections came into being had yet to be written, given that much of the literature on Mexico's national collections had taken some tropes very much for granted, especially the Museo Nacional de Antropología's claim to represent the nation and its cohesiveness. This collection of essays is the product of much collaborative discussion and debate, and we offer it as an invitation to continue to critically reflect on Mexico's national museum complex.

In addition to the editors' and authors' contributions, this book was made possible by many people. Christopher Fraga, with his sensitive attention to linguistic nuance and knowledge of the field of Mexican museums, art, and anthropology, provided exceptional translations for many of the texts written originally in Spanish. At the University of Arizona Press, Kristen Buckles has been an enthusiastic and supportive editor; Elizabeth Honor Wilder, editorial assistant, provided much needed guidance in response to our incessant questions. We are very grateful to both of them. We are mindful of how time consuming the reading of a manuscript is and express our deep appreciation to our anonymous reviewers, who provided careful and thoughtful feedback. We would also like to thank the various institutions that provided authors with funds for their research, travel, and essay translations, especially the Universidad Autónoma Metropolitana and the University of Texas at Austin, as well as the Dirección de Estudios Históricos of the Instituto Nacional de Antropología e Historia (INAH) and Haydeé López Hernández, who generously hosted our two-day workshop in March 2019. Thank you also to the many archives and institutions that provided authors with access and permissions for images included in this volume. We are particularly grateful to staff at the INAH for graciously and promptly helping us secure reproductions and permits in the particularly trying months of summer 2020: Antonio Saborit, director of the Museo Nacional de Antropología; Baltazar Brito Guadarrama, director of the Biblioteca Nacional de Antropología e Historia; Juan Carlos Valdéz Marín, director of the Fototeca Nacional; as well as archivists Vanessa Fonseca and Miguel Angel Gazca. We especially want to thank Mariana Castillo Deball, the artist who generously provided the design for the cover of *Museum Matters*, offering a visual rendition of the book's objectives. With her provocative sculpture *There Is a Space Later in Time Where You Are just a Memory* (2010), Castillo Deball not only destabilizes the history and practice of museum collecting, but beautifully twists, unravels, and distorts the famous Coyolxauhqui, one of Mexico's most emblematic pre-Hispanic monoliths on display in the Museo del Templo

Mayor, to show that the objects that make up these collections are far from static and unchanging.

The institutions that have held and cared for Mexico's national collections may have their shortcomings, many of which are central to the arguments developed by the authors in this volume. Nevertheless, the people who make up these institutions—museum professionals, scholars, curators, conservators, designers, and guards—as well as those outside these institutions, whose daily labor ensures the preservation of Mexico's collections, are key to the stories we tell. In the current context, where the very existence of these institutions is at stake, with budget cuts following government austerity packages, a vicious pandemic, and the recession that will surely follow, it is to them that we dedicate this book. Without them, research centers, museums, archaeological and historic sites, and the basic infrastructures that facilitate the protection of Mexico's collections would surely be lost. More importantly, we would also lose the incredible opportunity to reimagine these objects on different terms, taking into consideration the needs and claims of the many people and communities that coexist with them and all their fragments.

Museum Matters

Introduction

A Mexican Cabinet of Unlikely Things

MIRUNA ACHIM, SUSAN DEANS-SMITH, SANDRA ROZENTAL

This is a book about things—stones, relics, ruins, bones, mummies, mannequins, statues, photographs, inventories, fakes, instruments, and natural history specimens—that formed part of Mexico's national museum complex at different moments in the course of two centuries of collecting and display. Though today they might strike us as forming a rather heterogeneous, if not chaotic, assemblage, these objects shared a common space at different moments in the national collections and were symbolically and commercially commensurable with each other. It was not unthinkable, in this context, for the early museum to have exchanged local indigenous antiquities for African birds in 1828, or for a *malanggan* carving from New Ireland in the 1950s, for example.[1] In the course of the nineteenth century, many of these objects were studied by various scientific disciplines (archaeology, art history, geology, statistics, ethnography, anatomy, and pathology, among others), all of which were associated, practically and spatially, as well as intellectually, with the museum. Since the early twentieth century, however, the paths of the objects held in the national collections have diverged, and it is a measure of how much we have internalized that divergence that we might have a hard time imagining stones and bones or taxidermies and antiquities together in the same space again, as we attempt to bring them together within the confines of this book. Some objects, as is the case with pre-Hispanic antiquities, are matters of fact and faith, the building blocks that have come to sustain and bolster a modern national identity. They are featured in textbooks and widely reproduced on T-shirts, postcards, and souvenirs.[2] Meanwhile, others have been forgotten, lost, deaccessioned, forever relegated to storerooms, offices, corridors, or even destroyed, left outside the national canons and the narratives that have shaped them.

This book is meant as an experiment. We bring back together objects that have been separated for more than a century, not so much to re-create the surprising cabinet that would have greeted visitors for a large part of the nineteenth century, but to shed light on the interactions, affects, asymmetries, contingencies, limitations, agreements, and disagreements that have forged things into objects of science, aesthetics, and politics, making it hard to imagine today a mummy or the glass model of a jellyfish next to the emblematic Piedra del Sol. A key question, in doing so, is to ask how we got here. As we seek to understand how collections came into being or ceased to exist over time—or how things moved in and out of collections and museum spaces—we explore what it meant to move things physically and spatially, as well as conceptually and symbolically. *Museum Matters* thus takes as its starting point the conviction that there is nothing intrinsic about the meanings, values, or uses with which objects have been invested in the context of larger processes of nation building, nor about the particular spaces, arrangements, frameworks, or structures—the complex landscape of national museums—that store, display, and make claims about the nation's things today. Bruno Latour once reflected on the common root of the words "thing" and "parliament," to remind us that the body politic is "thick with objects" and that objects bring people together not because their meanings are fixed but because they continue to concern and divide their users.[3] Taking a cue from Latour, we seek to put things from Mexico's national collections back into the body politic; to reframe them as sites of parliament, that is, of debate and conversation; and to reflect on their usefulness for rethinking the nation and the various destinies of its collections today.

Collections on the Move

Like the objects they comprise, collections are not fixed entities. Objects come into collections but are just as easily removed, traded or exchanged, broken, misplaced, lost, or forgotten. In the case of Mexico's national museum complex, the sum of these gestures tells the story of how institutions were made and unmade, in response to disciplinary ambitions, political interests, rebellions and dissents, or simply financial limitations. A confusing palimpsest of names and acronyms, meant to make sense of changes and restructurings, maps out the institutional history of Mexican national collections.

Founded in 1825, four years after Mexico obtained its independence, the Museo Nacional de México was part of a larger wave that saw the establishment of national museums in various Latin American cities, from Lima to La Plata, from Bogotá to Santiago, all entrusted with the explicit mission to collect and display the most representative and valuable objects of the newly independent nations. What constituted Mexico's most representative objects could only be anyone's guess.[4] The museum began by bringing together objects that had been part of earlier viceregal collections—both state owned and private—specifically pre-Hispanic antiquities and natural history specimens.[5] Many of these objects also made their way abroad, despite an 1827 law that prohibited the export of Mexican antiquities.[6] Over the following decades, the museum collected silver ores from Chihuahua and canoes from the Pacific Northwest, portraits of U.S. presidents and of the French imperial family, meteorites from Oaxaca, and mammoth skeletons from the Estado de México, as well as pre-Hispanic antiquities. This reveals some degree of improvisation but also continuity with practices of collection and study developed under Spanish imperial rule, particularly during eighteenth-century scientific expeditions, which shaped the protocols for the collection of a wide range of objects and set up the sites associated with their study and care. As objects arrived at the museum, the resulting display was "a jumble of fragments of the past and present," in the words of Brantz Mayer, the U.S. ambassador who visited the museum in 1844.[7] Seemingly lacking visual order, objects sat in overcrowded proximity to each other in the makeshift space occupied by the museum in one room at the university, the first building that housed the museum. More often closed than open to the public, the museum even served at moments as military barracks. The institution's material conditions were a measure of how much or how little it was worth to governors and bureaucrats at a moment when the country was torn by civil strife and internecine wars, which Mexico paid for with the loss of half of its territory.

It was not until 1865, in the context of the Second French Intervention in Mexico (1861–67)—an ill-conceived attempt at extending French imperial interests in the Americas by imposing a Habsburg on the Mexican "throne"—that the museum was assigned a significantly more generous space, and more importantly, a symbolically charged place, on Moneda Street, in an area previously occupied by the mint, in the Imperial (now National) Palace, at the nation's political center. Emperor Maximilian understood that the museum could be fashioned into a source of political, cultural, and symbolic legitimacy for a government that was undoubtedly an outsider. He did not live to inaugurate the museum—many objects were still packed in boxes when he was executed in 1867—but his gesture was not lost on the Mexican liberal regime that succeeded him. The museum would become "one of the principal stages where the rituals of political autonomy were re-enacted through public commemoration ceremonies and special exhibits."[8] Over the following decades, as the country was pacified and unified under the Porfiriato (1876–1911), the museum developed into a relevant research center, a driving force behind scientific specialization and professionalization, and an important node in a dense network of national and international scholars and experts.[9] By the late nineteenth century, it was publishing scholarly journals, with articles and reports on its archaeological and natural history collections, the *Anales del Museo Nacional de México* and *Naturaleza*.

At the same time, even as disciplines as different as archaeology, ethnography, history, anthropology, comparative anatomy, teratology, botany, zoology, and paleontology shared space and funds at the museum, it was becoming increasingly clear that a rift was under way, which pitted the archaeological collection against all other types of objects in the Museo Nacional de México, to the detriment of the latter. It was, after all, pre-Hispanic monoliths in the Galería de Monolitos—inaugurated by President Porfirio Díaz in 1887—that welcomed visitors into the museum. Justo Sierra, the influential minister of public instruction, expressed just how much antiquities, especially large-scale objects—reflective of the advanced civilization reached by the ancients—meant to the Porfirian elites. In anticipation of the celebrations for the Centenario, the one-hundred-year anniversary of Mexico's independence, he urged his colleagues at the Ministry of Finance to allocate more funds to the care of antiquities: "For you, who are men of affairs and finance, this thing called archaeology is no more than a trivial and paltry thing, of little importance; but for us it is the only thing that distinguishes Mexico's personality before the scientific world; everything else exists elsewhere and is already being done [studied] by foreigners."[10] Among the beneficiaries of Sierra's petition was the completion of the reconstruction of Teotihuacan's massive Pyramid of the Sun, which became an obligatory pilgrimage site for Mexican politicians, foreign dignitaries, scholars, and high-placed personages, in the context of the centennial festivities.[11]

The alliance between the Mexican nation-state, Mexico's ancient past, and state-run archaeology was becoming increasingly tenacious. In 1909, it led to the displacement of the museum's natural history specimens to Chopo Street, in a (then) elegant and well-to-do neighborhood outside the strict confines of the city center. For the following half century, the Museo Nacional de Historia Natural, also known as the Museo del Chopo, occupied a glass-and-steel structure, initially built in Germany for a textile exhibition and imported piece by piece to Mexico.[12] The rest of the collection, constituted as the Museo Nacional de Arqueología, Historia y Etnología, remained in the country's symbolic and political center, on Moneda Street. By then, the archaeological collection alone boasted over ten thousand objects.[13] By 1939, the collection had grown significantly, leading to yet another excision. The objects corresponding to the colonial period and the nineteenth century went to Chapultepec Castle, to form the Museo Nacional de Historia. Material conditions undoubtedly influenced the decision to move objects out of the cramped quarters in the center. That the archaeological and ethnographic collections remained together in the Museo Nacional de Antropología, in the Moneda building, reflected postrevolutionary politics, which chose indigeneity, in both its ancient and its contemporary forms, as a unifying symbol for the nation.

The latest and most momentous change in the history of the national museum complex came in 1964. The collection of colonial-era artifacts at the Museo Nacional de Historia were moved to the Jesuit convent of Tepotzotlán, north of Mexico City, and integrated into the Museo Nacional del Virreinato. The natural history collection was also relocated, again, to a new building, specifically designed for it, in Chapultepec Park. The move implied tremendous loss of specimens and the demotion of the museum itself, which was no longer national but came under the jurisdiction of Mexico City as the Museo de Historia Natural de la Ciudad de México.[14] After some discussion, the ethnographic objects that were not of Mexican provenance remained at the Moneda Street location, reconstituted as the Museo Nacional de las Culturas.[15] The archaeological and ethnographic collections that were found within the country's territory were moved to a new building specially designed to house the Museo Nacional de Antropología, which has remained, to this day, Mexico's foremost museum, an experiment very much in line with the postrevolutionary state project that sought to consolidate the past, the present, and the future of the nation in a single narrative thread. The new Museo Nacional de Antropología was reimagined and reconstituted as an object in itself, a storehouse of collections presented as the collective heritage of a homogenous national whole.

The Museum as Object

In 1964, the Museo Nacional de Antropología was relocated from the city center, associated with the colonial past, to Chapultepec Park, an area with skyscrapers and innovative urban infrastructure that represented Mexican modernity.[16] The new museum presented itself as a "monument of monuments," a single space to encompass and consolidate Mexico's rich indigenous cultural heritage while providing Mexicans and foreigners alike with a sense of its national identity.[17] As Luis Aveleyra, a prominent archaeologist and one of the leaders of the museum's curatorial team, explained, the country's past and present indigenous civilizations were what gave Mexico its distinctive features on an international stage, the "essential component of its physiognomy as a nation." He further stressed the centralist mission of the museum by identifying its main goal as "the safeguarding, conservation, cataloguing, ordering, and restoration of its extensive archaeological, ethnographic and skeletal collections . . . housed in a single museum and relative to a single country."[18] Indeed, for more than five decades, the Museo Nacional de Antropología has been a stand-in for the nation.

The building, as well as its permanent collection and exhibition spaces, were carefully orchestrated to fulfill this ideological project. Together, they formed an instrument, a mirror that would simultaneously produce and reflect Mexicanness. This mission was very literally set in stone. One of the key government officials behind the new museum project, Jaime Torres Bodet, declared in a speech during the museum's inauguration, "People will find valor and confidence in the greatness of their past. Mexican, contemplate yourself in the mirror of that greatness. Foreigner, find evidence here of the unity of humankind's destiny. Civilizations pass, but the glories of other men who have fought to erect them will forever remain." These words are emblazoned in the white marble walls of the museum's entrance, along with a quotation from then-president Adolfo López Mateos: "The people of Mexico erect this monument in honor of the admirable precolumbian cultures that blossomed in the regions that are now territories of the Mexican Republic. Before the vestiges of these cultures, the Mexico of today pays homage to that indigenous Mexico in whose example it recognizes the qualities of its national originality." The 1964 museum was configured to be both a monument and a mirror that has reflected a very specific idea of the nation through its collections, while, we would argue, it has simultaneously obscured and distorted these collections' prior, oftentimes layered, complicated, and untold histories.

The 1964 building was purposefully designed to highlight Mexico's participation in the international avant-gardes of high modernism and the country's unique heritage through explicit citations of pre-Hispanic architecture and the use of local materials and crafts.[19] The museum followed the homogenizing premises of Mexican *indigenismo*, presenting contemporary indigenous expressions from all over Mexico as the corroded residues of different but related pre-Hispanic civilizations whose development was forever stunted by conquest. Although the team behind the making of this iteration of the museum boasted having worked on the first truly scientific effort to collect the nation, ethnographic collections were given much less importance than pre-Hispanic material culture.[20] Past and present indigenous artifacts were divided from each other and placed on two separate floors, following a stratigraphic logic that highlights real yet distant connections between contemporary indigenous forms of cultural production, framed as "folklore" or "tradition," and objects produced by Mexico's ancient civilizations, cast as high art.

In addition to this spatial separation, both the museum's architecture and exhibition design treated objects from the collection differently. Pedestals and glass cases with theatrical lighting were used to enhance each of the archaeological objects' forms and motifs, while baskets, earthenware pots, and colorful masks and textiles—many acquired by the museum for its early ethnographic collections in the nineteenth century and that could also have been classified as antiques—were incorporated into timeless lifesize dioramas offering visitors static tableaux of indigenous ways of life, festivities, and rituals.[21] Reminiscent of Kirshenblatt-Gimblett's famous essay on ethnographic displays, objects made and used by postconquest indigenous people were displayed on the top floor as anonymous and timeless artifacts, even when many, like the works of Wixarika artist José Benítez Sánchez or

Yɨkaɨye Kɨkame's yarn paintings, were not only dated and signed but also already circulating in the high art market.[22] For the museum's curators and planners, contemporary indigenous material culture was understood as being on the verge of disappearing, a process that the Museo Nacional de Antropología would somehow remedy through a kind of salvage operation. The "ethnographic present" was, therefore, mobilized to show living indigenous people as static and timeless purveyors of national identity.[23] The museum's conception of Mexican anthropology and ethnology did not consider urban or mestizo communities, let alone transnational migration, poverty, inequality, racism, human rights violations, and violence, or the struggles for land and sovereignty that define indigenous populations' everyday lives and claims. Thus, the museum reproduces forms of colonial violence, omitting or even purposely silencing stories that might disturb or disrupt its claim over the indigenous roots (both past and present) of Mexico's national identity.[24]

Since its opening, the museum in Chapultepec has undergone numerous renovations and curatorial reconfigurations, yet none has really challenged the museum's narrative. The halls have been renovated on a one-by-one basis, avoiding a comprehensive rethinking of the ways in which the museum continues to contribute to this narrative's reification. Renovations undertaken in the last thirty years have consisted largely of cosmetic facelifts, changing the names of galleries for more politically correct and up-to-date versions, in line with contemporary scholarly trends, and incorporating more contemporary exhibition design and audiovisual technologies.[25] Little has been done, however, to truly question the museum's ideological stance and its controversial portrayal of contemporary indigenous peoples. As a result, despite numerous renovation efforts, the Museo Nacional de Antropología has remained largely undisturbed, keeping a strong grip on the way collecting and objects have been imagined, not only at the museum, but also at other institutions housing national collections, in reference to the present as well as to the past.

The Museum's Black Box

The historiography on Mexico's national museums and their various iterations has also been slow to think critically about collections' complex history, mostly legitimating and naturalizing the powerful associations between pre-Hispanic antiquity and the Mexican nation-state. A handful of exceptions focus on the Museo Nacional's early history or look at very specific episodes of its more recent 1964 incarnation.[26] As in other contexts where the museum has become "muse" of institutional and postcolonial critiques, artists and writers have been the most fervent critics of the museum and the history of its collections, by shedding light on the museum's uses of science, specifically archaeology and anthropology, to reproduce vertical power relations.[27] They draw attention to how the Mexican state on the one hand exalts indigenous cultural manifestations, while on the other hand, it actively engages in the impoverishment, marginalization, and destruction of indigenous ways of life.[28] Other critiques have come from film, namely the broadly acclaimed *Museo*, by Alonso Ruizpalacios, which fictionalizes the famous 1985 heist by two university students, resulting in the theft of some of the museum's most prized pre-Hispanic artifacts; and *La Piedra Ausente*, by Sandra Rozental and Jesse Lerner, a documentary that focuses on the convoluted history and 1964 forced dispossession of the Coatlinchan monolith, popularly known as Tlaloc.[29] But the critical and dense historiography is sparse. Most of what has been published on the museum in its various embodiments has been in the form of coffee table books, the museum's own catalogs, and commemorative volumes celebrating each decade since the opening of the Museo Nacional de Antropología in 1964 and reminding the public of its symbolic place as the culmination of a long, forward-striving process.[30]

Ideology doubles as teleology in a narrative that bears the imprint of, first, liberal, then postrevolutionary, historiographies, to envision only one possible outcome: the creation, albeit with some detours, out of the initial chaos of the early Museo Nacional de México, of a world-class Museo Nacional de Antropología. To some extent, this process is understood to mirror that of the nation itself. Just as Mexico was taking urgent steps toward modernization, the national collections, increasingly and unequivocally associated with pre-Hispanic antiquities, would come to signify the ancient and ancestral past, the solid ground on which visions of the modern and homogenous nation would be built. If not patently false, this narrative is obviously too simple. It conflates the history of Mexican collecting and of the formation of its national museums exclusively with the ambitions—as wielded by political elites and their various regimes of power—to build a strong state, forge a coherent national identity, and shape a disciplined citizenry.[31] It forgets the rationales and justifications that operated in the selection of certain kinds of objects and the exclusions of others. Whether intentional or not, this form of amnesia means that the museum has reflected little on its own becoming, that is, on the material, cultural, and ideological forces and on the epistemological premises that shaped that becoming. More seriously, it has reflected little on how, in turn, collections have served as sites for enacting political, social, cultural, racial, intellectual, and scientific policies, ambitions, and anxieties. Assuming a smooth teleology between the jumbled national collection of the 1820s and the Museo Nacional de Antropología today also implies that the objects have been endowed with intrinsic meanings and uses all along, taking for granted the national museum complex today as guardian of the state discourses and practices regarding national patrimony wrapped around those meanings. In so doing, this story of the museum's smooth becoming has failed to recall the narrative fragments that are cancelled by these powerful discourses and practices.

The essays collected in this volume seek to historicize and complicate the emergence, consolidation, and dispersal of Mexico's national museum complex by telling the stories of the objects that were part of national collections at different moments.[32] Authors were invited to analyze particular case studies and processes of acquisition, ownership, study, display, reception, forgery, controversy, loss, and dispossession over time, to unravel and unsettle evolutionary narratives by framing how these materials became or stopped being "objects of the nation." In different ways, objects function as heuristic devices, which allow for more nuanced questions to be asked of the museum. Where did objects come from? Why and how were they taken out of their "original" contexts? Who brought them in? How were they studied, written about, and displayed over time? What role did their materiality play in the way they were collected, studied, and resignified? How were they made into objects of science, of art, of politics? How did they acquire value? How did fakes and replicas of Mexican collections become central to the very constitution of Mexico's national museums?[33] Why did some objects remain part of the national collections, while others were lost, dispersed, or forgotten? How did certain objects come to signify the nation while others did not, or stopped doing so at particular moments? What kinds of larger concepts, such as nature, culture, nation, landscape, race, ethnicity, science, religion, art, artifact, authenticity, and beauty, were and are taken for granted and reified by the very act of collecting and displaying particular kinds of objects?

This book proposes, then, to bring together, around a series of specific questions, some of the scholars who have engaged Mexican collecting from the perspective of objects and within a broad temporal scope, from the late eighteenth century until the present. It also brings together scholars from Mexican, U.S., and European academies, trained in a broad range of disciplines: history, anthropology, ethnology, archaeology, history and philosophy of science, and cultural and postcolonial studies. Only through such an interdisciplinary approach could we analyze the making of the museum and its collections as a whole over the course of two centuries. Much more than a mere exercise in Mexican or regional studies, this volume is also a contribution to a global history of collections. On a basic level, most of the objects showcased here traveled along circuits that were not exclusive to Mexico and were acquired, studied, and discussed in circles far beyond national boundaries. On a more complex level, the objects of Mexican collecting came to articulate and embody intellectual and political categories such as race, civilization, barbarity, modernity, progress, and technology, all of which were being contested in the arena of both national and international politics of the eighteenth through twenty-first centuries.

Overview

Rather than a chronological overview that would tell a kind of linear history of events, we have organized the volume into three thematic sections that address the main arguments of this book: Canons, Fragments, and Disturbances. "Canons" examines how different kinds of objects and institutions contribute to the construction of canons and in so doing illuminate how categories of inclusion and exclusion are configured and reconfigured over time as collecting practices, values, and tastes change. The section opens with Susan Deans-Smith's "'A History Worthy of the Grandeur of the Spanish Nation': Collecting Mexican Antiquity in the Viceroyalty of New Spain." Deans-Smith focuses on the collection of antiquities within the Spanish empire and the role played by the Royal Academy of San Carlos in Mexico City in interpretations of Mexican antiquity prior to Mexican independence in 1821. Her analysis traces the contestations and ambiguities generated by the valorization of Mexican antiquity and the categorization of its artifacts at the same time that the universal claims of neoclassicism and ideal beauty were also acknowledged. Despite such malleability of meanings, the pre-Hispanic objects housed in the academy were relocated to the newly established Museo Nacional de México in 1825. Their exclusion from the academy collections signified what they were not, which is to say, they were not considered worthy of the academy's collections and its concepts of ideal beauty based on classicism. The categorization of pre-Hispanic objects, however, was far from resolved, even in their new location in the Museo Nacional de México, and they remained unstable and fluid, depending on particular contexts and agendas for most of the nineteenth century.

In Miruna Achim and Bertina Olmedo Vera's "Forgery and the Science of the 'Authentic,'" they interrogate the understudied question of the relationship between Mexico's national museums and the acquisition, loss, destruction, or erasure of surviving archaeological fakes and forgeries. They place particular emphasis on how types and ideals are refracted through the diagnostics and valuations of archaeological fakes. They draw attention to how forgeries illuminate what curators, collectors, dealers, and scholars expected to see in the artifacts of ancient America, expectations influenced especially by different ideals of beauty across time and across cultures. The authors insist on the importance of recognizing the role fakes play in the construction of authenticity and of asking not what the criteria for identifying fakes are, but rather, how the criteria for identifying the "authentic" developed out of the effort to recognize fakes. What made something "authentic" at different moments in time?

Laura Cházaro, in "Body Objects in Transit: National Pathology between Anatomy Museums and the Museo Nacional de México, 1853–1912," focuses on the formation of collections and the circulation of medical objects (pathological anatomical specimens, skeletal remains, wax and papier-mâché models) between the Museo Nacional de México and two anatomy museums in the capital, one at the Escuela Nacional de Medicina, the other at the Hospital General de San Andrés. She explores how such objects became a source of both medical and anthropological inquiry, for the construction of national pathologies and national history, and how some of them ended up being displayed in the Museo Nacional de México in 1895. Cházaro places particular emphasis on how medical objects acquired new meaning as anthropological objects and were racialized when relocated to the space of the Museo Nacional de México.

What it means for objects to be lost, forgotten, relocated, and resignified is addressed in the second part of this book, "Fragments." In "The Tangled Journey of the Cross of Palenque," Christina Bueno traces how and why, after the three large rectangular limestone panels of the Cross of Palenque had been dismantled and separated in the nineteenth century, they were brought back together and reassembled in 1909 in the Museo Nacional de México. For decades, two panels remained in Mexico, but the third had been taken to the United States in 1842 to be subsequently displayed at the Smithsonian Institution in 1858. Bueno reconstructs the political agendas and power relationships that facilitated the removal of two panels from Palenque, destined for the Museo Nacional de México—the first (central) panel in 1884, the second (left) in 1909—and the return of the third (right) panel from the Smithsonian to Mexico in 1907. Central to understanding this remarkable case study are the larger questions of cultural diplomacy, cultural repatriation, and the national control of antiquities. By focusing on the process of return and reassemblage of the Cross of Palenque, Bueno provides a foil for other cases of fragmentation that involve disassembly, dispossession, and loss attendant on the museum's becoming.

Such was the case with the natural history collections in the national museum complex. In "Past and Present at the Museo de Historia Natural," Frida Gorbach takes as her starting point a handful of objects currently on display in the Museo de Historia Natural de la Ciudad de México that have survived a long history of loss and destruction after the 1909 expulsion of sixty-four thousand natural specimens from the Museo Nacional de México and their relocation to the Museo del Chopo. Her interest lies less in the reconstruction of the itineraries of these objects than on how they conjure what is missing and lost. What happened to all those collections that turn-of-the-century naturalists gathered, classified, and exhibited? How does one recover histories of disappearance and write about an archive that does not exist?

Haydeé López Hernández, in "Clues and Gazes: Indigenous Faces in the Museo Nacional de Antropología," shifts direction to focus on the Archivo Fotográfico de Etnografía del Museo Nacional de Antropología, especially to the photographic records of thirty-one ethnic groups, cataloged between 1963 and 1964. As López Hernández argues, these photographs were originally intended to endow the ethnographic halls at the newly opened Museo Nacional de Antropología with objects for exhibits and "authentic" visual evidence that would serve to craft narratives of Mexico's indigenous patrimony. These documents have been banished for the most part from the museum's halls today. The author insists on the need to understand the ramifications of their resignification, such as the erasure of their historicity and the fixing of the subjects photographed over half a century earlier into an atemporal limbo as "ethnic types" devoid of individuality. To deepen our understanding of that erasure, López Hernández reexamines the rationales behind the increasing inclusion of photography as part of the toolkit of anthropological fieldwork.

Carlos Mondragón, in "Unsettled Objects: The Pacific Collection at the Museo Nacional de las Culturas," focuses on the main protagonist behind the assembly of the Pacific Collection, Miguel Covarrubias, to reexamine how the concept of Mesoamerica as a culture area—so central to how the 1964 Museo Nacional de Antropología was designed—was created in relation to ideas about cultural diffusion emanating from anthropological engagements with the Pacific in the 1940s and 1950s. Focusing on the perishable nature of the objects from mostly Melanesian ritual worlds, in contrast with the solidity of the stone relics that made up most of the Museo Nacional de Antropología's pre-Hispanic collections, he explores how these objects were collected, interpreted, and exhibited over time, only to be slowly forgotten in the storerooms of what has become a rather marginal space within the national museum complex.

In the chapters of the final thematic section, "Disturbances," the authors address three case studies that expose the kinds of silencing and forms of historical violence that accumulate and come together in the museum's halls and collections. In "Tehuantepec on Display: Tlalocs, Theodolites, Fishing Traps, and the Cultures of Collecting in the Mid-Nineteenth Century," Miruna Achim reconstructs the removal of two pre-Hispanic ceramic urns from the island of Manopostiac in the isthmus of Tehuantepec, in 1843, as part of a state-sponsored scientific commission meant to inform about the feasibility of opening a canal through the isthmus. She explores the ways in which this collection was enabled by and in turn sustained positivist narratives built on the putative opposition between barbarity and civilization, superstition and science, fallowness and utility, which were integral to the vision of a modern Mexico in the nineteenth century. Contending that the Museo Nacional de Antropología has done little to reflect on the violence at the heart of its early collections and on the narratives used to justify collecting, Achim's rereading of the Tehuantepec survey reflects on the losses and erasures incurred by the process through which pre-Hispanic antiquities become the essence of Mexico's past.

Mario Rufer, in his "Conjuring Violence Away with Culture: The Purépecha National Emblem in the Museo Nacional de Antropología" addresses the pacification of contemporary indigenous peoples and their claims over land

and sovereignty implied in their transformation into ethnographic exotica. He focuses on the featherwork Purépecha National Emblem dating from around 1829, a replica of what was then the Mexican national coat of arms that has been recast as a folkloric handicraft in the museum's ethnographic halls. Rufer poses a series of questions unsettling the relationship between culture and violence, sovereignty and domination. The featherwork emblem's display shows how the Mexican nation-state works to silence and ignore the Purépechas' deep history of military resistance from pre-Hispanic to contemporary times.

Sandra Rozental's "A Monolith on the Street" scrutinizes the significance of the liminal location of the colossal pre-Hispanic monolith known as Tlaloc, the Mexica rain deity—even though the sculpture predates Mexica civilization by a millennium. Since its removal from the town of San Miguel Coatlinchan to the museum in 1964, the statue has stood as both a metonym for the museum and its collection of state-sanctioned national heritage and a monument in urban public space. This doubling has made the monolith ideal for appropriation by various actors and social movements that have used it to denounce the Mexican state's authoritarian politics. At the same time, it reveals the museum's foundations in histories of violence and forced dispossession.

In sum, the main objectives of *Museum Matters* are twofold: first, to challenge understandings of the museum and its objects as fixed ontological entities through an exploration of how the museum and its various iterations came into being over the *longue durée.* Such exploration requires understanding the particular materialities of objects and their trajectories and travel across various regimes of value. By focusing on the physical, spatial, and conceptual movement of objects, this volume makes visible the tangled webs of social and political relations that bring objects into being or throw them into oblivion.[34] In the Mexican case, charting these relations provides insights into colonial assemblages, national politics, expectations, and intellectual fashions that attest not only to how people and places have made objects, but also, and more importantly, to how objects have in turn made their collectors, caretakers, and users.

Our second objective is to dislodge some of the more entrenched narratives that have become attached to collections as objects of national patrimony. It is a call to recognize the objects hailed at different moments as Mexico's patrimony, and the containers that hold them, as vibrant and contingent sites of contention, dissent, discussion, and negotiation. Our overall purpose is political: if there is nothing fixed or intrinsic about the things collected in this volume or about those gathered in Mexico's national collections in the course of two hundred years, we hope the nation's objects can become truly public and inclusive sites for the expression of multiple forms of use, affect, and care.

Notes

1. Miruna Achim, "The Art of the Deal, 1828: How Isidro Icaza Traded Pre-Columbian Antiquities to Henri Baradère for Mounted Birds and Built a National Museum in Mexico City in the Process," *West 86th* 18, no. 2 (2011): 214–31. For a discussion of the *malanggans* in the collection, see Mondragón in this volume.
2. For more on patrimonio and its uses in Mexico, see Sandra Rozental, "On the Nature of Patrimonio: 'Cultural Property' in Mexican Contexts," in *The Routledge Companion to Cultural Property*, ed. Haidy Geismar and Jane Anderson (London: Routledge, 2017), 237–57. For the ideological project wedding archaeology and power in Mexico, see Ignacio Rodríguez, "Recursos ideológicos del Estado mexicano: El caso de la arqueología," in *La historia de la antropología en México*, ed. Mechthild Rutsch (Mexico City: Universidad Iberoamericana, Plaza y Valdés, Instituto Nacional Indigenista, 1996), 83–103; and Luis Vázquez León, *El leviatán arqueológico: Antropología de una tradición científica en México* (Mexico City: CIESAS, 2003).
3. Bruno Latour, "From Realpolitik to Dingpolitik: An Introduction to Making Things Public," in *Making Things Public: Atmosphere of Democracy*, ed. Bruno Latour and Peter Weibel (Cambridge, Mass.: MIT Press, 2005), 4–31.
4. For a history of the museum from its foundation to 1867, see Miruna Achim, *From Idols to Antiquity: Forging the National Museum of Mexico* (Lincoln: Nebraska University Press, 2017). For a panoramic view of collections in the late eighteenth and nineteenth centuries, see Luis Gerardo Morales, *Orígenes de la museología mexicana: Fuentes para el estudio histórico del Museo Nacional, 1780–1940* (Mexico City: Universidad Iberoamericana, 1994).
5. See Deans-Smith and Gorbach in this volume.
6. Sonia Lombardo de Ruiz and Ruth Solís Vicarte, *Antecedentes de las leyes sobre Monumentos Históricos (1536–1910)* (Mexico City: Instituto Nacional de Antropología e Historia [INAH], 1988), 31.
7. Brantz Mayer, *Mexico as It Was and as It Is* (Philadelphia, Pa.: G. B. Zieber, 1843), 90.
8. Shelley Garrigan, *Collecting Mexico: Museums, Monuments, and the Creation of National Identity* (Minneapolis: University of Minnesota Press, 2012), 88; see also Mauricio Tenorio-Trillo, *Mexico at the World's Fairs: Crafting a Modern Nation* (Berkeley: University of California Press, 1996).

9. For histories of the museum in the late nineteenth and early twentieth centuries, especially regarding questions of specialization and institutionalization, see Christina Bueno, *The Pursuit of Ruins: Archaeology, History, and the Making of Modern Mexico* (Albuquerque: University of New Mexico Press, 2016); Frida Gorbach, *El monstruo, objeto imposible: Un estudio sobre teratología mexicana, siglo XIX* (Mexico City: Universidad Autónoma Metropolitana–Xochimilco and Itaca, 2008); Haydeé López Hernández, *En busca del alma nacional: La arqueología y la construcción del origen de la historia nacional en México (1867–1942)* (Mexico City: INAH, 2018); and Mechthild Rutsch, *Entre el campo y el gabinete: Nacionales y extranjeros en la profesionalización de la antropología mexicana (1877–1920)* (Mexico City: INAH, 2007). See also Apen Ruiz Martínez, *Género, ciencia y política: Voces, vidas y miradas de la arqueología mexicana* (Mexico City: Secretaría de Cultura, INAH, 2016).
10. Justo Sierra to Roberto Núñez, vice secretary of finance, May 18, 1909, in Sierra, *Epistolario y papeles privados*, Obras Completas 14 (Mexico City: Universidad Nacional Autónoma de México, 1984), 289–90.
11. Bueno, *Pursuit of the Ruins*.
12. Gorbach, *El monstruo, objeto imposible*.
13. Eduard Seler, *Inventario de las colecciones arqueológicas del Museo Nacional, 1907*, ed. Bertina Olmedo Vera and Miruna Achim (Mexico City: INAH, 2018).
14. See Gorbach in this volume.
15. See Mondragón in this volume.
16. Relocating the museum to Chapultepec had been proposed since the late nineteenth century and more recently in the 1950s. See Ana Garduño, "La utopía construida: El museo en el Bosque de Chapultepec," in *Museo Nacional de Antropología: 50 aniversario (1825–1964)*, ed. Antonio Saborit and Carla Zarebska (Mexico City: Conaculta/INAH, 2014), 168–88.
17. The quotation is how then minister of education Jaime Torres Bodet referred to the museum on the day of its inauguration.
18. See INAH, *Museo Nacional de Antropología* (Mexico City: Artes de México, 1965), 16.
19. Artists from the various artistic trends that defined Mexican modernism—both the heirs to the Escuela Mexicana de Pintura associated with the muralists, and Mexico's more abstract painters associated with the Ruptura, were invited to contribute works of art to enrich the museum's displays. See Mary Coffey, *How a Revolutionary Art Became Official Culture: Murals, Museums, and the Mexican State* (Durham, N.C.: Duke University Press, 2012). For studies on the incorporation of pre-Hispanic elements and of local materials and crafts, see Cristóbal Andrés Jácome, "Palimpsestos constructivos: La impronta del pasado prehispánico en la modernización mexicana," *CAIANA: Revista de Historia del Arte y Cultura Visual del Centro Argentino de Investigadores de Arte*, no. 4 (2014): 1–14; Luis M. Castañeda, *Spectacular Mexico: Design, Propaganda, and the 1968 Olympics* (Minneapolis: University of Minnesota Press, 2014);

and Sandra Rozental, "La pátina de 'lo mexicano': Albañiles y artesanos en el Museo Nacional de Antropología," in *Object Notes: Extraño y cercano / Strange and Close*, comp. Santiago Da Silva and Malte Roloff (Mexico City: Labor Ipse Volutas, 2019), 103–8.

20. They claimed that this was the first time that specialists, namely archaeologists and anthropologists, were deployed all over the country to collect specimens to fully represent the country's diverse yet unique culture. See Pedro Ramírez Vázquez, *Museo Nacional de Antropología: Gestación, proyecto y construcción* (Mexico City: INAH, 2008).
21. Deborah Dorotinsky Alperstein, "Fotografía y Maniquíes en el Museo Nacional de Antropología," *Luna Córnea*, no. 23 (March–June 2002): 60–65; Sandra Rozental and Mario Rufer, "Río Congo: El corazón de las tinieblas en el Museo Nacional de Antropología," *Horizontal*, March 4, 2016.
22. Barbara Kirshenblatt-Gimblett, "Objects of Ethnography," in *Exhibiting Cultures: The Poetics and Politics of Museum Display*, ed. Ivan Karp and Steven D. Lavine (Washington, D.C.: Smithsonian Institution Press, 1991), 386–444. For a fascinating take on the museum's Wixarika collections in the Sala del Gran Nayar, see Paul Liffman, "Museums and Mexican Indigenous Territoriality," *Museum Anthropology* 30, no. 2 (2007): 141–60.
23. For more on the concept of "ethnographic present," see Johannes Fabian, *Time and the Other: How Anthropology Makes Its Object* (New York: Columbia University Press, 1983).
24. See Rufer in this volume.
25. Undertaken in 2016, the most recent renovation was of the Otopame Hall, previously renovated in 1998 and 2000. The hall was curated by a member of the museum's staff, Arturo Gómez Martínez, who identifies as Nahua. In interviews and press releases, Gómez Martínez stressed that this renovation would finally take indigenous self-representation seriously and feature only collections made by indigenous artisans and artists. Relying on the white-box model of art galleries, however, the hall continues to decontextualize contemporary indigenous expressions from history and politics, now treating them as aesthetic objects.
26. For examples on the museum's nineteenth- and early twentieth-century history, see Achim, *From Idols to Antiquity*; Gorbach, *El monstruo, objeto imposible*; López Hernández, *En busca del alma nacional*; and Rutsch, *Entre el campo y al gabinete*. For critiques of the museum's more recent history, see Néstor García Canclini, *Culturas híbridas: Estrategias para entrar y salir de la modernidad* (Buenos Aires: Editorial Sudamericana, 1992); and Federico Navarrete, "Ruinas y Estado: Arqueología de una simbiosis mexicana," in *Pueblos Indígenas y Arqueología en América Latina*, comp. C. Gnecco and P. Ayala (Bogotá: Centro de Estudios Socioculturales e Internacionales–Universidad de los Andes, 2010), 65–84.
27. Kynaston McShine, *The Museum as Muse: Artists Reflect* (New York: Museum of Modern Art, 1999). See Octavio Paz, "Critica a la Pirámide," in *Posdata*

(Mexico City: Siglo XXI, 1962), 103–55, for one of the earliest critiques of the museum. See also Mariana Castillo-Deball, *These Ruins that You See* (Mexico City: Conaculta, 2008).

28. See James Oles, "Museum Destruction," 58–76; Sandra Rozental, "Kit to Detonate a Monolith," 76–94; and Mariana Botey, "Mining the ISA and Revising Cultural Extractivism," 112–20, all in Eduardo Abaroa, *Total Destruction of the National Museum of Anthropology* (Mexico City: Athénée Press, 2017).
29. See Alfonso Ruizpalacios, dir., *Museo* (Mexico City: Detalle Films, 2018); Sandra Rozental and Jesse Lerner, dirs., *La piedra ausente / The Absent Stone* (Mexico City: Fondo para la Producción Cinematográfica de Calidad FOPROCINE México, 2013).
30. Many of the books on the museum were coordinated or even authored by the museum's architect, Pedro Ramírez Vázquez. See, for example, Pedro Ramírez Vázquez, *The National Museum of Anthropology, Mexico: Art, Architecture, Archaeology, Ethnography*, trans. Mary Jean Labadie and Aza Zatz (New York: Abrams and Helvetica, 1968); and *Museo Nacional de Antropología*. Two large volumes were published for the museum's fortieth and fiftieth anniversaries. The former includes a surprisingly critical essay exposing the questionable ethics of the museum's 1964 collecting strategies. See Roger Bartra, "Sonata etnográfica en no bemol," in *Museo Nacional de Antropología: Libro conmemorativo del cuarenta aniversario* (Mexico City: CONACULTA/INAH, 2004), 331–47.
31. The history of Mexican collecting has been informed mostly by scholarship on the history of nationalism and museums in Europe and in North America, where museums figure as sites for nation building. See especially Benedict Anderson, *Imagined Communities: Reflections on the Origins and Spread of Nationalism* (London: Verso, 2003); Tony Bennet, *The Birth of the Museum: History, Theory, Politics* (New York: Routledge, 1995); and Carol Duncan, *Civilizing Rituals: Inside Public Art Museums* (London: Routledge, 1995). For a similar approach to the history of the Mexican national museums, see Miguel Ángel Fernández, *Historia de los museos de México* (Mexico City: Promotora de Comercialización Directa, 1988); Enrique Florescano, "La creación del Museo Nacional de Antropología y sus fines científicos, educativos y políticos," in *El patrimonio cultural de México*, ed. Enrique Florescano (Mexico City: Fondo de Cultura Económica, 1993), 145–64; and Luisa Fernanda Rico Mansard, *Exhibir para educar: Objetos, colecciones y museos de la Ciudad de México (1790–1910)* (Mexico City: Ediciones Pomares/UNAM, 2004).
32. For recent scholarship on object-centered museum and collection studies, which has inspired our approach, see Samuel J. M. M. Alberti, *Nature and Culture: Objects, Disciplines, and the Manchester Museum* (London: Palgrave Macmillan, 2009); James Delbourgo, *Collecting the World: Hans Sloane and the Origins of the British Museum* (Cambridge, Mass.: Harvard University Press, 2017); Sandra Dudley, *Museum Materialities* (London: Routledge, 2010); Eliza-

beth Edwards, Chris Gosden, and Ruth B. Phillips, eds., *Sensible Objects: Colonialism, Museums and Material Culture*, vol. 5 (New York: Berg, 2006); Chris Gosden, Frances Larson, and Alison Petch, *Knowing Things: Exploring the Collections at the Pitt Rivers Museum* (Oxford: Oxford University Press, 2008); Ivan Karp and Steven D. Lavine, eds., *Exhibiting Cultures: The Poetics and Politics of Museum Display* (Washington, D.C.: Smithsonian Institution Press, 1991); Fred R. Myers, ed., *The Empire of Things: Regimes of Value and Material Culture* (Santa Fe, N.Mex.: School of American Research, 2001); and George W. Stocking Jr., ed., *Objects and Others: Essays on Museums and Material Culture* (Madison: University of Wisconsin Press, 1988). For similar approaches to collecting in Latin America and particularly Mexico, see Miruna Achim and Irina Podgorny, eds., *Museos al detalle: Colecciones, antigüedades e historia natural* (Buenos Aires: Colección Prohistoria, 2013); Daniela Bleichmar and Peter C. Mancall, *Collecting across Cultures: Material Exchanges in the Early Modern World* (Philadelphia: University of Pennsylvania Press, 2011); Elizabeth Hill Boone, *Collecting the Pre-Columbian Past: A Symposium at Dumbarton Oaks, 6th and 7th October 1990* (Washington, D.C.: Dumbarton Oaks Research Library and Collection, 1993); Stefanie Gänger, *Relics of the Past: The Collecting and Study of Pre-Columbian Antiquities in Peru and Chile, 1837–1911* (Oxford: Oxford University Press, 2014); Curtis M. Hinsley, "From Shell-Heaps to Stelae: Early Anthropology at the Peabody Museum," in Stocking, *Objects and Others*, 49–74; and Philip L. Kohl, Irina Podgorny, and Stefanie Gänger, *Nature and Antiquities: The Making of Archaeology in the Americas* (Tucson: University of Arizona Press, 2014).

33. For work on fakes and replicas and their relevance to the history of Mexican collecting, see Ronda L. Brulotte, *Between Art and Artifact: Archaeological Replicas and Cultural Production in Oaxaca, Mexico* (Austin: University of Texas Press, 2012); Justin Jennings and Adam T. Sellen, *Real Fake: The Story of a Zapotec Urn* (Toronto: Royal Ontario Museum, 2018); Sandra Rozental, "Stone Replicas: The Iteration and Itinerancy of Mexican Patrimonio," *Journal of Latin American and Caribbean Anthropology* 19, no. 2 (2014): 331–56; and Gabriela Zepeda, "Guardianes y moneros: Patrimonio arqueológico y supervivencia campesina en el sur de Nayarit" (master's thesis, Guadalajara, CIESAS de Occidente, 2000).

34. We are inspired in our approach by the concept of "relational museum" developed as an approach to the collections at the Pitt Rivers Museum at Oxford. See Gosden, Larson, and Petch, *Knowing Things*.

Part I
Canons

\\ 1

"A History Worthy of the Grandeur of the Spanish Nation"

Collecting Mexican Antiquity in the Viceroyalty of New Spain

SUSAN DEANS-SMITH

In 1825, Bernardo González wrote to the president of the Real Academia de San Carlos in Mexico City to inform him that "the pieces of Mexican antiquity which my father-in-law, don Manuel de la Mota, deposited in the academy on the orders of don Ciriaco Carvajal" had passed to his wife, his only heir. González had placed them at "the government's disposition for the adornment of the national museum."[1] The objects in question were four Postclassic sculptures (figures 1.1–1.4) discovered during the demolition of properties belonging to the Mayorazgo de Mota (located in the current streets of Carmen and Justo Sierra in downtown Mexico City).[2] What at first sight may appear to be a rather innocuous transfer of objects from one space to another, however, raises the question, why did a Spanish judge of the Audiencia of Mexico—Ciriaco González Carvajal—order pre-Hispanic objects to be placed in the Real Academia de San Carlos? Although the exact date of their deposit is unclear, it was no later than 1794. By that time the academy had established itself as one of Mexico City's flagship institutions designed to facilitate the Spanish Bourbon monarchy's reformist ambitions in both the sciences and the arts inspired by Enlightenment principles.[3] Renovation and innovation lay at the core of such ambitions to modernize Spain and its empire and reestablish its position as a global power. The Real Academia de San Carlos possessed extraordinary collections of paintings, prints, medals, and antique plaster casts that included some of the finest statues in the

Figure 1.1 José Antonio Polanco, "Human figure, possibly a standard bearer of Ancient Imperial Mexico" (*Indio triste*), 1794, ink and charcoal drawing. Guillermo Dupaix, "Descripción de monumentos antiguos mexicanos," Biblioteca Nacional de Antropología e Historia, Mexico City. Courtesy of the Instituto Nacional de Antropología e Historia.

classical canon, such as the Apollo Belvedere and the Borghese Gladiator, as well as an extensive library, all designed to facilitate the teaching of neoclassicism and inculcate concepts of ideal beauty.[4] The academy, however, like its counterparts in Spain, also trained artists to participate in Spain's scientific and antiquarian expeditions to provide accurate illustrations of sites

Figure 1.2 José Antonio Polanco, "Coyote" (*Ahuizote*), 1794, ink and charcoal drawing. Guillermo Dupaix, "Descripción de monumentos antiguos mexicanos," Biblioteca Nacional de Antropología e Historia, Mexico City. Courtesy of the Instituto Nacional de Antropología e Historia.

and specimens. This combination of the fine arts and scientific endeavors demonstrated the Spanish enlightenment's "understanding of the practical applications of art."[5] As such, the deposit of the four Postclassic sculptures in the Real Academia de San Carlos seems a logical choice, especially given the absence of a formally designated space for objects of Mexican antiquity. But what does their placement in a particular space—a "royal" and "academic"

Figure 1.3 José Antonio Polanco, "Rattlesnake" (*Gray Rattlesnake*), 1794, ink and charcoal drawing. Guillermo Dupaix, "Descripción de monumentos antiguos mexicanos," Biblioteca Nacional de Antropología e Historia, Mexico City. Courtesy of the Instituto Nacional de Antropología e Historia.

space—tell us, more broadly, about the valorization and collection of Mexican antiquity and contemporaries' understandings of it in the late eighteenth and early nineteenth centuries?

To address these questions, I provide a brief overview of the contexts in which institutional support for antiquities expeditions within the Spanish empire developed to better understand their political and cultural significance. I then shift focus to look more closely at the Mexican academy's role in the documentation and valorization of Mexican antiquity prior to Mexican independence in 1821, as well as the establishment of the Museo Nacional de México in 1825. Finally, I explore the contested assessments that pre-Hispanic objects provoked about their value and significance. I make three arguments. First, institutions such as the Real Academia de San Carlos were key sites in Spanish imperial and intellectual networks that supported the

Figure 1.4 José Antonio Polanco, "Monstrous Toad" (*Toad*), 1794, ink and charcoal drawing. Guillermo Dupaix, "Descripción de monumentos antiguos mexicanos," Biblioteca Nacional de Antropología e Historia, Mexico City. Courtesy of the Instituto Nacional de Antropología e Historia.

documentation, discussion, and illustration of Mexican antiquity. The Real Academia de San Carlos would come to play a comparable role to that of the Real Academia de San Fernando in Madrid in the visualization and valorization of Mexican antiquity, even as it promoted the new aesthetic of neoclassicism and its privileging of universal and ideal beauty.[6] The Bourbon monarchy's support for the study of antiquity demonstrated its recognition of the changing values of ruins and ancient artifacts as well as increasing global competition for what Irina Podgorny describes as "the possession of antiquity."[7] Second, the study and valorization of Mexican antiquity cannot be understood as an exclusively Mexican creole enterprise. Both peninsulares and Mexican creoles (as well as other European scholars and collectors) expressed appreciation of Mexican antiquity and its histories, albeit for very different reasons.[8] Mexican antiquity found its place in expressions of Spanish cultural patriotism and empire even as it was becoming foundational to expressions of Mexican creole patriotism and, subsequently, nationalism. As such, both Spanish and Mexican valorization of Mexican antiquity insisted on the value of local/national antiquities while acknowledging the universal claims of Greco-Roman classicism. Even as such valorization signified a tolerance of cultural diversity *avant la lettre,* however, connotations of idolatry marked the limitations of such tolerance.[9] Third, contemporaries' discussions about Mexican antiquity were characterized by contested claims about its significance and how to categorize its artifacts. The value of pre-Hispanic objects was neither intrinsic nor stable but fluid, depending on particular contexts. Such instabilities would continue to define the collection and conservation of pre-Hispanic antiquities well into the nineteenth century and after the creation of the Museo Nacional de México.[10]

Antiquities and the Spanish Nation

> *The Spanish have no clue what lies beneath their feet, nor do they understand the value of antiquities.*
>
> —José Francisco Ortiz y Sanz

The intensification of the study of antiquities in both Spain and New Spain derived in part from the broader need to challenge searing European critiques that portrayed the "Spanish nation" as barbarous and backward, and the inhabitants of its American colonies as inferior. "Scientific" study of antiquities indexed Spain's enlightened modernity as an active participant in the emerging disciplines of archaeology, art history, and the natural sciences. Interpretation and illustration of such discoveries provided material evidence for revisionist histories of the "glories" of the Spanish "nation," both past and present. As Gábor Klaniczay and colleagues argue, "There was hardly any project on modernity that was not accompanied by images, representations and constructions of the past, just as . . . there was hardly any reconstruction of Antiquity without reference to the projects of modernity and concepts related to the present or the future."[11]

The Bourbon monarchy's support of the study, collection, and conservation of antiquities began with Phillip V and Isabel Farnese. Charles III, however, set a major precedent for royal sponsorship when, as king of Naples and Sicily, he ordered excavations at the sites of Herculaneum (begun in 1738) and Pompeii and Stabiae (begun in 1748).[12] The startling discoveries were published in the eight volumes of *Le antichità di Ercolano Esposte* (Antiquities of Herculaneum exposed).[13] Subsequently, archaeological expeditions were conducted on both sides of the Atlantic that would produce discoveries of not one but multiple antiquities: Roman, Islamic, Celtic-Iberian, and American.[14] Scientific expeditions under Charles III's patronage generated instructions distributed throughout the Spanish empire in 1752 and 1776 that included the collection of "curiosities" and "antiquities."[15] In 1777, Antonio de Ulloa, a colonial official, scientist, and naval officer, compiled a special set of instructions for the collection of detailed information about Mexico's natural history and resources. Out of fifty-eight questions, nine related to antiquities. The Spanish monarchy also authorized archaeological and antiquities expeditions. The author of the lament that foreigners believed that "the Spanish have no clue what lies beneath their feet"—the Valencian scholar and antiquarian José Francisco Ortiz y Sanz—received royal permission to conduct a peninsula-wide survey of Spanish archaeological sites.[16] Although the survey never materialized, its projected scope and itinerary under Ortiz y Sanz's supervision—*Noticia y plan de un viage arquitectónico-antiquario*—was published in 1797. In 1804 Charles IV appointed a retired Flemish captain of dragoons, Guillermo Dupaix, to direct the first (and only) Royal Antiquities Expedition of New Spain. Three of four projected expeditions were completed between 1805 and 1809, when the project was suspended because of the Mexican insurgency.[17]

Royal sponsorship and the development of royal antiquities collections facilitated such expeditions, as well as what Jorge Maier Allende has referred to as the "institutionalization of archaeology."[18] Key institutions for the study of antiquity in Spain included the Biblioteca Real (1716), the Real Academia de la Historia (1738), the Real Academia de San Fernando (1752), and the Real Gabinete de Historia Natural in Madrid (1771). Both the Real Academia de la Historia and the Real Academia de San Fernando would play particularly influential roles in antiquities research.[19] The Real Academia de la Historia became the designated site for collection of information about Spain's American colonies and the project to write a revisionist history of the New

World directed by Juan Bautista Muñoz.[20] In 1792, Charles IV approved the creation of the Sala de Antigüedades in the Real Academia de la Historia to oversee official reports on excavations and antiquities.[21] The Real Academia de San Fernando also took a leading role in the evaluation and illustration of new discoveries, especially those of Spain's Islamic past and Al-Andalus. Begun in 1756, subsequent studies resulted in the illustrated publication of the *Antigüedades árabes de España*, issued in two parts in 1787 and 1805. The Real Academia de San Fernando also expanded its regulatory role over building construction and architectural design to include ancient sites, and in 1808 it announced that its supervision included "conservation of the old."[22]

Royal legislation targeted the collection and protection of antiquities, influenced not only by an increasingly aggressive arts and antiquities market (licit and illicit) but also by Napoleon Bonaparte's cultural predations in Italy and Egypt (and from which Spain would eventually suffer). A royal decree of 1803 provided landmark legislation that stipulated the "method of collection and conservation of antiquities discovered or to be discovered in the kingdom."[23] Although the antiquities law did not specify "American" antiquity, its main principles—discovery, interpretation, conservation, and ownership—may have influenced Charles IV's approval of the Royal Antiquities Expedition of New Spain in 1804 as well as the creation of an antiquities commission in Mexico City in 1808.[24] In 1812, the Cortes de Cádiz circulated a new set of instructions throughout the empire that included one dedicated to the documentation of antiquities. Provoked by Bonaparte's confiscations of artworks and antiquities throughout Spain, it anticipated destruction and displacement of artifacts within the crumbling empire.[25] With an eye to their preservation, if only on paper, the instruction ordered that gouache paintings be made of "all monuments, ruins, palaces, temples, graves, pyramids, hieroglyphs and other objects related to the antiquity of the people in their gentility" and sent in duplicate to Spain.[26] Regardless of the uneven effects of such laws (bordering on irrelevance), recognition of their need contributed to the making and marking of the significance of the study of antiquity and its artifacts.

Part of antiquity's significance resided in its uses for the construction of historical imaginaries of empires and nations. Anything but a monolithic concept, antiquity can take on multiple forms and meanings to support divergent agendas.[27] The "possession of antiquity" not only refers to ownership of the actual artifact or control over archaeological sites but control over its meanings. The instrumentalization of Spain's plural antiquities to create contested narratives of the Spanish "nation" and its histories is illustrated by the following examples.[28] In a critique of classicism's claims to universal forms and ideals of beauty that marginalized the local and the national, the noted Spanish collector and classicist José Nicolás de Azara y Perera suggested that classical mythological figures of the fountains of the gardens at the Royal Palace of La Granja de San Ildefonso should be replaced by "events of our history or our fables," which could include representations of "our own Endovélico (Endovelicus) or Vizlipuzli (Huitzilopochtli) the Mexican."[29] For Dupaix as well as for the creole antiquarian and astronomer Antonio de León y Gama (among others), Mexican antiquity also reflected "the Grandeur of the Spanish Nation . . . [and] to the extent that knowledge of the ancient Indians is increased so will their immortal conquerors' glory grow."[30] Multiple antiquities, however, could become "conflicted" antiquities as different interests staked their claims about the historical significance and expressions of Spanish imperial power.[31] In a vivid example of the entanglements of imperialism and classicism, Luis de Lorenzana submitted a design to the Real Academia de San Fernando for a new "Spanish" architectural order to express Spain's greatness. Intended to visually embed Mexico's conquered status into Spanish classical architecture, he sought to add to the canon of the five orders the "Spanish Order." Composed of a column with "its capitol girdled by a crown of feathers receiving water from a conch shell" and from which emerged a serpent, it represented "America discovered, conquered, and converted . . . the most illustrious, the most remarkable, and extraordinary enterprise of men."[32] Clearly, Mexican antiquity could mean different things to different constituencies at different times at both institutional and individual levels within the Spanish empire.

The Real Academia de San Carlos and Mexican Antiquity

> *The country abounds in monuments for which nobody cares, but which would be very useful to document its history.*
>
> —Ciriaco González Carvajal

Despite the move toward the "institutionalization of archaeology," decisions about where to house pre-Hispanic objects were characterized by their ad hoc and contingent nature and may help to explain how the four Postclassic sculptures came to reside in the Real Academia de San Carlos. Although the Royal University of Mexico became a prominent space for the study of Mexican antiquity, other institutional spaces in Mexico City, such as the academy and the Gabinete de Historia Natural, would also house pre-Hispanic artifacts.[33] Their placement in these scholarly and scientific spaces indicated that they were worthy of study and appreciation. Yet, the ambiguity of their categorization is illustrated by their juxtaposition with other types of artifacts and materials, such as the "soils" in Mexico City's Gabinete de Historia Natural and Greco-Roman antique plaster casts in the Real Academia de San Carlos.[34] So, where did pre-Hispanic antiquities belong? In natural history collections? In fine art collections? Somewhere else?

Several reasons may have influenced González Carvajal to order the four Postclassic sculptures' placement in the academy: his familiarity with institutional developments in Spain for the study of antiquity; the broader community of collectors and antiquarians represented in the academy's membership, as well as his own interests as an antiquarian and collector; and academy artists and officials' professional engagement with Mexican antiquity. As such the Real Academia de San Carlos provided a generative place for the study and illustration of Mexican antiquity.

González Carvajal's knowledge of the development of institutional support for the study of antiquities in Spain may have shaped his vision for the Real Academia de San Carlos to be a legitimate space for artifacts that could illuminate ancient Mexico's history and its arts.[35] He arrived in Mexico City to assume his position on the Mexican Audiencia at a pivotal moment for the academy and for the study of Mexican antiquity in the early 1790s.[36] In 1791 the Real Academia de San Carlos acquired its exquisite collection of antique classical plaster casts at the same time that the Plaza Mayor's renovation resulted in the discovery of some of Mexican antiquity's most spectacular examples. The lack of an official department for the study of Mexican antiquity comparable to that of the Real Academia de la Historia in Madrid most likely also influenced González Carvajal's proposal to Viceroy Iturrigaray to create an antiquities commission in Mexico City in 1808.[37]

The Real Academia de San Carlos's administrative structure facilitated the representation of officials from other key Enlightenment institutions, the Spanish colonial bureaucracy, and local elites in its governance and academic projects. Viceroys automatically held the position of vice-protector, the academy's highest-ranking official. Some of New Spain's most powerful officials occupied the next highest-ranking academy office, that of its president, such as Francisco Fernández de Córdoba, the superintendent of the mint. Two directors of the Royal Mining Tribunal—Joaquín Velázquez de León and Fausto Elhuyar—served on the academy's governing board, as did powerful royal officials, such as the intendant of Mexico City, Bernado Bonavía y Zapata, and González Carvajal himself, an Audiencia judge. Honorary academicians appointed included leading members of the scholarly and scientific literati, such as the physician and mathematician José Ignacio Bartolache, the auxiliary bishop of Michoacán and future archbishop of Charcas Benito María de Moxó y Francolí, and Antonio Batres (Leopoldo Batres's grandfather). They belonged to a small but enthusiastic circle of antiquarians and collectors in Mexico City with interests in Mexican antiquity, which included well-known creole scholars such as José Antonio de Alzate y Ramírez, and Antonio de León y Gama, as well as Guillermo Dupaix. González Carvajal and Elhuyar played particularly influential roles in the promotion of research on Mexican antiquity, especially by supporting Dupaix and the Royal Antiquities Expedition in New Spain.[38] González Carvajal's role as an antiquarian and individual collector may have also influenced his decision to place the Postclassic sculptures in the Real Academia de San Carlos. By the time he returned to Spain in 1809, he had amassed a significant Mexican antiquities collection.[39] In sum, academy officials' antiquarian interests, which extended to Mexican antiquities, provided an important statement to the broader public that pre-Hispanic artifacts were objects of desire, worthy of study and possession. Indeed, the academy's involvement combined with its cultural authority as a royal institution may have created a fashionable cache for the study of Mexican antiquity.

Academy artists, academicians, and students played an active role in the knowledge production about Mexican antiquity for both institutional and individual patrons. The two draftsmen recruited by Guillermo Dupaix to help him with the illustrations of pre-Hispanic artifacts—José Antonio Polanco and José Luciano Castañeda—both trained at the Real Academia de San Carlos.[40] The first and second academy director generals—Jerónimo Antonio Gil (engraver and academician of merit) and Rafael Ximeno y Planes (academician of merit in painting)—both worked on projects in Spain prior to their arrival in Mexico that included some of the most important visual renditions of Spanish antiquity and history.[41] After Gil's appointment in 1778 as principal engraver of the Royal Mint in Mexico City, the Real Academia de la Historia proposed that he engrave the indigenous hieroglyphs and maps collected by Lorenzo Boturini. Although this never materialized, as director-general, he oversaw the training and selection of academy students who accompanied scientific and antiquities expeditions. He would undoubtedly have been consulted on where the four Postclassic sculptures should be displayed in the Real Academia de San Carlos. Ximeno collaborated with the auxiliary bishop of Michoacán and honorary academician Moxó to illustrate the latter's collection of pre-Hispanic objects (figure 1.5) and tutored the Museo Nacional's future creator, Lucas Alamán.[42] Ximeno also became friends with González Carvajal and, at the latter's urging after his return to Spain in 1809, encouraged Dupaix to continue his work on the descriptions for the Royal Antiquities Expedition after its suspension in 1812.[43] The Real Academia de San Carlos's role and cumulative impact on the illustration of Mexican antiquity, as Leonardo López Luján has argued, "transcended the rural indigenous universe—where ruins served as landmarks—, to proliferate in the urban milieu, but in the form of prints and as evidence of a glorious past that was beginning to be reappraised."[44]

Academy architects also contributed to the documentation and analysis of pre-Hispanic objects. Miguel Constanzó, a military engineer, director of the Real Academia de San Carlos's Mathematics Department, and member of its governing board, worked with León y Gama on his study of pre-Hispanic objects.[45] On the intendant's orders (Bonavía y Zapata), Constanzó described the contents of an offertory cache to León y Gama in 1791, discovered during the ongoing renovation works of the Plaza Mayor.[46] León y Gama also sought Constanzó's help in his attempts to find a method to weigh the Coatlicue.[47] José Damían Ortiz, a city architect and academician of merit in architecture, provided the first information about the Piedra del Sol's discovery to the intendant.[48] Another academician of merit in architecture, Luis Martín, accompanied Pedro de Laguna to record the plan and elevation of the Palace of Mitla in Oaxaca. Subsequently, he worked with Alexander von Humboldt on his several geological excavations in the environs of Mexico City.[49] One can also speculate about the extent to which surveyors who had to be examined by the Real Academia de San Carlos also became a source of information about new discoveries as part of their daily work in Mexico City, especially during the urban renovations of the 1790s.[50]

Figure 1.5 Frontispiece, Benito María de Moxó's personal museum, 1804–1805, copperplate engraving by Armanino after Saávedra, original gouaches by Rafael Ximeno y Planes, from Benito María de Moxó, *Cartas mejicanas*, 1837. Courtesy of Harvard University.

When González Carvajal ordered the placement of the four Postclassic stone sculptures in the Real Academia de San Carlos in the early 1790s, it is unclear whether discussions had occurred with the Royal University as to whether they should be housed there. Recall that Bonavía y Zapata, the intendant of Mexico City and member of the academy's governing board, recommended that the newly discovered Coatlicue be moved to the Royal University. Although both institutions were close to the locations where the respective artifacts were unearthed, the stone sculptures' size made them a better fit for academy space, unlike that of the huge and heavy Coatlicue, which could be better accommodated in the space of the Royal University. To my knowledge, no public statement announced the placement of the four Postclassic sculptures in the Real Academia de San Carlos, which suggests that such information occurred by word of mouth. But where were they displayed? López Luján suggests that (referring to the academy's collection of classical statues) "alongside these European masterworks there were at least four Mexica sculptures."[51] What does "alongside" mean exactly? Shared space does not necessarily mean that artifacts within that space are valued or understood in the same way. We know very little about how these Post-classic sculptures were exhibited and consumed in academy spaces. Dupaix may have supervised his draftsman Polanco's drawings of them at the Real Academia de San Carlos, given the clear notation on the ink and charcoal drawing of the "Human Figure" (*Indio Triste*) that references the academy (figure 1.1).[52] That they were not exhibited in the same spaces as the classical antique plaster casts when Humboldt visited the academy in 1803 is indicated by his proposal that such an exhibition should be mounted. As he imagined it, "The remains of Mexican sculpture, those colossal statues of basalt and porphyry, which are covered with Aztec hieroglyphics . . . ought to be collected together in the edifice of the academy. . . . It would be curious to see these monuments of the first cultivation of our species, *the works of a semi-barbarous people* inhabiting the Mexican Andes, placed beside the *beautiful forms* produced under the sky of Greece and Italy."[53]

In an 1817 inventory of the Real Academia de San Carlos's collections and their locations, one entry lists "two American idols" (the other two are not accounted for) that shared space in a small room (possibly a storage room) located at the foot of a staircase with "three unframed canvases in disrepair, two small panels with paintings of Saint Nicholas, and various plaster molds also in disrepair."[54] How they were arranged is not specified. Granted, by

1817, the artifacts' location within academy space may be explained by a rearrangement of collections to cope with the Real Academia de San Carlos's increasingly dire state, caused by the withdrawal of royal funding after the outbreak of the 1810 Mexican insurgency. These "idols" may have been kept in a different space (as suggested by the inventory entry) separate from the classical sculpture galleries. If so, their location in different spaces may have suggested to viewers a different hierarchy of significance and value compared with classical works. Although little direct evidence of viewers' reactions to these objects at the academy exists, descriptions of two of the Postclassic sculptures by Dupaix and León y Gama convey their different responses. Dupaix commented on the size, purpose, and materials from which the "Human Figure" (*Indio Triste*) was made (figure 1.1). But he also commented on its form, noting, "This work of sculpture is original and very well made."[55] Decidedly less enthusiastic about the "Coyote" (*Ahuizote*), which he also described as a "wild dog" (figure 1.2), Dupaix observed "something monstrous in its configuration."[56] León y Gama, however, viewed the sculptures as historical objects, providing detailed descriptions of his understanding of their iconographic and ritual characteristics, but made no assessment of their aesthetic qualities.

What else can be said in broader terms about how individuals responded to the decontextualized artifacts of ancient Mexico in royal institutions such as the Real Academia de San Carlos and the university, or in private collections, or what they imagined after reading descriptions of such artifacts and the meaning making that became associated with Mexican antiquity? Did they inspire admiration and curiosity, or provoke revulsion, incomprehension, and frustration, or unsettling combinations of such reactions? Some scholars have interpreted the four Postclassic sculptures' placement in the Real Academia de San Carlos as signifying an openness to the aesthetic expressions of Mexican antiquity, in addition to those of classical antiquity.[57] Such assessments, moreover, take on a particular resonance within the cultural context of neoclassicism as the official aesthetic style, which valued restraint, clarity, symmetry, and proportion. Although some commentators demonstrate a suggestive openness to cultural diversity, a brief review of examples of contemporaries' assessments of Mexican antiquity reveals their contested and ambiguous nature. Openness to cultural diversity, however, reached its limits when observers perceived the idolatrous signification of Mexican antiquity, which overshadowed its antiquarian interest and value.

And it should not be forgotten that no additional pre-Hispanic artifacts were placed in the academy, one reason perhaps that González Carvajal complained to the viceroy that "nobody" cared about the monuments of antiquity in New Spain.[58] So, how were they understood and experienced?

Perceptions of Mexican Antiquity

> *You must agree that the Spanish found mysteries in our land that they did not understand. . . . What do you say to that?*
>
> —*Diario de México*

It is well known that Humboldt viewed Mexican antiquities and ruins as historical objects worthy of collection, preservation, and study, but "art" they were not.[59] Telling in Humboldt's imaginary exhibition that would place Mexican and classical antiquities side by side was its clear purpose to provide a visual didactic exercise that claimed the high ground for classicism and its "beautiful forms" compared to "the works of a semi-barbarous people" (the implication being that such works were not "beautiful"). For Humboldt the material residue and ruins of ancient Mexico pointed to "artistic infancy," and that "although they have learned, since the Europeans' arrival, how to render shapes with greater accuracy, there is no indication they are filled with a sense of beauty."[60]

Like Humboldt, Dupaix emphasized the need to document, conserve, and collect, warning against the imminent decay of many sites that he witnessed firsthand, soon to disappear without trace. Unlike Humboldt, even as he made similar comparisons across cultures and with classical antiquity as a baseline, his assessment of Mexican antiquities positioned them as worthy of "the attention of the connoisseur" and requiring "the intelligent examination of the lovers of antiquity."[61] Sprinkled throughout Dupaix's descriptions of pre-Hispanic artifacts and architecture are pointed references to how they exemplify "the rules of art," demonstrate "invention" (unlike Humboldt's "slavish copying"), "genius," "geometric correctness," and "good taste," all key academic terms that indexed aesthetic sophistication.[62] Dupaix acknowledged, however, that ancient Mexico did not achieve the "Greek state of perfection" but insisted that their artistic works "show that the ancient inhabitants of this country were not so rude and barbarous as some writers have falsely represented them. The same feelings of delicacy which suggested to the Grecian artist the attitude in which he has represented the Venus de Medici, guided the chisel of the Mexican sculptor."[63]

Humboldt and Dupaix capture a spectrum of reactions expressed by a variety of commentators. Although I have found no evidence of writings about Mexican antiquity by academic artists, some academy officials offer insights into their responses to pre-Hispanic objects. Both honorary academicians González Carvajal and the Benedictine bishop Moxó approximated Dupaix's interpretations, valuing the aesthetics of Mexican antiquity and, in so doing, expressing a degree of tolerance for cultural diversity. González Carvajal, in a letter to Viceroy Iturrigaray, noted the same "admiration" expressed by "the knowledgeable professors of the Royal Academy" when shown drawings from his personal collection from Mitla, "as they would [show for] Greek fragments and mosaics." He also emphasized their significance as historical documents and how they and other discoveries could contribute to the understanding of "the origin of the Indians and the first peoples of America."[64] Moxó described a "precious monument of Mexican antiquity" in his collection as exhibiting "such precision, fineness, and simplicity that it is almost as if it could have been made by a Greek or Roman artist."[65] Moxó, like Dupaix, reasoned that if examples of Mexican antiquity did not demonstrate a similar standard of perfection and beauty as that of the Greeks and Romans, it was because they were constrained by the visual expressions demanded by their superstitions and religion.[66]

The categorization of some pre-Hispanic artifacts as "idols" illuminates the contested discourses that swirled around them. Antiquarian and scientific value could be diminished with their characterization as idolatrous, an unwelcome reminder of Spain's failed "spiritual conquest." Classification of an object as "idolatrous," however, did not necessarily doom it to rejection. What mattered was the situational context. Two examples demonstrate such situational contingencies: the discovery of two Mexican monoliths during the Plaza Mayor's renovation in 1790 and the removal of a statue of Ferdinand VI.

After the discoveries of the Piedra del Sol and the Coatlicue, Bonavía y Zapata, the intendant, recommended to Viceroy Revillagigedo that the latter be moved to the Royal University, where it could be preserved for its antiquity and because of what "it can contribute towards [an] understanding [of those times]."[67] Along with Revillagigedo's approval of Bonavía's request, the Piedra del Sol was also placed on public display embedded in one of the

Mexico City cathedral towers. The Coatlicue's installation in the university's central patio, however, was short lived. After indigenous inhabitants began to leave offerings to her "that their elders used to present to their idols," Revillagigedo ordered the monolith's reburial. As Enrique Florescano asserts, this "demonstrated the moment in which enlightened inhabitants of New Spain attempted to convert a monument that was a living part of the beliefs and religious practices of the indigenous populations into an archaeological document that they could explain and understand."[68] Nothing comparable occurred with the Piedra del Sol which remained in public view until it was relocated to the Museo Nacional de México in 1885. Despite Revillagigedo's censorious order to rebury the Coatlicue, he nevertheless approved the publication of León y Gama's descriptions of both monoliths in his *Descripción histórica y cronológica de las dos piedras* (1792). With the exception of privileged visitors to Mexico City such as Humboldt and William Bullock, for whom the Coatlicue was unearthed so they could view it personally, the public's only access to the monolith was through León y Gama's illustrated description until it was finally displayed in the Museo Nacional de México in 1833.

Revillagigedo, as part of the Plaza Mayor's renovation, also ordered the removal of a statue of Ferdinand VI in 1791 (eventually to be replaced by Manuel Tolsá's neoclassical bronze equestrian statue of Charles IV). Provocative about the viceroy's decision to remove the statue of Ferdinand VI is the entanglement of perceptions of Mexican antiquity and its connotations of idolatry with "bad" art and "bad" taste, on which he based his decision. Revillagigedo justified the statue's removal because "the sovereign's image was sculpted by some poor ignorant Indian, executed without art, intelligence, and without any resemblance to the original. It had more of a gross and horrible form of the idols that the Indians made and worshipped in their paganism."[69] Whether the episode with the Coatlicue affected Revillagigedo's evaluations of pre-Hispanic forms is unclear, but his reasons for the removal of Ferdinand VI's statue expose his dismal assessment of indigenous artists' capabilities, past and present, as well as his revulsion for Mexican antiquity's aesthetic forms. The contradictions inherent in Revillagigedo's decisions to approve the publication of León y Gama's description of the Coatlicue but order the concealment of the actual monolith are all the more significant for how his decisions and statements as viceroy and spokesperson for the Real Academia de San Carlos as its vice-protector may have influenced public reception of Mexican antiquity.

Colonial periodicals and pamphlets also offer suggestive insights into opinions about Mexican antiquity. While the writings of León y Gama and Alzate published in the 1790s are well known, less attention has been paid to discussions about Mexican antiquity published by the *Gazeta de México* and the *Diario de México*.[70] The *Diario* in particular increased its coverage of Mexican antiquity especially during the politically volatile decade of 1810–21.[71] Common to many of the descriptions and discussions is an emphasis on the importance of producing knowledge about, as well as the revindication of, Mexican antiquity, its history, and its aesthetic expressions. Two commentaries that the *Diario* published stand out for their framing for readers of the dilemma of how and whether the "local" (Mexican antiquity) could be reconciled with the universal (classical antiquity). In 1808 readers opened the latest issue to find an anonymous "Dialogue" between "Cortés" and "Moctezuma." With its strikingly modern relativist impulse, it drew readers' attention to the concept of the autonomy of artistic expression that should be assessed on its own merits, not measured against a canonical classical art and antiquity. "Cortés" attempts to persuade "Moctezuma" of the "Americanos'" inferiority and argues that the Greeks and Romans invented the arts and sciences about which "the Mexica did not have the slightest idea." "Moctezuma" replies that "one does not always have to follow the Greeks' example." He points out to "Cortés" that the arts in America advanced without the Greeks and were "more admirable than even the arts in Europe. . . . You must agree that the Spanish found mysteries in our land that they did not understand . . . for example, monumental stones that they could not conceive of how to elevate without machines. . . . What do you say to that?"[72]

Two months after the publication of the "Dialogue" (possibly in response to "Moctezuma's" question), a Spanish translation of the exiled creole Jesuit Pedro José Márquez's *Description of Two Ancient Monuments of Mexican Architecture* appeared in the *Diario*.[73] Márquez's analysis complemented León y Gama's descriptions of the Piedra del Sol and the Coatlicue, building on Alzate's analysis of the ruins of Xochicalco. Márquez, through his well-honed classicizing optic, drew favorable comparisons between Roman and Mexican architecture, such as that between the pyramid steps at Xochicalco and the Roman amphitheater. But if Márquez, like Dupaix, stopped short of arguing for complete parity between the architectural works of ancient Mexican societies and those of the Greeks, that did not mean that they were any less admirable or should be excluded from a register of antiquity. Márquez analyzed Mexican antiquity within the context of the theory of the common origin of mankind to argue that Greece, Rome, and Mexico drew from the same source of knowledge, but that Mexico was at a different stage in its cultural development.[74] In so doing, Márquez challenged the concept of a singular, classic universal aesthetic that denied validity to other antiquities characterized by their particular forms and that did not conform to the canonical standard of universal beauty.

Validation of "national" and "local" antiquities also found expression in other contributions to the *Diario*. An anonymous contributor, for example, hoped to raise sufficient subscriptions to fund the striking of a medal to celebrate the creation of the Supreme Central and Governing Junta of Sevilla and its role to coordinate resistance to Napoleon's invasion and occupation of Spain. The medal's design would illustrate ancient Mexican ruins and place them alongside revered ruins of antiquity, so that "we are all witnesses to the ruins of Troy . . . the antiquities of Palmyra, the monuments of Herculaneum, the bas-reliefs and obelisks of Rome, the pyramids of Egypt, the enormous *masas* of Mexico. . . . We will be the envy and admiration of the world."[75] Similar to Dupaix's declaration to the viceroy in 1817 that the discoveries made during his antiquities expeditions provided material to write "a history certainly worthy of the grandeur of the Spanish nation," the writer sought to create a visual expression of the value of ancient monuments globally that included those of Mexico.[76]

If the revindication of Mexican antiquity that appeared in the periodicals signaled recognition of its cultural and historical value, the same could not be said for its economic value. There is little evidence of the development of a local market for pre-Hispanic artifacts in New Spain, with subscribers aiming to buy or sell such objects, as occurred in the case of mineral collections. Acquisition of pre-Hispanic objects occurred through informal, unregulated practices, in which exchange, gifting, or donation dominated. Collectors' networks facilitated knowledge about persons interested in acquiring such objects, as did the instructions distributed to officials throughout New Spain for scientific expeditions and especially those of the Royal Antiquities Expedition, and in which indigenous governors and informants played a significant role. The bishop-antiquarian Moxó, for example, recounted how some indigenous villagers brought him a "beautiful head made in the time of their gentility." Their governor had told them of Moxó's interest, and they had brought the objects to him without requesting any payment.[77]

Conclusion

Meaning making about Mexican antiquities occurred through competing discourses that could value them as objects worthy of the most outstanding antiquarian collections and scientific study, as historical evidence to support instrumentalized narrations of national glory or barbarism, as having aesthetic appeal, or rejected as hideous and idolatrous, and banished from view. As Daniel Crespo has argued "the revindication of pre-Hispanic artistic patrimony was not accompanied by a revolution in the comprehension of the beautiful, a concept that continued to be defined based on the principles of classicism."[78] In the wake of Mexican independence, the question of where to place Mexican antiquities was partially resolved with the founding of the Museo Nacional de México in 1825, even as they would continue to be placed next to a miscellany of materials in the museum's early years. The four Postclassic sculptures were duly removed from the Real Academia de San Carlos to the Museo Nacional de México as described by Bernardo González at the beginning of this chapter. But even as the Museo Nacional de México began its work to assemble its collections of Mexican antiquity in a centralized location, it contended with the opposing forces of dispersal and disappearance of pre-Hispanic objects. It is somewhat ironic that the very individuals who made significant contributions to the collection of Mexican antiquity also contributed to its dispersal, sometimes intentionally, sometimes not, as these two examples—Dupaix's draftsman, Castañeda, and the judge and antiquarian González Carvajal—demonstrate.

Desperately in need of money, Castañeda sold a major collection of antiquities and manuscripts "that included 180 'idols,' statues of serpents and other animals, and some reliefs pertaining to the Royal Antiquarian Expeditions; 120 drawings by Dupaix and Castañeda; and a notebook that had belonged to Boturini."[79] After Latour Allard bought the collection, he sold it to a Mr. Melnotte, after several failed attempts to sell it to the Louvre. Mr. Melnotte, in turn, eventually sold it to the Louvre.[80] When González Carvajal returned to Spain, taking his collections with him, his fading fortunes resulted in the sale by his widow of some of the most outstanding pieces of his antiquities collection to John Wetherell in the 1830s. Wetherell subsequently donated them to the British Museum.[81]

Postindependence edicts on the Real Academia de San Carlos's renovation enshrined classicism as the benchmark of beauty and taste. In an 1823 report on the academy's future, emphasis was placed on "the collection of statues and drawings that illustrate all of the marvels of Greek and Roman sculpture, and that has been the source of good taste of our Nation."[82] And, if the government committed to the advancement of Mexico's artists by sending them to Rome, it also committed to the "conservation of the monuments of arts." The example cited for such conservation was Manuel Tolsá's bronze equestrian statue of Charles IV. Absent from such discussions is any mention of Mexican antiquity having a place in the reincarnated national arts academy and sharing space with its classical sculptures.[83] Yet, the contingencies that affected the collection and location of objects in the wake of Mexican independence—vision, interest, space, money, or lack thereof—are eloquently expressed in Pietro Gualdi's lithograph of the interior of the university patio (figure 1.6). Instead of ordering the equestrian statue's removal from the Plaza Mayor to the national arts academy, Lucás Alamán selected the university, the fledgling Museo Nacional's designated location.[84] There, the equestrian statue—by this time gaining fame internationally as one of the

Figure 1.6 Pietro Gualdi, "Interior of the University." *Monumentos de Mejico, tomados del natural y litografiados por Pedro Gualdi* (Mexico City: Massé y Decaen, 1841). Courtesy of the Beinecke Rare Book and Manuscript Library, Yale University.

masterpieces of neoclassical art—shared the same space as a pre-Hispanic monolith (possibly the Coatlicue, depicted in a fenced enclosure at the patio's left side; figure 1.7), thus bringing Mexican and classical antiquity back into conversation with one another, if only temporarily, and into the same orbit of Mexico's embryonic cultural patrimony.

Figure 1.7 Detail, pre-Hispanic monolith, Pietro Gualdi, "Interior of the University." *Monumentos de Mejico, tomados del natural y litografiados por Pedro Gualdi* (Mexico City: Massé y Decaen, 1841). Courtesy of the Beinecke Rare Book and Manuscript Library, Yale University.

Notes

I wish to acknowledge my co-editors, Miruna Achim and Sandra Rozental; the participants in the two-day workshop; Peter Mason; and Jc'q Smith, all of whom provided constructive feedback and suggestions.

1. González to President of RASC, June 20, 1825, doc. 2167, Antigua Archivo de la Academia de San Carlos, Universidad Nacional Autónoma de México.
2. Note that for the captions for figures 1.1–1.4, I have retained Dupaix's original descriptions with their contemporary archaeological descriptions in parentheses. For an important critical reading of the erasure of Dupaix's descriptions of Mexican antiquities, see Miruna Achim, "Writing Lessons in the History of Antiquarianism: The Manuscripts of Guillermo Dupaix," *Colonial Latin American Review* (forthcoming). The first three sculptures are currently on display in the Sala Mexica in the Museo Nacional de Antropología; the toad resides in the Museo de Escultura Mexica "Dr Eusebio Dávalos Hurtado," in Santa Cecilia Acatitlan, north of Mexico City. See Leonardo López Luján, *El capitán Guillermo Dupaix y su album arqueológico de 1794* (Mexico City: INAH, 2015), 94–121.
3. Elizabeth Franklin Lewis, Mónica Bolufer Peruga, and Catherine M. Jaffe, eds., *The Routledge Companion to the Hispanic Enlightenment* (London: Routledge, 2019).
4. On these collections see Clara Bargellini and Elizabeth Fuentes, *Guía que permite captar lo bello, yesos y dibujos de la Academia de San Carlos, 1778–1916* (Mexico City: UNAM/IIE, 1989).
5. Daniela Bleichmar, *Visible Empire: Botanical Expeditions and Visual Culture in the Hispanic Enlightenment* (Stanford, Calif.: Stanford University Press), 26.

6. See Leonardo López Luján, "The First Steps on a Long Journey: Archaeological Illustration in Eighteenth-Century New Spain," in *Past Presented: Archaeological Illustration and the Ancient Americas*, ed. Joanne Pillsbury (Washington D.C.: Dumbarton Oaks, 2012), 69–105.
7. Irina Podgorny, "The Reliability of the Ruins," *Journal of Spanish Cultural Studies* 8, no. 2 (2007): 213–33; 228.
8. Although I cannot develop this point further due to limited space, it is important to note that the concept of creole patriotism does not adequately capture the motivations behind the collection and study of Mexican antiquity, which has a very long history. See, for example, Lia Markey, *Imagining the Americas in Medici Florence* (University Park: Pennsylvania State University Press, 2016); and Elizabeth Horodowich and Lia Markey, eds., *The New World in Early Modern Italy, 1492–1750* (Cambridge: Cambridge University Press, 2017).
9. See Daniel Carey and Sven Trakulhn, "Universalism, Diversity, and the Postcolonial Enlightenment," in *The Postcolonial Enlightenment: Eighteenth-Century Colonialism and Postcolonial Theory*, ed. Daniel Carey and Lynn Festa (Oxford: Oxford University Press, 2009), 240–80. For an incisive discussion of material culture and cultural translation, see Peter Mason, "Periculosae plenum opus aleae: The 'Mensa Isiaca,' Lorenzo Pignoria and the Perils of Cultural Translation," in *Beyond Egyptomania: Objects, Style and Agency*, Studien aus dem Warburg-Haus, ed. Miguel John Versluys (Berlin: Walter De Gruyter, 2020), 133–49.
10. Miruna Achim, *From Idols to Antiquity: Forging the National Museum of Mexico* (Lincoln: University of Nebraska Press, 2017).
11. Gábor Klaniczay, Michael Werner, and Ottó Gecser, introduction to *Multiple Antiquities—Multiple Modernities: Ancient Histories in Nineteenth Century European Cultures*, ed. Gábor Klaniczay, Michael Werner, and Ottó Gecser (Frankfurt: Campus Verlag, 2011), 9. For recent revisionist approaches to antiquarianism and antiquarians, see Benjamin Anderson and Felipe Rojas, eds., *Antiquarianisms: Contact, Conflict, Comparison* (Oxford: Oxbow Books, 2017).
12. Herculaneum and Pompeii set a new standard for the practice of "scientific" archeological practice (although far from the protocols that the discipline developed in the late nineteenth century). See Andrea Milanese, "Exhibition and Experiment: A History of the Real Museo Borbónico," in *The Restoration of Ancient Bronzes: Naples and Beyond*, ed. Erik Risser and David Saunders (Los Angeles: Getty, 2013), 13–29. See also Maria del Carmen Alonso Rodríguez, "La antigüedad al servicio del rey: La difusión del gusto Pompeyano en España en el siglo XVIII," *Cuadernos dieciochistas* 19 (2018): 105–37.
13. The eight volumes appeared between 1757 and 1792. In New Spain, descriptions of antiquity appeared as early as 1748. See Leonardo López Luján, "*Alia Herculanea*: Pre-Hispanic Sites and Antiquities in Late Bourbon New Spain," in *Altera Roma: Art and Empire from Mérida to Mexico*, ed. John M. D. Pohl

and Claire L. Lyons (Los Angeles: Cotsen Institute of Archaeology Press, 2016), 313–42.

14. Daniel Crespo Delgado, "El 'gran mapa de la humanidad' y las Bellas Artes prehispánicas durante la Ilustración," *Anuario de Estudios Americanos* 65, no. 2 (2008): 125–50.
15. Historia, vol. 110, exp. 2, fols. 17–41, Archivo General de la Nación (AGN).
16. Ortiz y Sanz quoted in José Miguel Morán Turina and Delfín Rodríguez Ruiz, *El legado de la antigüedad: Arte, arquitectura y arqueología en la España* (Madrid: Ediciones Istmo, 2001), 145. On Spain's antiquities expeditions and collections see Martín Almagro Gorbea and Jorge Maier Allende, eds., *De Pompeya al Nuevo Mundo: La Corona Española y la arqueología en el siglo XVIII* (Madrid: Real Academia de la Historia: Patrimonio Nacional, 2012); and José Miguel Morán Turina, *La memoria de las piedras: Anticuarios, arqueólogos y colecciones de antigüedades en la España de los Austrias* (Madrid: Centro de Estudios Europa Hispánica, 2010).
17. Dupaix's reports and illustrations were not published until after his death. See López Luján, *El capitán*; and Elena Isabel Estrada de Gerlero, *Guillermo Dupaix: Precursor de la historia del arte prehispánico* (Mexico City: Instituto de Investigaciones Estéticas/INAH, 2017).
18. Jorge Maier Allende, "La corona y la institucionalización de la arqueología," in Almagro Gorbea and Maier Allende, *De Pompeya al Nuevo Mundo*, 340.
19. The official post of "antiquarian" at the Real Academia de la Historia was created in 1763.
20. See Jorge Cañizares-Esguerra, *How to Write the History of the New World: Histories, Epistemologies, and Identities in the Eighteenth-Century Atlantic World* (Stanford, Calif.: Stanford University Press, 2001). Muñoz was especially interested in comparing New World pre-Hispanic ruins with those of Pompeii and Herculaneum. See also Antonio E. de Pedro Robles, "La real expedición anticuaria de México (1805–1808), y la representación del imaginario indianista del siglo XIX," *Anales del Museo de América* 17 (2009): 42–63.
21. This was one of four new offices into which the Real Academia de la Historia was divided. The other three were the Diccionario Geográfico, Historia de Indias, and Gobierno. Maier Allende, "La corona," 356.
22. Jorge García Sánchez, "La Real Academia de San Fernando y la arqueología," *Academia*, nos. 106–7 (2008): 30–32.
23. Export of paintings from Spain was prohibited in 1779, but the prohibition proved difficult to enforce. The Real Academia de la Historia drafted the document on which the 1803 royal decree to protect and preserve ancient monuments was based. See Jorge Maier Allende, "II Centenario de la Real cédula de 1803: La Real Academia de la Historia y el inicio de la legislación sobre patrimonio arqueológico y monumental en España," *Boletín de la Real Academia de la Historia* (2003): 439–73. The antiquities specifically stipulated were Roman, Punic, Christian, Visigothic, Arab, and Medieval. The decree did not prohibit

export of antiquities, require a license to excavate, or provide sanctions against violations of the law's provisions.

24. Maier Allende, "La corona," 357.
25. On the "indiscriminate sacking and pillage of works of art" following Napoleon's invasion of Spain in December 1808, see Ignacio Cano Rivero, "Seville's Artistic Heritage during the French Occupation," in *Manet/Velázquez: The French Taste for Spanish Painting*, ed. Gary Tinterow and Geneviève Lacambre (New Haven, Conn.: Yale University Press, 2003), 98–99.
26. Article 13, *Instrucciones que la Gobernación de Ultramar del Superior Gobierno . . . hace a los Diputaciones Provinciales*, quoted in Elena Isabel Estrada de Gerlero, "Carlos IV y los estudios anticuarios en Nueva España," in *1492–1992: V Centenario arte e historia*, ed. Xavier Moyssén Echeverría and Louise Noelle (Mexico City: Instituto de Investigaciones Estéticas; Universidad Nacional Autónoma de México 1993), 84.
27. Klaniczay, Werner, and Gecser, *Multiple Antiquities*. For discussion of "poles of curiosity" within antiquity—classical and the local or national—see Krzysztof Pomian, "Les deux poles de la curiosité antiquaire," in *L'Anticomanie: la collection d'antiquités aux 18e et 19e siècles*, ed. Annie-France Laurence and Krzysztof Pomian (Paris: École des Hautes Études en Sciences Sociales, 1992), 59–68.
28. On antiquities' capacity to "offer instruction to their viewers through the creation of a visible historical narrative," see Susan Crane, "Curious Cabinets and Imaginary Museums," in *Museums and Memory*, ed. Susan Crane (Stanford, Calif.: Stanford University Press, 2000), 75.
29. San Ildefonso lies fifty miles north of Madrid, in the province of Segovia, Spain. Note that Azara's point was not to reject classicism outright but to appreciate localized expressions of its forms. See Andrés Ubeda de los Cobos, "El mito de la escultura clásica en la España ilustrada," in *La Visión del mundo clásico en el arte español* (Madrid: Editorial Alpuerto, 1993), 330.
30. Dupaix to Apodaca, January 1817, Guillermo Dupaix Papers, 1804–1820, Benson Latin American Collection, General Libraries, University of Texas at Austin (BLAC).
31. I borrow the term from Elliot Colla's study of Egypt, *Conflicted Antiquities: Egyptology, Egyptomania, Egyptian Modernity* (Durham, N.C.: Duke University Press, 2008).
32. Delfín Rodríguez Ruiz, "De la Torre de Babel a Vitruvio: origen y significado de la arquitectura," in Morán Turina and Rodríguez Ruiz, *El legado de la antigüedad*, 111–12.
33. Enrique Florescano, "The Creation of the Museo Nacional de Antropología of Mexico and Its Scientific, Educational, and Political Purposes," in *Collecting the Pre-Columbian Past*, ed. Elizabeth Hill Boone (Washington, D.C.: Dumbarton Oaks Research Library and Collection, 1993). On the creole Jesuit and historian Francisco Javier Clavijero's lament about the lack of a professor of antiquities on the faculty of the Royal University of Mexico City, see David A. Brading, *The*

First America: The Spanish Monarchy, Creole Patriots, and the Liberal State, 1492–1867 (Cambridge: Cambridge University Press, 1991), 456.

34. Leonardo López Luján, "Archaeological Collections in Mesoamerica and New Spain," in *100 Selected Works: National Museum of Anthropology* (Mexico City: INAH/Artes de México, 2011), 21.
35. The Real Academia de la Historia argued that many of the antiquities discovered "belong to the fine arts" and as such should be assessed by the Real Academia de San Fernando. García Sánchez, "La Real Academia de San Fernando," 30–34.
36. González Carvajal sat on the Real Academia de San Carlos's governing board from 1797 to 1809 and was appointed as an honorary academician from 1793 to 1796 and 1810 to 1821. He served on the Mexico City Audiencia from 1790 to 1809. Among his many official positions and scholarly affiliations, he was a corresponding academician of the Real Academia de la Historia and its Junta de Antigüedades, and in 1819 he was named conservator of the ruins of Itálica.
37. Iturrigaray to Dupaix, June 3, 1808, Guillermo Dupaix Papers, BLAC. The Junta de Antigüedades' members included González Carvajal, Dupaix, the creole canon José Mariano Beristáin y Souza, and Ignacio Ignacio Cubas, archivist of the viceregal archives.
38. See López Luján, *El capitán*, and Estrada de Gerlero, *Guillermo Dupaix*, for further discussion of their roles. Dupaix referred to González Carvajal as "Father defender of the Expedition" and "Father Protector and Lover of the Arts," in letters to the judge on July 12, 1813, and March 28, 1813, respectively, Guillermo Dupaix Papers, BLAC. Dupaix appointed Elhuyar as the executor of his estate.
39. Several items from his collection were illustrated by Dupaix in his 1794 album. See Francisco Martín Blázquez, "Composición, trayectoria y vicisitudes ocurridas a la colección de objetos naturales y antigüedades prehispánicas del magistrado Ciriaco González Carvajal," in *Actas del I congreso internacional de jóvenes investigadores. Coleccionismo, mecenazgo y mercado artístico en España e Iberoamérica*, ed. Antonio Holguera Cabrera, Ester Prieto Ustío, and María Uriondo Lozano (Sevilla: Universidad de Sevilla, 2017), 772.
40. Dupaix noted Polanco's "affinity" for antiquities. Whether this indicated that Polanco owned a small collection of pre-Hispanic artifacts is unclear. See López Luján, *El capitán*, 74. Castañeda received one of the four academy scholarships designated specifically for indigenous students.
41. Both artists were academicians of merit of the Real Academia de San Fernando. Gil engraved the plates for the illustrations of the Visigoth ruins of Talavera la Vieja, the *Antigüedades árabes de España*, and the *Discurso sobre las monedas árabes y algunas inscripciones cúficas con tablas de estos monumentos* (1784). Ximeno's work appears in many of the most important historical works published in Spain in the second half of the eighteenth century, such as the *Historia General de España*, by Father Juan de Mariana (Valencia: Oficina de D. Benito Monfort, 1796).

42. Benito María de Moxó, *Cartas mejicanas escritas por d. Benito María de Moxó en 1805, dadas á luz á impulsos del Revmo. P. Fr. Andrés Herrero* (Genova: Tipografía Pellas, 1837). Moxó lived in Mexico in 1804 and 1805, during which time the Real Academia de San Carlos appointed him as an honorary academician. Ximeno painted the gouaches of Moxó's collection, on which several copper engravings were based that appeared in his *Cartas mejicanas* (first published in 1837). See López Luján, "First Steps," 97.
43. Dupaix to González Carvajal, March 28, 1813, Guillermo Dupaix Papers, BLAC.
44. López Luján, "First Steps," 98. Not all sophisticated interpreters of Mexican antiquity maintained a close relationship with the academy, most notably, Antonio de Léon y Gama and José Antonio de Alzate y Ramírez.
45. On the role of military engineers in the discovery and description of antiquities, see Podgorny, "Reliability of the Ruins."
46. Antonio de León y Gama, *Descripción histórica y cronológica de las dos piedras*, ed. Carlos María de Bustamante (Mexico City: Imprenta del Ciudadano Alejandro Valdés, 1832), 11–12.
47. León y Gama, *Descripción histórica*, 81.
48. León y Gama, *Descripción histórica*, 11.
49. Alexander von Humboldt, *Views of the Cordilleras and Monuments of the Indigenous Peoples of the Americas: A Critical Edition*, ed. Vera M. Kutzinski and Ottmar Ette, trans. J. Ryan Poynter (Chicago: University of Chicago Press, 2012), 320, 324.
50. Dupaix examined a polychromed ceramic musical instrument, possibly a flute or whistle, at the house of don Antonio Arriaga, a surveyor, in Coyoacán. López Luján, *El capitán*, 215.
51. López Luján, "Archaeological Collections," 22.
52. See López Luján, *El capitán*, 72–74.
53. Alexander von Humboldt, *Political Essay on the Kingdom of New Spain* (New York: AMS Press, 1966), 159–60, emphases added.
54. *Libro de Inventario de la Academia, 1817*, Acervo Histórico Gráfico Antigua Academia de San Carlos, Universidad Nacional Autónoma de México, Facultad de Artes y Diseño. No entries appear for any of the sculptures in the inventory of the academy's collections taken in 1808.
55. López Luján, *El capitán*, 96.
56. López Luján, *El capitán*, 104.
57. See, for example, Estrada de Gerlero, *Guillermo Dupaix*.
58. González Carvajal to Iturrigaray, August 1, 1803, fols. 1–125, Historia, vol. 116, AGN.
59. Humboldt, as George Kubler observed, distinguished "between works of art and monuments, the latter being inferior to the former and so was critical of Mesoamerican artistic production. . . . [H]is position remained ambivalent between aesthetics from above and below, unresolved between ideal and material study." See Kubler's *Esthetic Recognition of Ancient Amerindian Art* (New Haven, Conn.:

Yale University Press, 1991), 99–100. Eloise Quiñones Keber provides a more sympathetic interpretation of Humboldt's assessment of Mexican Antiquity in "Humboldt and Aztec Art," *Colonial Latin American Review* 5, no. 2 (1996): 277–97; see also Oscar H. Flores Flores, "Neoclassical Taste and Antiquarian Scholarship: The Royal Academy of the Three Noble Arts of San Carlos of Mexico, Alexander von Humboldt and Pedro José Márquez," in *The Routledge Handbook on the Reception of Classical Architecture*, ed. Nicholas Temple, Andrzej Piotrowski, and Juan Manuel Heredia (New York: Routledge, 2019), 110–34.

60. Humboldt, *Views*, 88, 280.
61. Guillermo Dupaix, "The Monuments of New Spain," in Edward King, *Antiquities of Mexico* (London: A. Aglio, 1830–48), 454, 432.
62. Dupaix, "Monuments," 433, 434.
63. Dupaix, "Monuments," 464.
64. González Carvajal to Iturrigaray, August 1, 1803.
65. Moxó, *Cartas*, 92.
66. Dupaix and Moxó most likely knew one another and discussed their collections. See Moxó's praise of Dupaix's collection of Mexican antiquities, *Cartas*, 92.
67. Bonavía to viceroy, September 5, 1790, Historia en General, vol. 2254, exp. 22, Archivo Histórico de la Ciudad de México.
68. Florescano, "Creation of the Museo Nacional de Antropología," 86.
69. Constanzó to Ignacio de Iglesias Pablo, March 10, 1795, Indiferente Virreinal, vol. 2865, exp. 7, AGN.
70. On these earlier writings, see Miruna Achim, "Signos y piedras: La literatura anticuaria en búsqueda de la historia Mexicana," in *Entre textos e imágenes: Representaciones antropológicas de la América indígena*, ed. Fermín del Pino-Díaz, Pascal Riviale, and Juan J. R. Villarías-Robles (Madrid: CSIC, 2009), 17–26.
71. As one of the *Diario*'s editors, Carlos María de Bustamante's patriotic commitment to Mexican antiquity undoubtedly influenced increased attention to it in the newspaper. On Bustamante's antiquarian interests, see Achim, *From Idols to Antiquity*.
72. "Dialogue between Cortés and Moctezuma," *Diario de México* (*DM*), May 24, 1808. When I first came across this anonymous "dialogue," I speculated that Dupaix had written it; however, it is excerpted from Bernard de Fontenelle, *Dialogues des Morts* (1684).
73. "Dos monumentos de arquitectura Mexicana: Tajín y Xochicalco," *DM*, July 27, 1808, taken from Pedro Márquez, "Las efemérides literarias de Roma," no. 29, July 19, 1806. Márquez corresponded regularly with the Real Academia de San Carlos and donated a series of classical prints for teaching purposes to it. See Oscar Flores Flores, ed., *El clasicismo en al época de Pedro José Márquez (1741–1820): Arqueología, filología, historia, música y teoría arquitectónica* (Mexico: Universidad Nacional Autónoma de México, Instituto de Investigaciones Estéticas, Real Academia de Bellas Artes de San Fernando, 2014); and his "Neoclassical Taste and Antiquarian Scholarship."

74. Juana Gutiérrez Haces, "Los antiguos mexicanos, Vitruvio y el padre Márquez," in *Historia, leyendas y mitos de México: su expresión en el arte* (Mexico City: Universidad Nacional Autónoma de México/Instituto de Investigaciones Estéticas, 1988), 194–96.
75. *DM*, February 18, 1809. The subscriptions did not materialize, so neither did the medal.
76. Dupaix to Apodaca, January 1817, G339, Guillermo Dupaix Papers, 1804–1820, BLAC.
77. Moxó, *Cartas*, 91.
78. Crespo Delgado, "El 'gran mapa,'" 144.
79. Achim, *From Idols to Antiquity*, 59–60.
80. See Marie-France Fauvet-Berthelot, Leonardo López Luján, and Susana Guimarâes, "The *Real Expedición Anticuaria* Collection," in *Fanning the Sacred Flame: Mesoamerican Studies in Honor of H. B. Nicholson*, ed. Matthew A. Boxt and Brian D. Dillon (Boulder: University Press of Colorado, 2012), 461–88. Although the French commission assigned to assess the collection recommended its acquisition, it would be for its historical value, not as "art objects . . . as they are the product of a civilization that became stationary after its first tries of Art" (473).
81. Wetherell's catalog itemized ninety-five artifacts, nine of which were illustrated in Dupaix's album of 1794. Blázquez, "Composición, trayectoria y vicisitudes," 773. Wetherell's father, Nathan, also contributed to the dispersal of Spanish antiquities with his purchase of a large collection of archaeological artifacts from Itálica. Cano Rivero, "Seville's Artistic Heritage," 102.
82. Sonia Lombardo de Ruiz and Ruth Solís Vicarte, *Antecedentes de las leyes sobre monumentos históricos (1536–1910)* (Mexico City: INAH, 1988), 34–35.
83. Lombardo de Ruiz and Solís Vicarte, *Antecedentes*, 36–38.
84. As Ministro de Relaciones Interiores e Exteriores, Alamán ordered the bronze equestrian statue's relocation in 1823 to protect it from possible destruction. Presumably, this was also a pragmatic decision given the academy's temporary closure and deteriorated condition, as well as the statue's size. The statue would be moved in 1852 and again in 1979 to what is now its permanent location in the Plaza Tolsá, in front of the Museo Nacional de Arte. On the peripatetic history of the equestrian statue, see Seth Dixon, "Mobile Monumental Landscapes: Shifting Cultural Identities in Mexico City's '*El Caballito*,'" *Historical Geography* 37 (2009): 71–91.

\\ 2

Forgery and the Science of the "Authentic"

MIRUNA ACHIM AND BERTINA OLMEDO VERA

Vast storerooms sprawl in the basement of the Museo Nacional de Antropología. Out of sight of the public, in the museum's inner sanctuary, tightly packed on movable compact shelving, sit crates full of bones, mummified bodies, and human-made artifacts, corresponding to the cultural periods and regions that organize the display rooms of the museum above. Other objects, smaller and more fragile—clay seals, silex arrowheads, obsidian tools, jadeite jewelry, and small ceramic fragments—are stored in drawers, gingerly encased in protective material. Each object comes with its own inventory label, and in some cases with two or more time-weathered labels—speaking to the history of the object in the museum, as it underwent various inventories—sometimes with numbers and place of origin recorded directly onto it, as was common practice until the mid-twentieth century. In May 2019, after completing the entrance protocol with the police guard, we made our way into the archaeology storeroom. This time we were not here to admire those exemplars of national patrimony that spill over from the exhibit space above; we had come to look at things that most of the museum's curators have lost interest in: fakes.[1] Unlike the museum's "authentic" objects, its fakes sit crammed together on ten shelves in the back of the archaeology storeroom, in no apparent order, certainly not organized by culture or type—for what culture or type or provenance can be assigned to an object made in the nineteenth or twentieth centuries? Most of them lack inventory labels, although some do have them, which means that, at some point, they were part of the museum's collection and only later deemed to be forgeries and segregated to form part of this gathering of outcasts. To make matters more confusing, there are possibly authentic objects, of uncertain provenance, among them, temporarily awaiting a curator's verdict.

We walk toward the corner with a mixture of fascination, horror, and condescension, with a sense, coming only in retrospect, that we would have never been duped by a fake, that we knew better. In some cases, we did: the representation of a rather misshapen monkey-like creature with obsidian encrusted into its chest and amber beads into its eyes; a "deity" with incongruous medieval crown-like gear on its heads; a female figurine grinning its perfect set of teeth; a mother and child composition of porous volcanic stone, amorously embracing, harking back to images of Virgin Mary with child; carved details that immediately betray the use of metal tools; and many, many paperweight-like heads of stone, eyes squinting, mouths gaping in horror (figure 2.1). Many of these objects form a class of their own, incomparable, unique, different from any other artifact, both among fakes and among authentic artifacts. "Why didn't forgers at least make them agreeable or beautiful?" wonders Bertina, the archaeologist and curator of the Sala Mexica in our team of two. "Maybe because, for a large part of the nineteenth century, pre-Hispanic objects were considered ugly, deformed, or bizarre, so making them 'ugly' might have been a way of imbuing them with the air of an ancient pre-Hispanic past," ventures Miruna, the historian. We stop to wonder how the criteria for telling not the fake but the authentic came about, what made something plausibly authentic at different moments.

In many cases, discovering why or whether an object on these shelves is a fake is taxing. To our eyes, many look "authentic." In other cases, "something simply doesn't feel right." Ultimately, a thin line separates the "authentic" from the "fake"—so thin and porous, in fact, that we keep placing certain objects back and forth, now on one side of the divide, now on the other. Make the criteria for differentiation too rigid, and there is no room for regional variation or for human agency—that is, for the ancient artisan with a personal signature style or for the artisan in the periphery, striving to reproduce objects made for the elites. And, of course, there is no room for the unique, for that one artifact that is different from all others, which could be a fake but could also be a masterpiece. But then, too many objects of the same kind

Figure 2.1 Objects of undetermined provenance—possibly archaeological fakes—at the Museo Nacional de Antropología. Archivo Digital de las Colecciones del Museo Nacional de Antropología. INAH-CANON. Reproduction authorized by the Instituto Nacional de Antropología e Historia.

can also be a reason for alarm. As Eliseo Padilla, the curator of the Sala de Occidente, succinctly puts it, "How many ceramic dogs from Colima are too many? Did people in Western Mexico do nothing for hundreds of years but make these cute and chubby dogs, to inter them in shaft tombs, where they would be discovered in the late nineteenth century, starting a collection craze that endures to our days?"[2] When the criteria for authenticity are too broad, many fakes pass as authentic. Besides these more subjective stylistic calls, chemical and physical analyses, involving increasingly sophisticated technologies, have contributed to developing a science of authenticity. But, like style, "scientific" methods have revealed that the line between the fake and the authentic is far from rigid. In some cases, certificates of authenticity based on new techniques of analyses are not enough to persuade researchers in a field that an object is authentic.[3] The bottom line, as restorer Sergio González at the Museo Nacional de Antropología suggests, is that all objects of unknown provenance or lacking strict excavation protocols and records are suspect.[4] Of course, not all of them are fakes.

How, then, is one to proceed in telling the authentic from the fake? This is a question asked since the nineteenth century by museums, collectors, dealers, and often the forgers themselves. It is a question whose answers are intimately entangled with ideas about aesthetic and commercial value, proof making, scientific authority, expertise, and institutional credibility. The problem with fakes was not a problem until fakes were perceived as a threat, economically, to the antiquities market; epistemically, to the scientific disciplines that were becoming consolidated in the second half of the nineteenth century; and institutionally, to national museums that staked their authority on their capacity to collect and display the "authentic" as "synonyms for cultures congealed in historical time."[5] Fakes have always been part of museums, yet most museums treat their fakes with little care, proportionally inverse to the care and attention they enjoyed when they were thought to be authentic. A fake speaks of gullibility or ignorance. Once something is exposed to be a fake, its inventory number is discontinued, and the object is banished out of sight, into a basement. Until recently, alleging limited space, most museums have gotten rid of their fakes altogether, forgetting thereby how fakes entered their collection in the first place; how they were studied, classified, and displayed; as well as the individual and collective decisions that banished them.[6] Specific fakes have sometimes fared better, finding a place in scholarly literature, as early as the nineteenth century, because they make for fascinating detective stories and enlightening case studies with provocative theoretical implications.[7] But in general, fakes are simply forgotten. In the case of the Museo Nacional de Antropología, there is no history of its fakes.[8] In fact, there is little awareness among the museum's employees about when and why fakes began accumulating at the back of the archaeology storeroom, and, more importantly, about what happened to the rest of the fakes held by the museum at different moments.

This chapter is a first approach to the collections of archaeological fakes accrued and lost at Mexico's national museums over the course of almost two centuries, as the museum peregrinated from place to place, probably taking each move as a pretext to rid itself of what it took to be fakes. We are interested in thinking through how to tell the story of the museum not only through its personnel, publications, and choice specimens, but through its relationship with forgery. First, this mundane and practical kind of relation tied the museum with the world of forgers and traffickers in fakes, not only because the museum sought to separate itself from this underworld, but because it was implicated at different times in the production and acquisition of forgeries, both knowingly and unknowingly. Second, there is an epistemological connection between fakes and "authentic" objects at the museum. The "authentic" is that which is not "fake." So, while the burden of proof has mostly consisted in determining whether something is fake (and not whether it is authentic), the methods and protocols for exposing a forgery—many of which come from the natural sciences—have contributed to shaping and reinforcing the methods for studying authenticity, for instance, by generating stylistic taxonomies and by examining marks of fabrication and processes of aging by different materials. Finally, the criteria for telling a fake apart have changed over the course of two hundred years, and those changes are not just a matter of better and more objective methods but have to do with aesthetic, political, and cultural projections and expectations about the pre-Hispanic past. As art historian Esther Pasztory has suggestively put it, "Fakes tell us what we want to see in the authentic. . . . If we want to understand how collectors saw Aztec art, we have to interrogate the forgery that was made to fit their tastes and interests."[9] What did the museum, and more widely, dealers, private collectors, and scholars, want to see in Mexico's ancient past at any specific moment? What were their expectations regarding the technical expertise, manufacturing practices, aesthetic ideals, and cultural provenance of Mexico's ancient peoples?

The Grotesque, the Ugly, and the Beautiful

Fakes at the Museo Nacional de Antropología are not a new phenomenon, not even a twentieth-century one. Leopoldo Batres, at the head of the Inspectorate for Archaeological Monuments between the late nineteenth and the early twentieth centuries, traced falsification to the sixteenth century and located it in the Mexico City barrio of Tlatelolco, which had specialized in ceramic production since pre-Hispanic times. In the years following the conquest, Tlatelolco's kilns began turning out ceramic ware for the Spanish conquistadors, and at that moment, according to Batres, Tlatelolco became an "emporium for fantastic and imitative ceramics."[10] Responding to Spanish taste, local artisans made all sorts of "fantastic" objects: pots "decorated with gods, their lip replete with as many whistles as notes on the chromatic scale," jars with snake-shaped handles, human figurines imitating gods, coiling serpents, flutes shaped like clarinets, lizards, and monsters.[11] Sometimes ancient molds, or molds made from original ancient pieces, were used. This industry persisted into the 1860s, when, Batres writes, Tlatelolco became increasingly mestizo and European.[12] It is difficult to know why Batres thought of these locally produced ceramics as falsifications and not simply as the persistence of an artisanal tradition, which struggled to keep up with and to adapt to new demands for everyday ware. Batres's concern, clearly, has to do with the ensuing confusion and distortion of evidence once these artifacts began to pass for original pre-Hispanic ceramics. These same concerns led Batres to reject all objects produced in the postconquest years as fakes, including colonial codices.

It is unlikely that sixteenth-century ceramics were made to pass for pre-Hispanic ware in the colonial period. Instead, for the origins of mass falsifications, we need to look at the turn of the nineteenth century, which saw, on the one hand, a new intellectual involvement with the vestiges of long-gone worlds, leading to the formation of cabinets and collections of antiquities, such as the one at the Museo Nacional de México. On the other hand, Mexico's aperture, as an independent nation, to foreign investment, commerce, diplomacy, and travel saw an influx of foreign merchants, speculators, diplomats, and tourists, some of whom took a scholarly or commercial interest in antiquities. As early as the 1820s, Jean Frédéric de Waldeck, a French artist and collector of Mexican antiquities—who would make a name for himself as draftsman for the Museo Nacional de México and as one of the earlier and more systematic explorers of Palenque—expresses doubts that Carl Nebel, a fellow artist, might have been peddling him fakes to test his acumen. Nebel had presented Waldeck with fragments of codices and with a small ceramic version of the Piedra del Sol, the famous so-called Mexican Calendar. "Is it a fake?" Waldeck asks himself. Under a magnifying glass, he discerns traces of color—blue, red, yellow, and brown—but he suspects that, though the pigments seem old, they could have been polished down to give them patina. "What if the relief is of Nebel's making, to take me by surprise and mock me afterwards? If this is the case, he was successful in achieving a perfect imitation, but not in deceiving me."[13] Unlike Waldeck, most foreigners did not come to Mexico to collect antiquities, and they were far less discerning. They took up collecting on the side, which brought them into competition with each other and with the Museo Nacional de México. Forgers stepped in to satisfy demand.

By the midcentury, the museum owned a collection of fakes. In a rare gesture, rather than hiding them away, and despite lacking exhibit and storage space, the museum, under the direction of José Fernando Ramírez (1804–71), one of its most competent directors, decided to put its fakes on display sometime in the midfifties. There is no record of the museum's fakes in institutional archives at that moment; the only description of this early display survives in the writings of Englishman Edward Burnett Tylor (1832–1917), who would later become associated with the foundations of cultural anthropology. His impressions of the museum—which Tylor visited in 1856, in the context of his year-long travels through Mexico—were mostly unfavorable, with extended comments on the chaos that reigned within, even as he had words of praise and admiration about specific objects. He found himself especially intrigued by the presence of a "particularly instructive shelf" there, which contained "numbers of sham antiquities." Their manufacture was "a regular thing in Mexico, as it [was] in Italy"—he felt compelled to add, in response to those who insisted there was no manufacturing of pre-Hispanic fakes in Mexico.[14]

For Tylor, the telltale sign of fakes was their departure from pre-Hispanic representations of Amerindian physiognomies. By careful examination, Tylor came up with a list of the more common errors committed by forgers:

> The foreheads of Mexican races are all very low and their painters and sculptors even exaggerated this particularity, to make the faces they depicted

> more beautiful, so producing an effect which to us Europeans seems hideously ugly, but which is not more natural than the ideal type of beauty we see in the Greek statues. After the era of the Spaniards, we see no more such foreheads; and the eyes, which were drawn in profiles as one sees them in the full face, are put in their natural position. . . . Short, squat figures become slim and tall. It is very seldom that the modern counterfeiter can keep clear of these and get back to the old standard. Among the things on the condemned shelf were faces too correctly drawn to be genuine, grotesque animals that no *artista* would . . . have designed who had not seen a horse, headdresses and drapery that were European and not Mexican.[15]

At stake in Tylor's—and the museum's—characterization of fakes is the recognition of different ideals of beauty, as centered on the representation of the human figure. What Amerindians considered beautiful—low foreheads and short, squat figures—is simply hideous and ugly to the eyes of Europeans, who take the nude Greek male body as their ideal. So, any human figurine that conforms to what a Westerner would consider beautiful or correct or "natural" is a potential fake. In his short description, Tylor does not side with one set of conventions over the other, suggesting they are both equally arbitrary. But he does identify one of the more important aesthetic criteria that has shaped approaches to the pre-Hispanic since the late eighteenth century and continues to do so today: the divide between the beautiful and the ugly.

In the 1810s, Alexander von Humboldt published *Vues de cordillères et monuments des peuples indigènes de l'Amérique*, an album of sixty-nine illustrations and descriptions of American "monuments," both natural and human made. On the whole, Humboldt qualified the vestiges of America's ancient past as bizarre, hideous, and singular, and saw them as embodiments of larger forces: the sublime and agitated topography of the Americas (for emphasis and comparison, Humboldt placed pre-Hispanic antiquities side by side with volcanoes and other grand geological formations), and the political and religious structures that limited individual freedom. Even if American antiquities seemingly lacked aesthetic worth, Humboldt did not consider them "unworthy of attention"; their worth was as objects of the science of humanity's past: "The grossest of works, the most bizarre of forms, those masses of sculpted stone, which impose themselves only through sheer bigness and by the high antiquity one attributes to them, those enormous pyramids that show the coming together of a multitude of workers, all this can be connected to the philosophical study of history. . . . They offer to our eyes a picture of the uniform and progressive march of the human spirit."[16]

The vestiges left behind by America's ancient peoples made manifest its place in universal histories of progress—where Western European civilization occupied the highest rung—that were the hallmark of Enlightenment historiography. Humboldt was not the first European to identify the productions of the American other with the grotesque, but his *Vues* became an obligatory reference for the study of American antiquities and certainly reinforced that stereotype, especially at a time when the study of American antiquities lacked a set of conventions—a language and a visual syntax—for their description and interpretation. Although not everyone agreed with Humboldt's aesthetic dictum (see Deans-Smith in this volume), many collectors and museum curators, well into the nineteenth century, continued to see the vestiges of America's ancient past as grotesque. In due time, forgers did their best to cast this vision of the authentic onto their creations.

One of the more notorious episodes in the history of Mexican fakes is the mass production of black ceramic ware, epitomized by a type of vase, of "notable form, . . . modelled in dark clay, and bristling with a superabundance of figures in relief, which gave a castellated effect," a possible take on the black ceramic ware made at Tlatelolco over centuries (figure 2.2).[17] The vase enjoyed lavish popularity among collectors in the second half of the nineteenth century, to become the object of scholarly vituperation by the late century. In 1886, W. H. Holmes, a geologist and archaeologist specializing in North American antiquities, who later became head of the Bureau of American Ethnology at the Smithsonian, wrote a short essay, "The Trade in Spurious Mexican Antiquities," where he presents one of the earliest descriptions of the vase:

> The body of these vases is usually a short, upright cylinder, mounted on three feet, and is profusely decorated with incised patterns and with a variety of ornaments, including human and animal figures in the round. A row of figures surrounds the rim, giving a battlemented effect; and a high conical lid, surmounted by a human figure, is usually added. The body of the vessel is modelled by hand. The attached figures are formed separately in molds, and afterwards set in their places. Certain parts are further elaborated by means of figured stamps.[18]

Holmes was among the first to document the bustling traffic in black ceramic ware. In the 1880s, he was working as a geologist for the Central Mexican Railway, and his travels around Mexico convinced him that there was a tight connection between fakes and trains, which brought ruins, especially those in the vicinity of Mexico City, even closer to it. Trains made the ruins at Teotihuacan, some forty-five kilometers from Mexico City, into a center for the production and distribution of black ceramic ware.[19] Holmes paints the following scene of the "antiquities" market at Teotihuacan:

EXAMPLE OF MODERN-ANTIQUE MEXICAN VASE (HEIGHT, 11 IN.).

Figure 2.2 Black ceramic ware. From W. H. Holmes, "The Trade in Spurious Mexican Antiquities," *Science* 7, no. 159 (1886): 172. Reprinted with permission from the American Association for the Advancement of Science.

> In passing back and forth by the railway, I found that each train was met by one or more of the venders, who were careful to expose but a limited number of the pieces, and that this method of sale was systematically practiced. Wishing to secure a piece, I waited until the train was about to move off, when I held out a silver dollar, and the vase . . . was quickly in my possession. The price asked was five dollars, and in the city of Mexico would have been three times that amount. At the rate of purchase indicated by my experience at San Juan [Teotihuacan] at least one piece per day was carried away by tourists, making hundreds each year.[20]

Hundreds of these objects most likely ended up on mantelpieces as family heirlooms, but some passed as "authentic" and made their way into museum collections, as donations or acquisitions, as was the case with the "miniature stone fort" or the "Chinese pagoda in clay"—as Holmes derisively calls two black ceramic vases that ended up at the Smithsonian.

By the end of the nineteenth century, many museums—in Mexico City, Vienna, London, and Washington, D.C.—owned too many vases of this kind: "It is not wonderful that museums in all parts of the world are becoming well stocked with this class of Mexican antiquities," wrote Holmes. His concern was above all intellectual: fakes distorted the understanding of the past. Though he did not doubt that "they will be detected in time and thrown out," he was worried that "in the meantime, they will have made an impression upon literature." Holmes's article is meant as an antidote of sorts against forgers' ruses to make these vases pass for genuine pre-Hispanic antiquities. He urged collectors not to fall for an aged look, which forgers achieved by burying the piece in moist earth to prepare it for the market or by washing it with a thin solution of clay. Ancient ceramics, by contrast, "are thoroughly discolored, and every crack and cavity . . . will be completely filled with sediment."[21] But, for Holmes, the most important feature for telling apart fakes was their "incongruousness": in the case of black ceramic ware, their pastiche were "not even imitations of genuine [ancient] work [but] compositions made up of unrelated parts, derived, maybe, from ancient art, and thrown together without rhyme or reason." As Holmes concludes, "Fraud is stamped upon every contour and written in every line." By contrast, "True native art is consistent: each part bears an intelligible relation to all other parts."[22]

Three quarters of a century had passed since Humboldt qualified American antiquities as grotesque. By the time Holmes studied them in the late nineteenth century, American antiquities had become more familiar to scholars and collectors. It was clear, Holmes suggested, that the ancients were masterful artisans, who made their objects with "rhyme and reason," in accordance with coherent iconographic, stylistic, and technical conventions. Black ceramic vases of the sort purchased by Holmes on the train to Teotihuacan would no longer do or would raise an eyebrow among high-end collectors. The deformed and incongruous might still appeal to those whose vision of the exotic indulged in fantasies of the tasteless look of primitive crudity. But authenticity had a different look. As scholars like Holmes sought to teach their contemporaries in the science of the authentic, forgers took note as well. Fakes were becoming increasingly "beautiful," well made, and hard to tell apart.

A Taxonomy of Fakes and the Science of Authenticity

In 1910, Leopoldo Batres (1852–1926) published the most extensive and apparently the only attempt, to date, to create a record of fakes at the Museo Nacional de México: *Antigüedades mejicanas falsificadas* [*sic*], a thirty-page booklet, followed by an annex with photographs of over two hundred objects at the museum. Batres begins with an anecdote from Paul Eudel's *Trucs et truqueurs: Altérations, fraudes et contrefaçons dévoilées* (1907), about a certain Professor Berg from Christiania (Oslo), who "discovered" a twelfth-dynasty Egyptian sarcophagus under the floor of a peasant's hut. A hefty sum secured the object, which arrived at the university museum two months later. Scholars gathered excitedly around it, but doubts and suspicions arose immediately: the solid "sycamore wood" of the coffin made a hollow sound; the prayer to Osiris lacked style; the paint was recent; the fabric wrapping the mummy, rough muslin; the mask's eyes were made of glass. Despondent, Professor Berg "starts doubting himself and . . . no longer answers his colleagues' questions; he has no energy left to argue, and like a man condemned to death, his eyes sunk in his orbits, awaits his condemnation."[23] This came in the form of X-rays, a new technology that made the contents of the wrapped bulk visible without destroying them—contact with air would pulverize the mummy. Only, there was no mummy but a "horrible simulacrum, the most vulgar of shadows, a straw mannequin."[24]

With Eudel's story—which has all the ingredients of a great crime mystery, from the scene in the hut in Egypt to the gathering of experts in Oslo; from the construction of incriminating evidence to ruined reputations—Batres disposes the reader toward his own booklet. Fakes, Batres affirms, plagued the study of prehistory, ancient Egypt, Babylonia, and medieval France. But their presence among archaeological artifacts at the Museo Nacional de México was especially detrimental to the study of Mexico's ancient past because "it was hard enough to know it," even when dealing with authentic artifacts. Fakes made that study so much harder. At stake, as Irina Podgorny has succinctly put it in a study on fakes and the consolidation of archaeology as a scientific discipline, is whether it was the archaeologist or the forger who got to create new types.[25] The fabrication, by a forger in Oaxaca, of "idols" made of clay and lead, with a singular resemblance to Hindu divinities—at a moment when archaeologists were looking for the Oriental origins of New World civilizations—shows fakes were of crucial concern for Mexican archaeology.[26] In his *Antigüedades mejicanas falsificadas,* Batres sets out to address this concern by doing for Mexican antiquities what Eudel had done for the antiquities of the Old World. He was especially suited for the task.

Since 1885, Batres had served as general inspector of archaeological monuments, a post created *ex professo* for him by President Porfirio Díaz. His broadly defined duties included collecting archaeological artifacts on behalf of the museum and the inspection, conservation, and reconstruction of archaeological sites. By 1908, his assignments were expanded to subsume the examination of "each acquisition [by the museum] in order to determine its authenticity, its culture of origin, and whether it had been severed from the ruins."[27] Acting, as he did, as broker between the museum and collectors, dealers, Mexican and foreign archaeologists, and people working at archaeological sites, Batres had profound practical knowledge of Mexican archaeology and would have inevitably had his run-ins with fakes and their makers—his photographs of forgers standing proudly by their kilns at Teotihuacan is telling in this regard (figure 2.3). Furthermore, since 1907, he had been working on a new inventory for the archaeological collection at the

Figure 2.3 Barrios brothers from San Juan Teotihuacan, exhibiting their ceramic molds. In Batres, *Antigüedades mejicanas falsificadas,* plate 30, Biblioteca Nacional de Antropología e Historia, Mexico City. Reproduction authorized by the Instituto Nacional de Antropología e Historia.

Museo Nacional de México.[28] It is possible that his small book of fakes was a byproduct of this much larger task and that the separate collection of fakes was part of his effort to record the museum's authentic artifacts.

Antigüedades mejicanas falsificadas is not a complete inventory of the museum's fakes. Batres shows only the more notorious ones. Still, the book gives a sense of the diversity of things that were being faked—vases, jewelry, masks, statuettes, and codices—as well as of the surprising range of materials used to make them: black clay, bone and human skulls, shell, obsidian, gold, silver, paper, coconut, and alabaster. Alabaster came from Italy, as vases and columns, to furnish bourgeois homes; when an alabaster object broke, forgers purchased the material and modeled it on objects in the museum. Batres also registers the tools used by forgers, such as a remarkable collection of eighty electroplated molds of hieroglyphs copied from codices, which were used to produce the "famous Chiapas bricks" in the museum's collection of fakes (figure 2.4).[29] Batres had intimate knowledge and appreciation for the fabrication of these molds, which combine precision, delicacy, and sturdiness: the reliefs, which imitate glyphs in ancient codices, are made of fine white wax; the wax is then subjected to galvanoplasty with copper, to ensure the molds would be robust enough to be pressed on wet clay and produce the "bricks."

Figure 2.4 Mold for the so-called Chiapas bricks. In Batres, *Antigüedades mejicanas falsificadas*, plate 10, Biblioteca Nacional de Antropología e Historia, Mexico City. Reproduction authorized by the Instituto Nacional de Antropología e Historia.

At the same time, Batres's book is a who's who of sorts in the world of forgery; an instruction manual, for the unsuspecting buyer or collector, on how to tell a fake by examining aspects as diverse as style and manufacturing techniques; and a scathing reckoning with scholars and high-ranking museum officials—many of whom Batres considered his bitter enemies—who fell for fakes. Alfredo

Chavero, the by-then-deceased director of the Museo Nacional de México, is the object of Batres's deepest scorn, for having published studies of fakes—which Chavero took for authentic metalwork—in the museum's journal *Anales del Museo Nacional de México*. Batres does not name others, although how hard could it have been for a contemporary of Batres's to guess the identity of the professor at the Museum of Natural History in New York and at Columbia University, who purchased fake Zapotecan antiquities (Marshall Saville)? Or that of the Mexican scholar (José Fernando Ramírez) who published studies of what Batres considered fake postconquest codices, only to have his work immediately criticized by a colleague, which resulted in the end of their friendship?

Forgery, as Batres describes it, is a wide, systemic phenomenon, which is not limited to the artisan working a kiln or chipping away at an obsidian block, to sell the product to the unsuspected buyer on a train to Teotihuacan. Rather, Batres describes forgery as collaborative work that brings together many people, of diverse social standing, each person bringing specific skills to the making of a fake, from its conception and its fabrication to passing it off as "authentic." This dense network includes, obviously, the artisan, but also the dealer, a "cynical individual, insinuating and suggestive, who employs all his art to convince his victims that white is black," and reaches as far up as "the directors of local museums, who, profiting from their situation, reproduce with astonishing fidelity the objects in their custody, to launch them on the market as genuine prehispanic artefacts."[30] Forgery, Batres seems to be saying, starts with the museum itself, which, to the eyes of its personnel and of forgers, provides a valuable archive of models and molds. One cannot stop wondering how much he, so intimately associated with the museum, knew.

Artisans form the most diverse group in this flowchart of forgers. There are, among artisans, those who enjoy high social standing, as is the case of the "dangerous forger," whom Batres does not name, who produced copies of Fray Bernardino de Sahagún's work held at European libraries; having fine knowledge of the originals and "an extraordinary ability" to reproduce them, his offensives are error free and unflinching, warns Batres. There is also another unnamed artist, from Oaxaca, a "true genius for forgeries of Zapotec and Mixtec antiquities."[31] On the other hand, Batres names don Elías Amador, a prestigious lapidary—and a patriot in the republican army at the time of the French intervention, who took seven bullets and was left for dead—who took up obsidian carving after the war, as an experimental project, seeking to understand and reproduce ancient manufacturing processes.[32] Most forgers, however, were lowlifes, "uncouth peons" and "counterfeiters whose ability [did] not go beyond confection," and whose connections with the crime world went beyond the forgery business. For instance, Batres warns his readers, "there just returned to Mexico City one of the most capable forgers of obsidian antiquities, who had been deported to the penitentiary islands of Tres Marías for being a recalcitrant thief. Almost all the men who dedicate themselves to this ignoble industry are alcoholics and waste their time in taverns."[33]

If Batres's text, with its cast of "dangerous" draftsmen, "cynical" traffickers, "recalcitrant thieves," and unscrupulous museum directors, sounds like a criminology manual—titles such as *Los criminales en México* (1904) and *Crímenes sexuales y pasionales* (1906), by Carlos Rougmanac, Batres's contemporary, come to mind—the resemblance is not at all casual. Like the criminologist, the archaeologist is called to the scene of a crime, to reconstruct and determine what happened. In a classical essay, Carlo Ginzburg identifies the configuration, toward the end of the nineteenth century, of an "indiciary paradigm," that is, the turn, by art connoisseurs, detectives, and psychoanalysts, to physical, chemical, biological, or morphological traces and clues, as an epistemological strategy for detecting the mark of a criminal or the brush of a famous artist.[34] Batres's methods for telling the fake from the authentic—as he strives to find the "something off" that separates the copy from the original—are based on the assumption that there is no such a thing as a "perfect copy," just as there is no "perfect crime." Procedures that were becoming increasingly routine in the study of crimes, such as the careful reading of traces with a trained eye and with the help of sophisticated instruments, were being adopted by archaeologists, who also worked with fragments and clues to build credible narratives about the past. Of course, Batres insists, it was indispensable for the critic to have thorough knowledge of the style, composition, form, symbolism, and dress used by pre-Hispanic peoples in their productions. He applies this kind of formal knowledge, for instance, to contrast pre-Hispanic and colonial codices: the use of perspective and arches in the latter were telltale signs. But knowledge alone is not enough; something more is needed for a critic to tell a fake: acumen ("penetración para juzgar").[35] He certainly believed he had it: "In front of my eyes have passed as imitations, or as the product of fantasy, fakes of incontrovertible merit; some of them were so perfect that only an eye with a lot of experience in this kind of defects can recognize the falsehood of an object."[36]

Metalwork and obsidian at the museum offered Batres good opportunities to test and show off his acumen. He published photographs of a fair number of gold fakes in the collections, from small figurines to beading and low reliefs. He also snidely included engravings of fakes that Chavero had taken to be authentic (figure 2.5). Some decades earlier, Batres thought, it would have been easy to distinguish between authentic and fake metalwork because forgers used soldering to bind parts of an object with metal alloys. Pre-Hispanic metalworkers did not use alloys; they cast the objects, sometimes achieving admirable thinness. But later forgers began to imitate the techniques of the ancients, so it was becoming increasingly difficult to tell a fake apart. Batres recommended that experts observe the trace left by tools on the object. Steel burnishers created a highly polished surface; by contrast, ancient polishing techniques, with agate, rendered a muted sheen.[37]

In the last section of his booklet, Batres turns to obsidian fakes. When Tylor described the market of fakes in Mexico City half a century earlier, he suggested that obsidian was a good investment because it was likely to be "authentic," for "the art of working obsidian [was] lost and there [could] be no trickery about that."[38] By the time Batres published his *Antigüedades mejicanas falsificadas*, the Museo Nacional de México owned the world's largest collection of obsidian fakes, consisting of masks, small amulet-type objects, vessels, faces, and animals. Batres found them technically admirable—"I have seen fake obsidian idols that are marvelous both in their carving and in their polish"—and especially difficult to tell apart as fakes.[39] As with metalwork, tool marks and manufacturing techniques are helpful. Contemporary artisans, Batres writes, grind obsidian blocks with emery, carve them with steel punches and chisels, and give them form with a mallet, before polishing the object with petroleum and an emery board. These instruments leave behind a noticeable trace. Pre-Hispanic artisans used stone tools to carve and grind obsidian, producing different kinds of marks. Would nineteenth-century obsidian carvers learn to work the material using the same techniques as ancient carvers, as metalworkers did? This was a common fear among connoisseurs and collectors. As Gordon Ekholm, the curator of Mexican archaeology at the American Museum of Natural History, wrote sometime later, curators were reticent to describe their experiences with fakes because they feared revealing their "secrets" to forgers, resulting in improved forgeries.[40] By the 1960s, communication between museums, collectors, connoisseurs, dealers, and forgers continued to map (as it does to this day) the contours of a vast underground network.

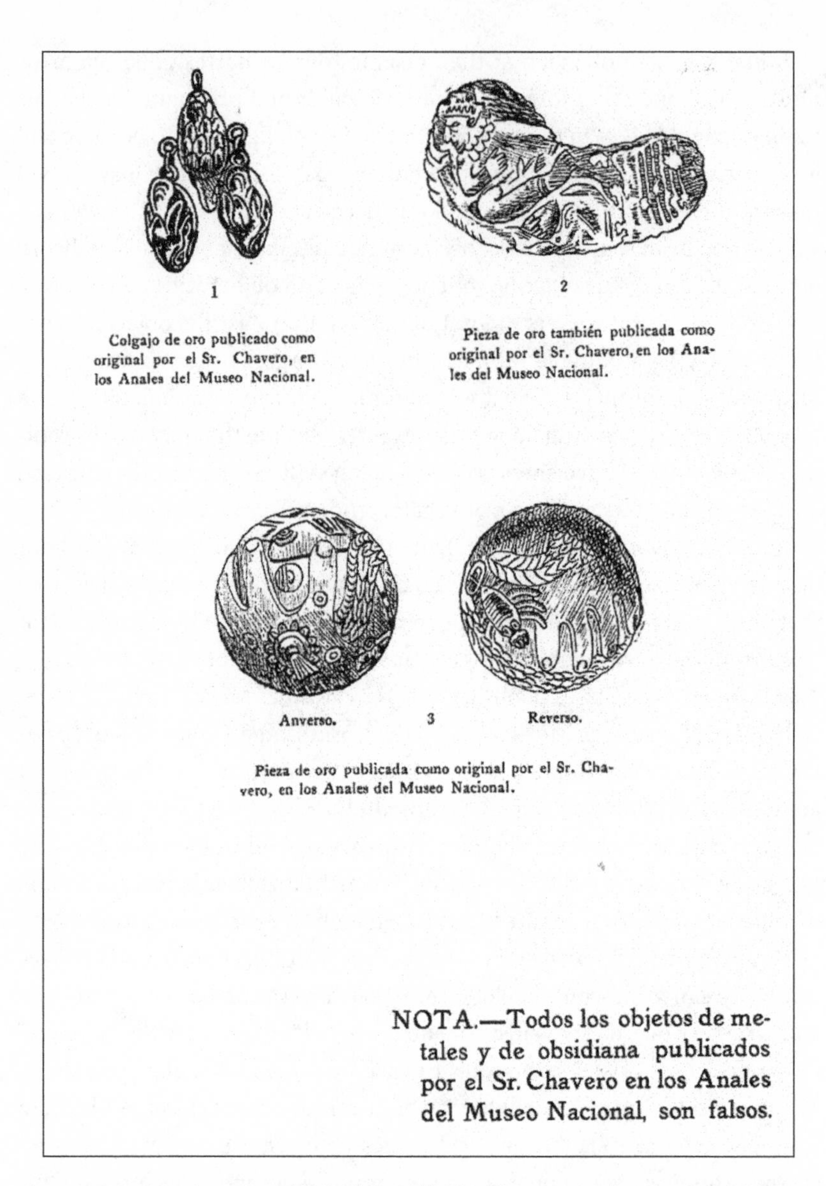

Figure 2.5 Metalwork, published by Alfredo Chavero in the *Anales del Museo Nacional de México*. In Batres, *Antigüedades mejicanas falsificadas*, plate 37, Biblioteca Nacional de Antropología e Historia, Mexico City. Reproduction authorized by the Instituto Nacional de Antropología e Historia.

There emerges, in the writings of Holmes, Batres, and Ekholm, the sense of a constant and intimate interplay between the museum curator and the forger, between the authentic and the fake, each shaping the understanding of the other. By the beginning of the twentieth century, to produce proof of forgery, collectors and connoisseurs looked for telltale traces and incriminating details: the use of clay washes to simulate aging, the mark of a steel burin or a mallet, the presence of alloys, a stain of petroleum, or a style that was "somewhat off." Taxonomies of mistakes made no sense, however, without a more thorough and systematic knowledge of what the authentic looked like: how pots and bones aged over hundreds of years; how and what materials and tools were used by ancient potters, carvers, sculptors, and jewelry makers to fashion their artifacts; what styles and iconographic programs gave meaning to different objects at different moments. Is it possible, then, that the necessity to tell the authentic from the fake shaped the way authenticity was studied? Did archaeology receive a boost from the kinds of protocols and technologies—from magnifying glasses to microscopes and X-rays, which someone like Batres might have borrowed, in both a literal and a conceptual sense, from the natural history laboratory at the Museo Nacional de México—that were being used to discard fakes? Can we trace the genealogies of methods and techniques for the production of evidence in Mexican archaeology to the study of fakes and further back, to the natural sciences? This is only a hypothesis, and a lot more research would be needed to confirm it. In any case, even if the extensive use of technologies in archaeology did not originate first with the study of fakes, it is difficult to disentangle questions about manufacturing techniques and styles, provenance, and chronology, which are the hallmark of contemporary archaeology, from early attempts to tell the fake from the authentic.

The Little Obsidian Monkey

At the beginning of the twentieth century, the turn to the methods of more established scientific disciplines, such as criminology, botany, and anatomy, as well as the reliance on scientific instruments, were key for the consolidation of archaeology as a scientific discipline and of the museum as a guardian of Mexico's authentic past. Still, a century later, excavation in controlled circumstances remains the consummate guarantee for authenticity. Suspicions still linger about the source of some of the more beloved and representative objects of the Museo Nacional de Antropología. Neither stylistic nor technical analyses suffice to produce consensus about their provenance or chronology among archaeologists.

Such is the case with the obsidian vase lovingly called the "little obsidian monkey" (*monito de obsidiana*), which has become one of the metonyms for the Sala Mexica and, more broadly, for the preciosity and the superb carving skills of the pre-Hispanic dwellers of Mexico's central valleys. Made of golden obsidian from the Sierra de las Navajas, in the present-day state of Hidalgo, the vase, 15.0 cm tall × 16.5 cm wide × 17.3 cm deep, has a globular shape and extremely thin walls.[41] As one of its first admirers, antiquities collector Eugène Boban, described it in 1884: "It is carved in the image of a kneeling monkey, which folds its tail, which surrounds the lip of the vessel, with both its hands."[42] The monkey, apparently blowing or whistling through its mouth, could be a personification of Ehécatl Quetzalcóatl, the Mexica deity associated with the wind and the underworld (figure 2.6).

Figure 2.6 *Monito de obsidiana*, Sala Mexica. Museo Nacional de Antropología. Archivo Digital de las Colecciones del Museo Nacional de Antropología. INAH-CANON. Reproduction authorized by the Instituto Nacional de Antropología e Historia.

References to the little monkey first appear in the documentation of the Museo Nacional de México on January 31, 1876, when, together with a gold "idol," it was sold to the museum for 600 pesos, by Dr. Rafael Lucio.[43] In 1882, the vase is included in the catalog of the archaeological and historical collections at the Museo Nacional de México, which specifies that "the precious obsidian vessel, found in an ancient tomb in an hacienda close to Texcoco," was being exhibited in a room on the top floor of the museum, together with obsidian mirrors, ritual vessels, and domestic utensils.[44] Two years later, Boban published a more detailed description of the vase, associating it, for the first time, with the god Quetzalcóatl and praising the "admirable regularity" of its carving, especially of its walls, "so thin that at first it resembles a glass bottle."[45] Boban also gave an elaborate account of its provenance: Dr. Lucio had obtained the vase from a sick patient, who in turn had bought it for the price of a donkey (estimated at 12 reales, or 7.5 francs) from a peasant who had found it in a tomb on his land, close to Texcoco. Stories like these, which had little chance of being confirmed, are common in the history of collecting. In any case, the little monkey has no excavation record associated with it. This has been one reason that its authenticity has been considered doubtful.

Boban's controversial place in the history of antiquities collecting does little to put those doubts to ease; indeed, his association with the piece raises red flags. Boban, who moved with certain ease between Mexico and France, was an antiquities dealer who accrued and sold numerous collections in the course of his life. He was, by necessity, a student of fakes, who rendered service to his contemporaries by displaying his forgeries, for illustrative purposes, at international exhibits.[46] Above all, though, he was a master forger, the mind behind the creation of the Aztec crystal skulls, some of the greatest forgeries in Mexican archaeology.[47] It comes as no surprise, then, that Boban moved with ease and familiarity among forgers, especially among lapidaries. In his correspondence with W. H. Holmes, for instance, Boban refers to a certain Juan Bobadilla, an expert carver of obsidian and jadeite. Though Bobadilla's skill might have been matchless, he and other master carvers incriminated themselves by producing obsidian figures and idols, writes Boban, when the "ancient Mexicans never made figures or idols of obsidian, but [used it] only for masks, adornments for lips and ears, eyes for stone idols, and pendants in the shape of animal heads." Boban categorically adds, "All obsidian objects with bodies, arms, and legs can be considered fakes."[48] If he had incriminating evidence about the obsidian monkey, he kept it to himself. Obsidian artifacts continue to raise doubts, even as they continue to be sought after; as Ekholm has suggested, they are beautiful and have a "fatal" appeal to collectors.[49] Lately, a series of studies revealing the presence of obsidian fakes in topnotch collections have confirmed these misgivings.[50]

If these reasons were not sufficient to call into question the authenticity of the obsidian monkey, its theft from the Museo Nacional de Antropología, together with other emblematic objects, on December 25, 1985—a theft that shocked Mexico and was the topic of the recent commercial film, *Museo*, starring Gael García Bernal—has contributed to raising some doubts about it. The monkey was eventually returned to the museum, but the fact that such a delicate object survived the incident unharmed made many wonder if the object that was returned was the same as the one that was stolen. As recently as 2011, archaeologist Leonard López Luján called for an "analysis of the monkey in order to confirm its authenticity," in the context of a catalog that includes it among the hundred most representative objects in the museum.[51]

The analysis was carried out in 2015 as part of the ongoing project "Estilo y tecnología de los objetos lapidarios en el México Antiguo" (Style and technology in lapidary objects in ancient Mexico). Led by archaeologist Emiliano Melgar Tísoc, the project seeks to advance knowledge about the provenance and chronology of pre-Hispanic artifacts by studying the technologies used to produce them. Based on the premise that "every culture has particular ways of making objects" and is reticent to changing those ways, the project looks for tool marks and manufacturing techniques—the way Batres had a century before.[52] In the case of the obsidian monkey, Melgar Tísoc used magnifying glasses, a stereoscopic microscope, and a scanning electron microscope to study the topology, roughness, and porosity of the piece—that is, the superficial characteristics that compose manufacturing marks. The analysis concluded, first, that there are no traces of metallic or electrical instruments in the manufacturing of the vase; second, that the traces found correspond to the use of pre-Hispanic tools, such as flint chippings (for incisions), reeds and animal skin (for smooth surfaces), and flint burins (for ear perforations); and, third, that the carving techniques coincide with those used by ancient artisans from Texcoco. In other words, the technical analysis of the piece corroborates nineteenth-century accounts of its provenance.[53]

This last assertion has proved controversial. Various archaeologists we have interviewed for this chapter have misgivings about rigidly associating a particular manufacturing technique with a specific place; this allows no room for an artisan's personal agency, that is, for their taste and training, or for the possibility that they could have traveled freely between Texcoco and other places. At the same time, there remains the possibility that nineteenth-century artisans could have used ancient manufacturing techniques to carve the vase, just as experimental archaeologists do nowadays; in fact, to analyze the tool traces obtained from the vase, Melgar Tísoc compared them with those produced by experimental archaeologists, who study ancient manufacturing techniques by reproducing them. Of course, none of these objections prove that the vase is not from Texcoco or that it is a fake. But they do show that authenticity is not an easy thing to prove. Despite some misgivings, the little obsidian monkey remains in the Sala Mexica. After all, the object has beauty to its advantage and reminds visitors of the sophistication reached by Mexico's ancient civilizations.

Conclusions

Over the course of their history, Mexico's national museums have lost most of their fakes, although there are no records of how this happened. Nor has there been much scholarly interest or curiosity to find out. There are some refences left of the fakes themselves, such as those gathered at the Museo Nacional de México by Ramírez in the 1850s or those documented by Batres in 1910. Archaeological fakes are not the only objects to have been periodically expelled from or made invisible by Mexico's national museums; they share this fate with things—such as natural history specimens or ethnographic photographs—that are no longer considered to embody the present's vision of Mexico's past or of its patrimony (see Gorbach and López Hernández, both in this volume). Yet, even as the Museo Nacional de Antropología has chosen to forget its fakes, they have been integral to the construction of the authenticity of the objects that the museum chooses to display. Some decades ago, Ekholm advised compiling historical catalogs of pre-Hispanic fakes, classified by styles and tastes, of the kind Batres also produced, to help curators distinguish forgeries in their collections.[54] We follow up on Ekholm's proposal to suggest that a catalog of fakes at the Museo Nacional de Antropología today, or—may we hope for it?—an exhibit of its fakes could be valuable in different ways as well. Such an exhibit could help forge new narratives of Mexican collecting and of the broader premises that have shaped expectations about the aesthetics of Mexico's past and of its value and uses as national patrimony.

Notes

1. We use a broad definition of "fake," as an object that is made to pass as "authentic," for the purpose of economic or intellectual gain.
2. Personal interview, May 2019.
3. For the controversy surrounding the fourth Mayan Codex, see Michael Coe, Stephen Houston, Mary Miller, and Karl Taube, "The Fourth Maya Codex," in *Maya Archaeology*, vol. 3, ed. Charles W. Golden, Stephen D. Houston, and Joel

Skidmore (San Francisco: Precolumbia Mesoweb Press, 2016), 116–67. Coe et al. strongly believe the codex is authentic.

4. Personal interview, June 2019.
5. Irina Podgorny, "Sobre la constitución de los objetos etnológicos en los inicios del siglo XX: Museos, falsificaciones y ciencia," *Museologia and Interdisciplinaridade* 2, no. 5 (May–June 2014): 23.
6. For an insightful book-length study of a museum's collection of fakes, see Justin Jennings and Adam T. Sellen, *Real Fake: The Story of a Zapotec Urn* (Toronto: Royal Ontario Museum, 2018). See also Mark Jones, *Fake? The Art of Deception* (Berkeley: University of California Press, 1990), for the catalog of an early exhibit on fakes organized by the British Museum.
7. For specific works on pre-Hispanic Mexican fakes, see W. H. Holmes, "The Trade in Spurious Mexican Antiquities," *Science* 7, no. 159 (1886): 170–72; Leopoldo Batres, *Antigüedades mejicanas falsificadas: Falsificaciones y Falsificadores* (Mexico City: Imprenta de Fidencio S. Soria, 1909); and Gordon Ekholm, "The Problem of Fakes in Pre-Columbian Art," *Curator* 7, no. 1 (1964): 19–31. For more recent literature, see Jane Maclaren Walsh, "The Dumbarton Oaks Tlazolteotl: Looking Beneath the Surface," *Journal de la Société des Américanistes* 94, no. 1 (2008): 7–43; Jane Maclaren Walsh and Brett Topping, *The Man Who Invented Crystal Aztec Skulls: The Adventures of Eugène Boban* (New York: Berghahn Books, 2019); Esther Pasztory, "Three Aztec Masks of the God Xipe," in *Thinking with Things: Towards a New Vision of Art* (Austin: University of Texas, 2005), 209–24; and Jennings and Sellen, *Real Fake*.
8. For an early twentieth-century account of the collection of fakes at the Museo Nacional de México, see Batres, *Antigüedades*. See also Nancy L. Kelker and Karen O. Bruhns, *Faking Ancient Mesoamerica* (Walnut Creek, Calif.: Left Coast Press, 2010), which addresses specific fakes at the Museo Nacional de Antropología in the context of a broader study of fakes in Mesoamerica.
9. Esther Pasztory, "Truth in Forgery," *RES: Anthropology and Aesthetics* 42 (Autumn 2002), 159.
10. Batres, *Antigüedades*, 8–9.
11. Batres, *Antigüedades*, 7.
12. Batres, *Antigüedades*, 24.
13. Waldeck, January 15, 1831, "Journal, in French, of Baron Jean Frederic Maximilien de Waldeck, 14 oct., 1829—21 aug. 1837," Add MS 41684, the British Library.
14. Edward Burnett Tylor, *Anáhuac: Or, Mexico and the Mexicans, Ancient and Modern* (London: Longman, Green, and Roberts, 1861), 230.
15. Tylor, *Anáhuac*, 230.
16. Alexander von Humboldt, *Vues des cordillères et monuments des peuples indigènes de l'Amérique* (Paris: Schoell, 1810–1813), 2.
17. Holmes, "Trade," 170.
18. Holmes, "Trade," 172.

19. Holmes, "Trade," 171.
20. Holmes, "Trade," 171.
21. Holmes, "Trade," 170–71.
22. Holmes, "Trade," 172.
23. Batres, *Antigüedades*, 4.
24. Batres, *Antigüedades*, 5.
25. Podgorny, "Sobre la constitución de los objetos," 24.
26. Batres, *Antigüedades*, 9.
27. Christina Bueno, *The Pursuit of Ruins: Archaeology, History, and the Making of Modern Mexico* (Albuquerque: University of New Mexico Press, 2016), 76–77.
28. He was charged with the task by museum director Genaro García, who was dissatisfied with the inventory produced by German archaeologist Eduard Seler in 1907. See Miruna Achim and Bertina Olmedo Vera, eds., *Eduard Seler: Inventario de las colecciones arqueológicas del Museo Nacional, 1907* (Mexico City: INAH, 2018).
29. Batres, *Antigüedades*. We have not been able to identify what "bricks" Batres refers to.
30. Batres, *Antigüedades*, 14.
31. Batres, *Antigüedades*, 14.
32. Batres, *Antigüedades*, 30.
33. Batres, *Antigüedades*, 14–15.
34. Carlo Ginzburg, "Clues: Roots of a Scientific Paradigm," *Theory and Society* 7, no. 3 (1979): 273–88.
35. Batres, *Antigüedades*, 27.
36. Batres, *Antigüedades*, 6.
37. Batres, *Antigüedades*, 25–26
38. Tylor, *Anáhuac*, 229.
39. Batres, *Antigüedades*, 30.
40. Ekholm, "Problem of Fakes," 21.
41. Obsidian can be traced to its source by identifying its chemical composition and characteristics, such as color. Every volcano produces a different obsidian.
42. Eugène Boban, "La vase en obsidienne de Tezcoco au Musée National de Mexico," *Revue d'ethnographie*, 1882, 71.
43. Vol. 1, exp. 47, fol. 164, Archivo Histórico del Museo Nacional de Antropología.
44. Gumesindo Mendoza and Jesús Sánchez, "Catálogo de las colecciones histórica y arqueológica del Museo Nacional de México," in *Anales del Museo Nacional de México* 65 (1882): 476, https://mna.inah.gob.mx/docs/anales/65.pdf.
45. Boban, "La vase en obsidienne," 71.
46. Exposition Universelle Internationale, *Catalogue spécial de l'Exposition des Sciences Anthropologiques* (Paris: Imprimerie Nationale, 1878), 27.
47. Walsh and Topping, *Man Who Invented Aztec Crystal Skulls*. See also Pascal Riviale, "Eugène Boban ou les aventures d'un antiquaire au pays des américanistes," *Journal de la Société des Américanistes* 87 (2001): 351–62.

48. Boban to Holmes, cited by Walsh, "La vasija de obsidiana de Texcoco," 67.
49. Ekholm, "Problem of Fakes," 29.
50. Walsh, "Dumbarton Oaks Tlazolteotl." As Walsh has shown, the Tlazolteotl statuette is also associated with Boban.
51. Leonardo López Luján, "Monito de obsidiana," in *100 obras: Catálogo esencial, Museo Nacional de Antropología* (Mexico City: CONACULTA/INAH, 2011), 186.
52. Emiliano Melgar Tísoc, Reyna Beatriz Solís Ciriaco, and Bertina Olmedo Vera, "Análisis tecnológico del mono de obsidiana de la Sala Mexica," in *Actas del Workshop de Arqueometría de la Universidad Tecnológica de Valencia* (Oxford: Archaeopress, forthcoming).
53. Melgar Tísoc, Solís Ciriaco, and Olmedo Vera, "Análisis tecnológico."
54. Ekholm, "Problem of Fakes," 25.

\\ 3

Body Objects in Transit

National Pathology between Anatomy Museums and the Museo Nacional de México, 1853–1912

LAURA CHÁZARO

Those who are familiar with museums know that collections result from the movement of objects from one place to another, and that they are the product of many different hands, expert or otherwise, and of quite varied intentions. But an object's mobility tends to be forgotten as soon as it is acquired, donated, or purchased; it is then regarded as immobile, as if being locked away in a display case or held in storage were its final destination. Some objects do, however, escape such confinement and, further still, go on to have other existences, being capable of undergoing transformation in terms of their materials and forms. In this chapter I discuss how the culturally and politically marked materiality of *life* reveals its ontological and temporal multiplicity through the case of anatomical pieces in nineteenth-century Mexico. In the brief timespan from 1853 to 1912, such specimens circulated intensively between the Museo Nacional de México; the Museo de Anatomía Patológica (founded in 1853), affiliated with the Escuela Nacional de Medicina (founded in 1833); the Hospital General de San Andrés (1823–1905); and its own Museo de Anatomía Patológica (1895–1900), forerunner to the Instituto Patológico (1900–1915).[1] As Dutch philosopher Annemarie Mol has shown, the living and by extension the corporeal acquired multiple existences, expressed in different values and materialities.[2]

These specimens—fragments of bodies—were also objects of knowledge, traveling across various regimes of value and commodification. In principle they were meant to exemplify what was normal and what was pathological, but through their movement and mutability, they created (and now re-create) different historicities: those of the patients through the histories of their diseases, as well as all that is implied by bodies in the national memory, especially racial differences. Indeed, anatomical pieces embody processes through which race became a material part of bodies and intervened in the valuing and commercialization of the living. Here I aim to show how those materialities embodied a multiple existence in Mexico. They were objects, byproducts of bodies, or pieces made of wax or papier-mâché, meant for clinical observation of the pathological forms in spaces like the Museo de Anatomía Patológica at the Escuela Nacional de Medicina and the Hospital de San Andrés. At the same time, those same specimens served as anthropological objects and testimonies of racial conditions at the Museo Nacional de México.[3] In the latter case, I focus on skulls and bones that could just as easily have been anatomical preparations from a morgue, or "discoveries" from an excavation of an archaeological site.[4] I explore how, despite their differences, the medical museums and the Museo Nacional de México materialized medical conditions (and indeed life itself) in pursuit of cures to "national" pathologies and to identify a normal political anatomy for the nation.

The anatomy collections that I analyze here had a brief, fragile existence. For a variety of reasons, there is practically no trace of them left today: they deteriorated over time, were donated to other museums, or simply got lost. The twist to this story is that they did not disappear entirely: they had a notable capacity to mutate, preserving marks of their previous existence in their new forms. Starting off as anatomical objects, some mutated into materials for bacteriology and histology laboratories. Others went from being anthropological pieces to becoming tables of measurements and anthropometric indices at the end of the nineteenth century. The Museo Nacional de México moved the unmeasured pieces to other museums to make space for its archaeological collections. Race endured through all these forms and materials—bones, photographs, and paper—to form part of the current medical and anthropological culture of bodies and objects. The anatomy specimens are not timeless fetishes or repositories of ideas (or identities). Rather, as Georges Didi-Huberman has observed about museum objects in general, they interrogate our own historical present, intertwining it with both the past and the future in their contingent forms of existence. As a result, and depending on their materials and the ways in which they are produced and circulated, anatomical pieces are combinations of temporalities.[5]

To illustrate the multiplicity of living objects, I focus on the circulation and production of pathological anatomical specimens from the Escuela Nacional de Medicina and the Museo Nacional de México.[6] Between 1853 and 1912, there was an intensive production of anatomical specimens that circulated through local and global exchange, not only as commodities, but also as material for cultural and cognitive processes. As Arjun Appadurai and Igor Kopytoff argued, objects produce values that are merged with or subtracted from affective exchanges (gifts) or purely commercial ones. Reconstructing the circulation of those objects allows us to see how living beings were reified, albeit not in an arbitrary way, nor with universal meanings. I follow the incremental mutations of those pathological pieces in transit as they express a multiplicity of histories—sometimes unanticipated—including those of patients and a racialized nation.[7]

Museological Spaces and Pathological Objects

During the colonial era, anatomy and surgery were practiced at the Hospital Real de Naturales, founded in 1553. In 1764 the Hospital Real opened an anatomical amphitheater, which held public presentations on dissection, but Mexico did not boast any anatomy collections like those of the Englishmen William (1718–73) and John Hunter (1728–93) at the Hunterian Museum.[8] Dissection and anatomizing were done by surgeons rather than medical doctors, but this situation changed in 1838 when the Escuela de Cirugía became part of the Escuela Nacional de Medicina. It was then that the doctors began tending to patients at hospitals and dissecting cadavers, especially at the Hospital General de San Andrés.[9]

In 1853, under the regime of clinical medicine, the Escuela Nacional de Medicina opened the Museo de Anatomía Patológica as an instructional museum to teach doctors how to autopsy cadavers and analyze pathological processes.[10] It was conceived as a space for bolstering the practice of medicine and doing away with its "bookish" aspect—at least such was the intention of Pablo Martínez del Río and Francisco Ortega, faculty in the department of pathological anatomy.

Between the time it was founded and 1870, the anatomy museum was a modest space. It occupied the terrace of the former Palacio de la Inquisición, a space it shared with the laboratory for the physiology class, which housed shelves of glass cases displaying specimens.[11] The head of the museum was a preparator who confined himself to teaching students to dissect, anatomize, and preserve anatomical specimens.[12] It was overseen by a *junta calificadora* (qualifying board) made up of faculty from the schools of pathological anatomy, internal and external medicine, topographical anatomy, and gynecology. Students and assistants at those schools were required to present an anatomical specimen a month, which, if it was approved by the *junta,* was then exhibited in the museum.

Although it occupied a small space, the anatomy museum encompassed the amphitheater at the Hospital General de San Andrés, where professors and students from the Escuela Nacional de Medicina practiced operations, autopsies, and pathological and histological analyses. The Hospital General de San Andrés also supplied the cadavers from which they produced their anatomical specimens. The doctors had no complaints about a lack of cadavers but did find fault with the spaces available for operating on and administering them. At the time the amphitheater at the Hospital General de San Andrés was regarded as a dirty, overcrowded space suffused with putrid odors.[13] The specimens being produced there were nevertheless fundamental to learning about, understanding, and controlling pathologies.

Given the importance of pathological anatomy, the director of the Hospital General de San Andrés, Rafael Lavista (1839–1900), championed the creation of a second Museo de Anatomía Patológica at the hospital in 1895. The second museum indirectly expanded the space of the Escuela Nacional de Medicina's museum. According to Lavista, if the goal was "to put Mexican pathology on a sound basis" and advance the study of "our diseases," clinical practice had to be reinforced by histological and bacteriological research.[14] In that regard the Museo de Anatomía Patológica of the Hospital General de San Andrés was a success. In 1900 it evolved into the Instituto Patológico, where pathological anatomy became the basis of experimental research.[15]

These experiences contrast with the life and spaces of the *natural* objects at the Museo Nacional de México.[16] Starting in 1867, the natural history wing of the museum in the Palacio Nacional on Moneda Street held anatomical specimens along with taxidermy and animal skeletons.[17] In addition to stones, minerals, and herbaria, there were birds, mammals, crustaceans, and cetaceans, many of which had been provided by collectors from outside the capital, most of whom were amateurs.[18] The most important influx of acquisitions of anatomical specimens and animals came between 1872 and 1889, during the directorships of Gumesindo Mendoza (1876–83) and Jesús Sánchez (1883–89). These acquisitions included human skulls and bones as well as comparative anatomies of animals. In 1896 the natural history collection was divided into five galleries: comparative anatomy (mammals and birds), botany, zoology, a herbarium, and teratology, located on the mezzanine of the Moneda Street building. All told, according to Alfonso L. Herrera (1868–1942), a pharmacist, naturalist, and conservator at the Museo Nacional de México, from 1889 to 1899 there were 22,694 pieces in the zoology collection alone, in addition to fifty-seven teratological specimens (human and animal) that were classified by Román Ramírez in 1895.[19] Starting in 1888, some of the anatomical specimens (skulls and bones) and teratological pieces were moved to the recently created Anthropology and Ethnography Halls, located on the top floor.[20] These specimens originated far from the medical amphitheaters, associated more with the hunter-gatherers, travelers, and ethnologists who collected the skulls and skeletal remains of Mexico's different populations.

Starting in the 1890s, at the Museo Nacional de México, directed by Manuel Urbina, there was pressure to remove natural history pieces, including bones and both normal and pathological anatomical specimens of humans and animals. In 1900, Urbina spearheaded an initiative that would confine the Museo Nacional to "Anthropology, Archaeology and History" and "*remove* all other Natural History, which [was to] be placed in another building with botanical [and] zoological annexes."[21] This removal of the natural history collections was carried out in 1908, when they were relocated to the Museo del Chopo.[22] Before that, however, despite the overcrowding and threat of being removed to make room for archaeological pieces, the natural history pieces held an important place in the public interest, garnering the attention of foreign travelers and collectors, antiques dealers, the press, and even the government itself.[23]

The pieces in the Escuela Nacional de Medicina's anatomy museum, by contrast, occupied more space over time, expanding into different spaces such as the Museo de Anatomía Patológica at the Hospital General de San Andrés. That said, for the first twenty years of its existence, the Escuela Nacional de Medicina's collection could be seen only by doctors. The 1853 regulations of the museum reserved the right not to open to the public until it held an "interesting" number of pieces. It did eventually open to the general public in 1875. Even so, in 1905 it reported receiving only five hundred visitors, almost all of whom were medical students.[24] The pieces at the respective anatomy museums of the Escuela Nacional de Medicina and Hospital General de San Andrés occupied a peripheral, almost marginal place in public life, but this did not stop them from gaining value as scientific objects or from opening spaces at the Museo Nacional de México as a result of medical knowledge and technologies.

Production and Temporality of Anatomical Specimens

Most of the specimens in the pathological anatomy collection came from actual human bodies; that is, they were fragments of cadavers. Others were made of wax or papier-mâché. Why was there this interest in reproducing the traces of pathology in the material form of cadavers themselves? Modern medicine depended on an order "based on the gaze," and the specimens of pathological anatomy played a central role therein by making visible what had remained invisible while the patient was alive—namely, the effects of the pathology in question.[25]

According to Miguel F. Jiménez (1813–75), professor of internal and external medicine at the Escuela Nacional de Medicina from 1850 to 1870, the museum's purpose was to help teach how to make diagnoses based on *clinical data*.[26] On the patient's headboard at the hospital, doctors recorded a clinical history, which described the patient's symptoms, diagnosed the disease, and suggested a treatment. The crucial feature of clinical practice was to record a history of the pathology and differentiate it from the normal state. If the patient died, the anatomist allowed the doctor to verify or correct the diagnosis recorded in the clinical history. Taking specimens of pathological anatomy revealed what had happened inside the body, which the doctor's gaze had been unable to penetrate while the patient was alive, and thereby allowed for comparison with the clinical history. As Jiménez pointed out, when a clinician cuts a body open, the effects of the pathology become visible in three dimensions. Each specimen in the collection therefore captured physical details that would disappear shortly after death.[27]

The "natural" specimens of anatomy were produced by doctors who turned body parts into collectible objects. These "natural" anatomical objects were marked by a peculiar temporality: they captured actions from the past to preserve them for the future. It was otherwise with artificially produced anatomies, that is, models of normal and pathological anatomy made out of papier-mâché, wax, or plaster, most of which were acquired from abroad via catalogs. Artificial objects do not retain the memory of a patient's tissue, that is, a name, a history, a past. Mexican doctors/collectors seem to have been largely uninterested in artificial pieces. They did not start collecting them until the 1870s, in contrast to European anatomy collectors, who were enthusiastic about artificial models.[28] In Mexico there was a preference for the vivid detail of "natural" pieces, the idea being perhaps that they offered more faithful exemplars of *national pathologies*. The instructional museum nevertheless acquired such pieces from European artisans, the most notable of which came from the French wax artist Raymond Vasseur-Tramond in 1874.[29] Like most wax artists, Vasseur-Tramond sold his pieces through catalogs, which circulated at universal exhibitions, advertising the prices and conditions of his pieces (figure 3.1).

A third kind of object of pathological anatomy consisted of photomicrographs (printed on glass slides) and tissue samples for histological analysis,

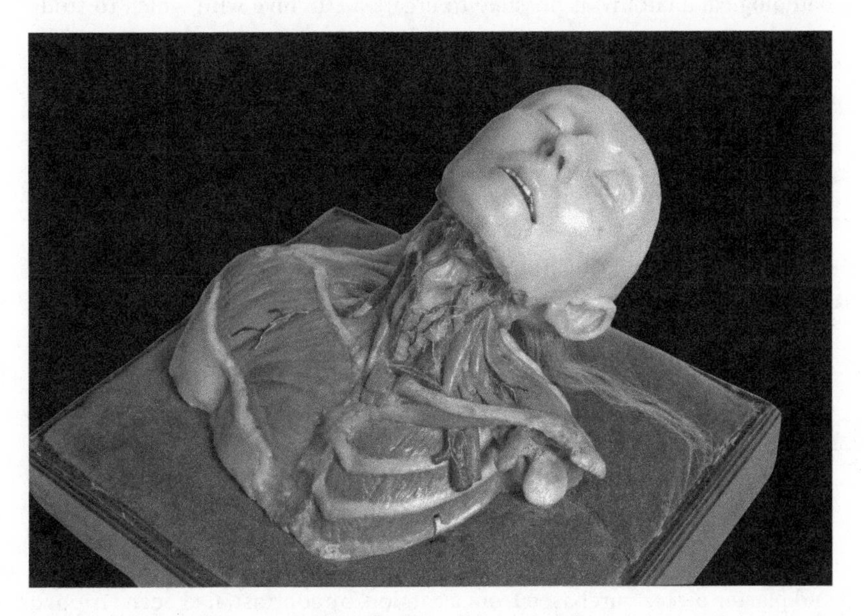

Figure 3.1 Anatomical wax model of the thorax, frontal view. Made by Vasseur-Tramond in the mid-nineteenth century, polychrome waxes such as this also used bone, teeth, hair, and thread. It is one of the artificial models that survive and are on display at the Museo de Historia de la Medicina Mexicana. Courtesy of the Facultad de Medicina, Patrimonio Universitario, UNAM.

meant to be viewed with a microscope. Produced in experimental settings, these techniques were another way of preserving and displaying pathologies. They arose in tandem with histology, bacteriological experimentation, and microscopes in the late nineteenth century. Some were purchased from abroad, while others were prepared at the anatomy museum at the Hospital General de San Andrés. There, under Lavista's directorship, doctors investigated the causes of diseases like yellow fever, tuberculosis, and typhoid, all common pathologies in Mexico at the time. These pieces had the advantage of favoring a microscale view that made it possible to identify how microorganisms acted on different tissues, unlike the macroscale view of a three-dimensional anatomical specimen. Different moments or states in a disease's development could also be reconstructed. But, as with artificial models, photomicrographs and tissue samples erased the patient's past.[30]

Of course, all anatomical pieces refer to time: to the history of the patient and of the disease. In Mexico, those times also seem to be folded into national history. Lavista and his colleagues aimed to collect as many specimens of pathological anatomy as possible to create an archive with which to study "our diseases." Like many other doctors of his day, Lavista was convinced that diseases found "special conditions" in Mexico: given "our climate and . . . the elevation at which we live, microorganisms evolved in a special way, [we must learn] how the Flora and Fauna peculiar to us evolve."[31] They were convinced that the country's geographical and racial features demanded a "national" pathological anatomy.

These three types of anatomical pieces are distinguished by different temporalities corresponding to different regimes of production and circulation. Although they had some similarities and shared the same fate, the social lives of the natural specimens, artificial models, and photomicrographs in the instructional anatomy collection were stamped with different origins and materialities. Drawing on Didi-Huberman, we could say that this collection involved a "combination of heterogeneous temporalities and materialities." The specimens taken from cadavers bore the clinical histories of the autopsied patients that registered their specific peculiarities.[32] The wax and plaster pieces purchased from a catalog, by contrast, had been stripped of personal memory. They came to Mexico via commerce with France or Germany, negotiated by price. These different materialities illuminate the different political temporalities through which specimens of pathological anatomy moved.

Classifying Anatomical Specimens, Producing Racial Difference

The inventories of the Escuela Nacional de Medicina's anatomy museum testify to what that museum used to be. An inventory has the effect of making a collection appear as a closed set, a smooth, a complete totality. These administrative artifacts nevertheless disclose the material substance and values of the inventoried pieces, along with their movements.[33] In other words, we can use these inventories to identify the different regimes of production and circulation of the pieces therein, as well as the values that ordered their social lives.

In 1870, the anatomy museum of the Escuela Nacional de Medicina named its first conservator, Juan María Rodríguez Arangoiti (1828–94), a renowned obstetrician and collector of specimens of pathological anatomy and teratology. The following year, the board of directors of the Ministerio de Instrucción prepared a new set of regulations for the museum, requiring the chair/conservator to care for, describe, and generate "the best classification" with which to administer any new acquisitions.[34] Rodríguez compiled the museum's first inventories in 1872 and 1873, thereby ordering the collection according to a classificatory scheme that persisted almost unchanged until 1912, and that spanned the careers of three successive conservators.[35]

Rodríguez devised twelve categories of pathological anatomy to sort the museum's collection (table 3.1, column 2). Each category included as many anatomical exemplars as there were varieties of ailments or afflictions recognized by pathological anatomy at the time. Rodríguez's taxonomy did create differences, seeking to make the details of each pathology visible. The inventories distinguished between normal and pathological anatomy. They began with the heading of "Normal Anatomies," normal anatomical specimens of entire bodies and systems, such as mummies, bones, or organs (column 1, row 1). The next categories referred to the pathological anatomy pieces (column 1, rows 2–4); and at the end was a section on teratology. Table 3.1 includes examples related to bones and teratology, the pieces that most circulated between the Museo Nacional de México and the medical museums.

Although Rodríguez did not cite it, he had adopted the taxonomy of the Musée de l'École de Médicine in Paris (1826), now the Musée Dupuytren.[36] This repetition of French taxonomy connects the anatomy museum at the Escuela Nacional de Medicina to European doctors but also reveals

Table 3.1 Inventory of the Museo de Anatomía Patológica of the Escuela Nacional de Medicina

Category	Types of pieces by category, examples	Number of pieces
1. Normal anatomies	Cranial cross-sections (nasal cut); injected kidney (arteries and veins), mummified adult male	8
2. Pathological anatomy of tumors and degenerative conditions (cancers)	Cerebral hydatids (cysts), malignant breast tumor, model tumor in plaster	10
3. Fractures	Maxillary bones, long bones, skulls	16
4. Pathological lesions of the bones		14
5. Teratology section	Ectromelias, cleft lips, spinae bifidae, "heart-shaped" pelvises	50

Source: "Inventarios, Museo de Anatomía Patológica" (1872), AHFM-FEMyA Appendix, doc. 497, ff. 17–23; "Informe pedido a varios empleados en la Escuela: Informe del Museo Anatómico" (1873), AHFM-FEMyA, file 140, doc. 36. This table is excerpted from both inventories. The one from 1873 records donations, marking the name of the donor and the history of each piece.

its peculiarities. Like the collection at the École de Médicine, the museum's pieces bear the name of the doctor who prepared them and the date of their creation. They also record the material of the piece, distinguishing between natural preparations (dry or liquid), models (in wax or plaster), photographs, and drawings. In the category of "Tumors and Degenerative Conditions," for example, the list includes "1 white tumor, modeled in plaster"; "encephaloid labial cancer (photograph); stomach cancer."[37] Once they had been registered in the inventory, the pieces became part of a whole, while also becoming distinguished from one another, lending each its own value. Like anthropological and archaeological collections, anatomy collections traveled across different regimes of value. This can be perceived in the materials themselves and in the marks left on them by affects and prices.[38]

Indeed, the inventories under discussion included many pieces, mostly from the teratology section, that stood out for having been donated by this or that prestigious doctor. These constituted the largest subset within the collection until the late 1870s. In general, they were accompanied by a brief description of the clinical history from which they had originated; they were memorializations of pathological events. Aside from Rodríguez himself, other renowned doctors from the Escuela Nacional de Medicina donated pieces to the museum, including Manuel S. Soriano, who donated sixty-seven annotated pieces and eleven histological photomicrographs of blood vessels in 1872; the physicians Gabino Barreda and Nicolás San Juan; and Gumesindo Mendoza, director of the Museo Nacional de México from 1876 to 1883.[39] With these attributions, the pieces were no longer anonymous: the prestige of the doctor who prepared them imbued them with value, while the clinical description of the patient turned the ailment into something exceptional. For example, one entry reads, "Portrait of the hemimele Don José María Alegre, a Portrait of the macrocephalic Idiot José and one of the masculine Hermaphrodite 'Micaela Martínez,' both from Dr. Rodríguez."[40] The names of both patient and doctor added affective rather than monetary value: the pieces were neither bought nor sold, circulating instead through a gift economy.[41] Doctors could build their relationships with their colleagues by bequeathing such objects to the museum. These were offered up not in commercial transactions but through an affective calculus of sociability, given out of "gratitude to the Escuela Nacional de Medicina," or "for the merit of the pieces" if they warranted publication in a medical journal.[42] Through these teratological specimens, all of which were from cases reported in Mexico, that affective regime contributed to the memory of what those doctors referred to as national pathologies.

Starting in the 1880s, the inventories also recorded the prices of the pieces collected, whether natural or artificial. For example, a cranial cross-section was valued at 1.50 pesos, an injected kidney (showing arteries and veins) at 1 peso, a thorax at 20 pesos, a wax model of the large sympathetic (autonomic) nervous system at 400 pesos.[43] In a different way from the regime of the gift and affect, these valuations alter the similarity between pieces. The doctor-collector would distinguish the appreciative value given to the pieces made by the doctors and students at the Escuela Nacional de Medicina, from the value assigned to the pieces acquired through purchase, within Mexico or abroad. Indeed, the wax and plaster models and photomicrographs were marked by the purchase prices at which they had been acquired, as specified in the commercial catalogs of the craftsmen who made them. Such is the case with the pieces by Tramond-Vasseur, acquired for 4,490 francs.[44] The difference seems to be significant, for after those pieces left Paris, they were distinguished neither by the name of the artist who manufactured them nor by their place of origin. No one praised their beauty or their powerful ability to represent the finer details of different pathologies. They were standardized products with no more history than that of the sale itself, products of international trade with an impersonal memory.

The teratological specimens are noteworthy in relation to these price-bearing pieces. The former are distinguished by the name of the doctor who performed the autopsy and have no price, but these were the pieces that circulated most. Of local origin and identified with national diseases, they are invaluable (in both senses of the term). Such is the case of the "heart-shaped" (*acorazadas*) pelvises (as they were called by Rodríguez and other obstetricians at the time), which were characterized by a long sacrum and a narrow subpubic arch, resulting in a heart-like shape. In these doctors' view, some Mexicans developed an abnormally long pubis—"abnormally long" in relation to European pelvises, that is—as a result of "racial atavisms," producing a shape that could result in difficult births. Other human and animal specimens also presented pathologies that were associated with race, extreme cases being janiceps and "monster maize."[45]

The pieces in this collection, ordered according to the same principles of pathological anatomy, brought together two regimes of value and time that were different but not mutually exclusive: gifts and affects on the one hand, and interchangeable commodities on the other. The pelvises that reached the Museo Nacional de México were priceless; they were valued as embodiments of national memory, referring to the past and to Mexicanness in racial terms.

In the early twentieth century, the inventories of the anatomy museum at the Escuela Nacional de Medicina all but erased the references to the doctors who had donated the anatomical specimens; their prices, however, remained. The inventories came increasingly to resemble the catalogs of merchandise for sale by the anatomical craftsmen and the makers of medical instruments (figure 3.2). In the 1905 inventory, the anatomy museum at the Escuela Nacional de Medicina reported that its collection was valued at 12,046 pesos, the highest value ever reached by the collection prior to the 1910 Revolution.

So what do we learn from the relationships between the doctor-collectors and the circulation of their specimens of pathological anatomy? According to Walter Benjamin, a basic condition of the relationships between collectors and their objects is the desire to ensconce them in their collection. Only thus

MÉDAILLES DE 1re CLASSE

Exposition 1855. Médaille 1re classe.

VASSEUR

NATURALISTE

Préparateur et Fournisseur de la Faculté de Médecine de Paris

CATALOGUE.

OSTÉOLOGIE HUMAINE.

Les différents prix des squelettes sont basés sur leurs qualités, qui consistent dans la dureté, la blancheur, le développement des os, le plus ou moins de graisse qu'ils contiennent à leurs extrémités, ou de son absence complète.

(*Cette observation peut s'appliquer à toutes les pièces d'ostéologie.*)

	fr.
Squelettes désarticulés. . . . . 50 à	80
Demi-squelettes désarticulés, composés de la tête, la colonne vertébrale, le sternum entier, un membre supérieur, un membre inférieur, dont la main et le pied sont enfilés avec corde à boyau. . . . . 35 à	50
Squelettes articulés (mâle)[1]. . . . . 75 à	160
Squelettes articulés (femelle)[1]. . . . . 75 à	160

1. Aux squelettes d'un prix supérieur, les articulations des phalanges sont faites à mouvements.

1

Figure 3.2 Vasseur-Tramond, page from *Catalogue de M. Vasseur-Tramond: Successeur. Naturaliste, préparateur d'Anatomie* (Paris: Éditions de l'auteur, 1875). Courtesy of the Bibliothèque nationale de France.

do they possess them, revealing what they know of them and thereby giving them a raison d'être, a destiny. In that act, the collector withdraws the collected objects from the logic of the market, frees them from their utility, and turns them into "broken-down matter."[46] That condition is translated into the permanent concern that the objects might escape from the collection, differentiate themselves, and be transformed. In other words, Benjamin tells us how other values are generated in the process of circulation, modifying the material that has been collected. Objects in a collection are caught up in a tension between breaking down among similar objects or moving from one collector-proprietor to another, acquiring other values and entering into circulation anew. Some of the pieces at the anatomy museum of the Escuela Nacional de Medicina did not break down definitively in their display cases but went back into circulation: namely, the pieces that embodied pathologies associated with a racial origin. As anatomical pieces, some acquired a new existence as pieces with anthropological value, for their pathologies were supposedly explained in terms of racial variation. Such pieces were displayed in racial terms at the Museo Nacional de México, where they acquired the values of objects destined for national memory. Moving beyond anatomical taxonomy, those specimens disclose the history of Mexican people: pathological anatomy became an anthropological specimen and, in so doing, positively affirmed fragments of national history.

Pathological Anatomy as Anthropological Specimens

According to the archives on the Museo Nacional's acquisitions, its Natural History Hall had collections of skeletons and anatomical preparations (normal and pathological), as well as the teratological collection reported in Román Ramírez's *Catálogo*.[47] In the 1870s, "ancient" skulls and bones were acquired along with animals, plants, and minerals. Although some of their origins are unknown, most came from excavations in and around archaeological sites.[48] At first these bones had no special place or classification, but that changed around 1887, when Jesús Sánchez was director of the museum. He was behind the creation of the Anthropology and Ethnology Hall, which he entrusted to Francisco Martínez Calleja in 1888.[49] The project was unsuccessful, but the skulls and skeletal remains were prepared to be preserved and incorporated into collections. They were categorized not as anthropological pieces but as anatomical testimonies of races, some classified as physiological, others as pathological, atavistic, or deformed.[50]

In 1895 the idea of an Anthropology Hall was revived with the aim of showing it to the participants in the Eleventh International Congress of Americanists. The Anthropology and Ethnology Hall was assigned to the assistant naturalist Alfonso L. Herrera and to Ricardo Cícero (1869–1938). We have some information about the way they organized it thanks to their *Catálogo de Antropología del Museo Nacional* (1895).[51] According to Herrera and Cícero, the order of the exhibition mirrored that of the discipline of anthropology. The exhibition opened with an Ethnology Hall consisting of photographs of Mexican villages, followed by pieces of physiological and anatomical anthropology, as defined by Jesús Sánchez. In total, 1,322 pieces were exhibited.[52]

If we compare the pieces from the anatomy museum at the Escuela Nacional de Medicina to the skeletal remains at the Museo Nacional de México, it becomes clear that the material taken from dead bodies constituted a highly variable combination of temporalities. The pathological anatomical specimens at the Museo Nacional de México came not from cadavers in the morgue but from bodies exhumed from graves and archaeological sites. Bones, skulls, and other highly deteriorated human remains were cast in plaster to preserve them. Tables of measurements were also drawn up, similar to those by the Frenchman Ernest Théodore Hamy (1842–1908), a naturalist at the Musée d'Histoire Naturelle.[53]

As in the medical museums, there was an attempt to preserve material remains that were destined to disappear, but the taxonomy employed in pathological anatomy was not adopted. Like Jean Armand de Quatrefages and Hamy at the Musée d'ethnographie du Trocadéro, Herrera and Cícero used these skulls and their measurements to familiarize themselves with physical, moral, and historical variation across the races. Although they saw themselves as following in the footsteps of the European naturalists, they also sought to distinguish themselves so as to recalibrate the anatomical order from a Mexican point of view. In *Crania ethnica* (1882), Quatrefages and Hamy proposed a comparative racial anatomy in which they referenced some sixty "Mexican" skulls, in addition to those cited in Hamy's *Mission scientifique au Mexique et dans l'Amérique Centrale* (1885). Those works had informed Herrera and Cícero's study of the races, but Quatrefages and Hamy's conclusions were sorely in need of revision. The Museo Nacional's collections presented an opportunity to rectify and expand on existing knowledge of osteological anatomy. Unlike the inventories from the Escuela Nacional de Medicina's anatomy museum, then, the *Catálogo de Antropología* produced something new: other existences and categories that established relationships, via anatomical pieces, between races, their histories, and their pathologies (table 3.2).[54]

The collection of anatomical anthropology comprised a combination of different collections: the Museo Nacional's natural history collections, pieces from private collections, and pieces from the teratological section of the Escuela Nacional de Medicina's anatomy museum. With no more classifying information than the name of the collector, the pieces were listed with their geographical origin (sometimes confused with "racial origin"), with further annotations on the relevant pathology, as determined by the collector, and references to measurements or indices (table 3.2, column 4). Thus, through the order of resemblance and contiguity, these pieces were turned into objects of ethnology and anthropology.

Whereas the clinical-anatomical procedure was to associate clinical histories with pathological anatomies, at the Museo Nacional de México the skulls expressed race and were connected to the history of the towns from which they were taken, not to say "produced." In other words, as anthropological objects, the anatomical pieces acquired new existences. At the Museo Nacional de México, the fragments of Mexican bodies (male or female) whose anatomies varied with respect to European or mestizo bodies (whether in terms of excess or lack) expressed their racial origins. The basic hypothesis of the doctor-collector was to draw associations or equivalences between clinical histories, where their pathologies and the histories of the Mexican peoples confirmed each other. In this way, the temporal reference associated with medicine is clearly tied here to national history. Indeed, those pieces refer to the past in at least two ways: as objects discovered in "ancient" places (graves or archaeological sites); and as evidence of the present speaking to biological reminiscences of the past, as in the case of the heart-shaped pelvises brought to the Museo Nacional de México.[55] In that same sense, the *Catálogo de Antropología* features tables of the cranial indices of indigenous people who were incarcerated at the Puebla Penitentiary, published in *Estudio de antropología criminal* (1892) by Manuel Martínez Baca and Manuel Vergara. Skulls and pelvises challenged conclusions reached in Europe about "female," "criminal," and

Table 3.2 **Comparative racial anatomy**

Provenance				
Location / race	Collection	Type of piece	Atrophies, deformities associated with race	Number of pieces
Michoacán, "Tarascan"	Nicolás León/Plancarte	Natural (burial)	Mutilation or sulciform atrophy	2
Neanderthal, Engis, Quichua, Aymara, Caribbean, Mexican	MNM	Plaster casts / tables of cubic measurements	"Inferior" cranial indices	39
State of Hidalgo, Chichimec	Collection of Protasio Tagle	Natural (excavations)	Cranial indices	39
Santiago Tlatelolco ST*; Huexotla, Nonoalco, San Juan Teotihuacan	MNM, by Manuel Ticó (1893)	Natural (exhumations)	Cranial indices, pathological lesions	80
Cerro de Xico, Lago de Chalco, Valle de México, Chalco, San Miguel Anacuco	Herrera and Cícero / MNM	Natural (excavations)	Cranial indices, deformities	100
San Francisco, San Lázaro, ST*, Mexico City, San Luis Potosí	Dr. P. Maury / Baumgarten Collection	Natural (excavations)	Cranial indices	39
Puebla Penitentiary	Collection of Drs. Martínez Baca and Vergara	Tables of cranial indices comparing indigenous and European criminals	Racial atavism	3 tables
Escuela Nacional de Medicina Hospital de Maternidad and Escuela Nacional de Medicina anatomy museums	José de J. Sánchez, Ignacio Flores	Comparative table of indices from 50 pelvises	Racial atavism	1 table
Ancient gravesites, ST*; Belen, Tulyahualco; modern pieces from San Andrés, Matzahua Otomíes, Mixteco	Mission Scientifique du Mexique; Musée de l'Homme	Tables of cranial capacities from 19 skulls	Cranial indices	3 tables

*ST = Santiago Tlatelolco

"indigenous" anatomies. According to Herrera and Cícero, the crux of the matter was whether it was possible to conclude that race implies pathologies given the limited number of skulls and bones that had been measured at that point. In addition to such anatomical questions, Mexican doctors raised doubts about the status of craniological knowledge, from the Dutch physician and racial anthropologist Petrus Camper (1722–89) to Hamy. Their aim was not to critique the concept of race but to enrich it with more anatomical evidence taken from and analyzed in Mexico.[56]

The *Catálogo de Antropología* does not mention the cost of acquiring and preparing those pieces, but like the collection at the Escuela Nacional de Medicina's anatomy museum, the pieces at the Museo Nacional de México did have prices associated with them. Some came from Mexican as well as foreign collectors involved in the market for plant, animal, and archaeological objects. For example, acquiring an "Aztec skull" cost the museum 7.50 pesos.[57] The values of the human remains, like those of the other objects at the Museo Nacional de México, depended not only on costs but also on negotiations between several kinds of actors: amateurs, doctors, Mexican officials, and European colonial museums. An exemplary case comes from bone pieces prepared by Francisco del Paso y Troncoso, director of the Museo Nacional de México, exhibited at the 1892 Exposición Histórica-Americana, in Madrid, which he then gave to Hamy in 1895 to be displayed at the Musée de l'Homme in Paris, whence they did not return.[58]

At the turn of the twentieth century, the collections of pathological anatomy at the Museo Nacional de México and the anatomy museum of the Escuela Nacional de Medicina disappeared from public view, although some of the pieces were salvaged from the shadows of their respective warehouses. Nevertheless, the values and racial identities inscribed on those anatomical pieces were not erased, and they continued to circulate with the same values but in other forms and materials.

Nicolás León (1859–1929) replaced A. L. Herrera as the naturalist at the Museo Nacional de México from 1900 to 1929. He participated in the relocation of the natural history collection to the Museo del Chopo in 1908.[59] With regard to the anthropology collection, from 1900 to 1911 León continued to collect skulls and skeletal remains, which he measured and classified, and many of which he cast in plaster. These pieces were no longer identified with pathological anatomy as a medical discipline. They became materials for a course in ethnology and anthropology that León started teaching in 1903.

The anatomy specimens themselves did not disappear but were concentrated in medical institutes and hospitals. The collection at the Escuela Nacional de Medicina's anatomy museum was transformed as the anatomy museum at the Hospital General de San Andrés evolved into the Instituto Patológico in 1900. In 1905, the Hospital General de San Andrés and the Instituto Patológico sent 1,306 specimens of pathological anatomy and 500 microscopic preparations to the anatomy museum of the Escuela Nacional de Medicina.[60] This shift transformed that museum. The shared production of anatomies by the hospital and the escuela ended, and the circulation of pieces decreased until it ended entirely around 1920.

In the early twentieth century, most anatomy objects were "broken-down," stranded in the display cases at both museums as *valuable* vestiges of medicine's and anthropology's past, alien to those disciplines and practices in the present. But, as Walter Benjamin pointed out, "broken-downness" is only one moment in the fragile lifetime of a collection. Although many anatomical pieces were no longer produced and in circulation, their values and materials continued existing, transmuted and re-created, in other forms and objects. Made with medical instruments and apparatuses rather than collected, these objects afforded other modes of existence: being re-created in other materialities and temporalities and circulating with other values, they preserved the regime of racial difference associated with them.[61] Such is the case of the bones and skulls that were measured and turned into indices (angular measures) that were then arranged in tables (figure 3.3). Cranial anatomies survive as tables of measurements that provide an account, through race and place, of greater or lesser cranial capacity, their shapes, and their anatomical defects.

To be sure, the anatomies continued to exist in other modes, thanks to investments in other materials, generating new regimes of exhibition and circulation. Currently, those other forms appear as evidence of scientific modernity, standardized matter available for global exchange. Indeed, they lost all reference to the histories of specific persons with ailing bodies to which they belonged, to the doctors who dissected them, and to the anthropologists who measured them. Although they seem to be unrelated to the old three-dimensional pathological anatomies, marked with local characteristics and tied to the past, today the anatomies of Mexican people continue to be associated with racial marks. Statistical tables and photomicrographs of "Mexican" tissues continue to course through the circuits of the medical market, making race a part of the commodification of human life.

Cráneos de los sepulcros antiguos de Belem, Tulyahualco, Medellín y cráneo moderno de San Andrés.

Medidas del cráneo.	Belem. 1 hombre	Tulyahualco. 3 hombres	Tulyahualco. 1 mujer	Medellín. 1 mujer	San Andrés. 1 hombre
Capacidad craneana aproximada	"	"	"	"	1375
Proyección — anterior — total	97	93	89	"	97
Proyección — anterior — facial	24	22	21	"	17
Proyección — posterior	85	85	79	"	82
Diámetro — antero-posterior máximo	169	171	157	167	166
Diámetro — transverso — máximo	142	145	139	139	139
Diámetro — transverso — bitemporal	137	134	134	"	138
Diámetro — transverso — biauricular	120	126	124	120	130
Diámetro — transverso — bimastoideo	99	101	102	"	104
Diámetro — transverso — frontal máximo	118	116	111	114	109
Diámetro — transverso — frontal mínimo	92	94	94	96	90
Diámetro — transverso — occipital máximo	112	110	104	106	106
Diámetro — vertical basilo-bregmático	135	130	128	"	134
Curva — horizontal — total	491	497	473	474	494
Curva — horizontal — preauricular	230	226	214	210	233
Curva — transversa — total	449	431	418	454	443
Curva — transversa — supra-auricular	310	315	290	310	300
Curva — frontal — cerebral	100	96	93	100	93
Curva — frontal — total	121	120	116	123	116
Curva — parietal	123	114	110	118	127
Curva — occipital	102	118	104	119	103
Longitud del agujero occipital	30	35	36	40	34
Anchura	28	28	29	32	30
Línea naso-basilar	102	96	91	92	100
Línea basilo-supra-nasal	110	107	102	106	112
Circunferencia media total	465	469	445	483	469
Índice — Longitud = 100 — Anchura	84.02	84.79	88.53	83.25	83.73
Índice — Longitud = 100 — Altura	79.87	76.02	81.55	"	80.72
Índice — Anchura = 100 — Altura	95.07	89.65	92.08	"	96.40

Medidas de la cara.	Belem. 1 hombre	Tulyahualco. 3 hombres	Tulyahualco. 1 mujer	Medellín. 1 mujer	San Andrés. 1 hombre
Cara. — Anchura — biorbitaria externa	106	106	100	103	104
Cara. — Anchura — interorbitaria	25	27	21	23	24
Cara. — Anchura — bizigomática máxima	133	130	129	"	135
Cara. — Anchura — bimaxilar mínima	60	62	53	60	68
Órbitas — Anchura	39	39	37	36	39
Órbitas — Altura	34	34	33	32?	36
Nariz — Anchura de los huesos nasales — superior	17	16	11	"	13
Nariz — Anchura de los huesos nasales — mínima	10	16	7	"	9
Nariz — Anchura de los huesos nasales — inferior	22	"	"	"	21
Nariz — Anchura máxima de la abertura	29	27	23	"	27
Nariz — Longitud — media de los huesos nasales	24	"	"	"	21
Nariz — Longitud — total de la nariz	51	46	46	49	50
Cara. — Altura — sub-cerebral de la frente	21	23	24	21	23
Cara. — Altura — intermaxilar	18	19	"	20	19
Cara. — Altura — total de la cara	90	"	"	90	92
Cara. — Altura — de los pómulos	24	23	19	"	25
Cara. — Altura — órbito-alveolar	41	38	"	"	40
Bóveda palatina. — Longitud	50	56	"	"	54
Bóveda palatina. — Anchura	41	43	40	"	46
Bóveda palatina. — Distancia de la espina nasal posterior al agujero occipital	51	38	41	"	40
Línea basilo-alveolar	104	93	"	"	94
Ángulo facial — sub-nasal	74	78	72	"	74
Ángulo facial — alveolar	61	63	62	"	64
Ángulo facial — dentario	"	"	"	"	60
Índice — orbitario	87.18	87.18	89.18	88.88	92.30
Índice — nasal	56.86	58.69	50.00	"	54.00
Índice — facial	67.66	"	"	"	69.17

Dr. Hamy. Mission Scientifique au Mexique et dans l'Amérique Centrale. Première partie. p. 31.

Figure 3.3 Luis Alfonso Herrera and Ricardo E. Cícero, table of measurement indices, *Catalogo de Antropología del Museo Nacional* (Mexico City: Imprenta del Museo Nacional, 1895), 123. Personal collection.

With the authority of science and of the museums that administer these transmuted anatomical specimens, we consume them. In their frayed edges and contradictions, however, we can see that that they are the products of experimental techniques, loaded with the values of the past, objects whose calling is to circulate like commodities, and at the same time to embody race, the founding origin of the nation.

Conclusions

The pathological and normal anatomies I have analyzed here reveal how objects possess multiple existences, depending on where and how they were produced; who collects them; the other objects with which they cohabitate; and the museums through which they move. Rather than ambiguity, we can think of this in terms of multiple existences. Instead of attempting to define those multiple existences, I have sought to reflect on the nature of objects. Pathological specimens are the starting point of future analyses. They show that body objects—like other objects—are not immutable things. They teach us that they are the result of different interests on the part of institutions and their collectors, but also of the memories and histories of the materials that constitute them, hence the mutations that they undergo in the course of their movements.

Thus, the movement of pathological anatomies between the medical museums and the Museo Nacional de México enabled us to recognize them as the result of multiple productions: of dissection practices, of forms of clinical knowledge and the skill to distinguish the normal from the pathological, and of the medical interest in measuring in accordance with the anthropometric knowledge of the time. Nor we can forget that the material nature of the anatomical pieces intervened in their production: pieces made from cadaverous material at the Hospital General de San Andrés are not the same as skeletal remains exhumed by antiquities collectors, which in turn are different from the wax and papier-mâché anatomies produced by European artisans. All these materials underwent changes as a result of the contingencies of exchange and trade, and of the spaces as well as the values with which they were exchanged. Perhaps the most relevant lesson of this circuitous journey through the details of body objects is a reflection on their political life, not only because they are the bearers of some of the history of racial politics in modern Mexico, but also because these objects show that they do not have fixed attributes: they are processual and relational; they express and create histories. In this case, medical and anthropological practices produced and circulated racialized body objects, making anatomy into material with political value, able to be exchanged, negotiated, and commodified. In the twenty-first century, those pathological anatomies actualize a past associated with race. At the same time, they are the future, evidence of the sciences of normality, pathology, and anatomy.

Notes

I am grateful to the editors for their suggestions and critical comments, which helped me expand and deepen the arguments in this text.

1. The Museo de Anatomía Patológica at the Hospital General de San Andrés opened on the occasion of the Segundo Congreso Médico Pan American in 1896. Joaquín Baranda to the Director of the Escuela Nacional de Medicina, October 28, 1896, doc. 3, folio 5, file 266, Archivo Histórico de la Facultad de Medicina de la UNAM, Fondo Escuela de Medicina y Alumnos (AHFM-FEMyA).
2. Annemarie Mol, *The Body Multiple: Ontology in Medical Practice* (Durham, N.C.: Duke University Press, 2002).
3. I draw inspiration from Walter Benjamin, *The Arcades Project*, trans. Howard Eiland and Kevin McLaughlin, ed. Rolf Tiedemann (Cambridge, Mass.: Belknap Press, 1999); Arjun Appadurai, ed., *The Social Life of Things: Commodities in Cultural Perspective* (Cambridge: Cambridge University Press, 1986); Lorraine Daston, ed., *Things that Talk: Object Lessons from Art and Science* (New York: Zone Books, 2004); Susan Leigh Star, "This Is Not a Boundary Object: Reflections on the Origin of a Concept," *Science, Technology and Human Values* 35, no. 5 (2010): 601–17; and Jean Baudrillard, *The System of Objects*, trans. James Benedict (London: Verso, 1996).
4. Miruna Achim, *From Idols to Antiquity: Forging the National Museum of Mexico* (Lincoln: University of Nebraska Press, 2017); Nicholas Thomas, *Entangled Objects: Exchange, Material Culture, and Colonialism in the Pacific* (Cambridge, Mass.: Harvard University Press, 1991), 16–17; Ivan Karp and Steven D. Lavine, eds., *Exhibiting Cultures: The Poetics and Politics of Museum Display* (Washington, D.C.: Smithsonian Institution Press, 1991); José Pardo Tomás, Alfonso Zarzoso, and Mauricio Sánchez Menchero, eds., *Cuerpos mostrados: Regímenes de exhibición de lo humano, Barcelona y Madrid, siglos XVII-XX* (Mexico City: Siglo XXI/UNAM, 2018); Irina Podgorny, "L'inquiétante étrangeté des musées ambulantes et des collections d'anatomie populaire du XIXème siècle," in *Les savoirs-mondes: Mobilités et circulation des savoirs depuis le Moyen Âge*, ed. Pilar González Bernaldo and Liliane Hilaire-Pérez (Rennes: Presses Universitaires de Rennes, 2016), 99–107.
5. Georges Didi-Huberman, *Devant le temps: Histoire de l'art et anachronisme des images* (Paris: Minuit, 2000), 43.

6. Mechthild Rutsch, *Entre el campo y el gabinete: Nacionales y extranjeros en la profesionalización de la antropología mexicana (1877–1920)* (Mexico City: INAH, 2007), 49–59; Luis Gerardo Morales Moreno, *Orígenes de la museología mexicana: Fuentes para el estudio histórico del Museo Nacional, 1780–1940* (Mexico City: Universidad Iberoamericana, 1994), 33–34.
7. Igor Kopytoff, "The Cultural Biography of Things," in Appadurai, *Social Life of Things*, 64–91.
8. John H. Teacher, *Catalogue of the Anatomical and Pathological Preparations of Dr. William Hunter in the Hunterian Museum* (Glasgow: James MacLehose, 1900).
9. On surgical practices and knowledge of doctors and surgeons, see Rafael Heliodoro Valle, *La cirugía mexicana del siglo XIX* (Mexico City: Tipografía SAG, 1942).
10. It was officially called the Museo de Anatomía Normal, Comparada y Patológica, but was known as the Museo de Anatomía Patológica de la Escuela Nacional de Medicina. Clinical practice is the basis of modern medicine and is understood as research designed to identify, record, and analyze the symptoms presented by disease. This information is used to determine degrees of deviation from the normal, and to propose a therapeutic intervention. Anatomy was one of the orientations of clinical practice and involved autopsying cadavers to identify the pathologies that afflicted a patient prior to death.
11. Xóchitl Martínez Barbosa and Jorge Zacarías Prieto, *Libro de juntas de profesores de la Escuela Nacional de Medicina, 1851–1883*, Archivalia medica 10 (Mexico City: UNAM, 2015), 32, 57.
12. The museum opened without a conservator. Positions for a prosector and a head of descriptive anatomy were created in 1855. "Sesión del día 10 de diciembre de 1855," in Martínez Barbosa and Zacarías Prieto, *Libro de juntas de profesores*, 77.
13. La Redacción, "Un mal anfiteatro," *La escuela de medicina, periódico científico, dedicado a las ciencias médicas* 2 (1880–1881): 343.
14. A conservator was not named. Instead there was a doctor of pathological anatomy (Manuel Toussaint), a bacteriologist (Ángel Gaviño), and a preparator of anatomical specimens. Xóchitl Martínez Barbosa, *El Hospital de San Andrés: Un espacio para la enseñanza, la práctica y la investigación médicas, 1861–1904* (Mexico City: Siglo XXI/Hospital General, 2005), 147, 173.
15. Rafael Lavista, "Discurso pronunciado en la inauguración del Museo Anatamo-Patológico en el Hospital San Andrés presidida por el Señor Presidente de la República," *Revista quincenal de anatomía patológica y clínicas y quirúrgica* 1, no. 1 (1896): vii–xxix. Histories of the museum include Isaac Costero, "El Instituto Patológico Nacional y su antecesor, el Museo Patológico," *Anales de la Sociedad Mexicana de Historia de la Ciencia y de la Tecnología* 1 (1969): 84–96; Martínez Barbosa, *El Hospital de San Andrés*; and Ana María Carrillo, "La patología del Siglo XIX y los institutos nacionales de investigación médica en México," *LABO-acta* 13, no. 1 (2001): 23–31.

16. Hugo Arciniega Ávila, "La galería de las Sibilas: El Museo público de historia natural, arqueología e historia de México," *Boletín de monumentos históricos* 14 (2008): 35–54. On the natural history collections, see also the chapters in this volume by Miruna Achim and Frida Gorbach.
17. "Compra de diferentes animales para el Departamento de Historia Natural," vol. 2, doc. 35, ff. 123–27, Archivo Histórico del Museo Nacional de Antropología (AHMNA).
18. There were veterinarians and doctors from the provinces, but above all amateurs who knew how to desiccate and mount pieces. "Relacionado con la adquisición y disección de animales para el Departamento de Historia Natural," February 1874, vol. 2, doc. 33, ff. 114–21, AHMNA.
19. A. L. Herrera, "Informe del ayudante naturalista, julio–septiembre 1898," vol. 236, doc. 9, f. 69, AHMNA; Román Ramírez, *Catálogo de la anomalías coleccionadas en el Museo Nacional, precedido de unas nociones de teratología* (Mexico City: Imprenta del Museo Nacional, 1896).
20. I am unsure exactly how many pieces were moved and what they were, having found only general mentions of them. Manuel Rivera Cambas, "El museo nacional" (1880), in Morales Moreno, *Orígenes de la museología mexicana*, 76; and Jesús Galindo y Villa, *Breve noticia histórico-descriptiva del Museo Nacional de México* (Mexico City: Imprenta del Museo Nacional, 1896), 12–15.
21. "Reunión de trabajo, 9 de octubre de 1900," vol. 236, doc. 28, f. 132, AHMNA.
22. "El Subdirector comenta problemas de espacio" (1908), vol. 266, doc. 42, f. 281 and vol. 266, file 43, ff. 282–83, AHMNA. For more on the Museo del Chopo and natural history, see Frida Gorbach's contribution to this volume.
23. Achim, *From Idols to Antiquity*, 70ff.
24. "Programa para el año escolar 1874," file 266, doc. 1, f. 4, AHFM-FEMyA; "El Museo Anatamo-Patológico abrirá diario" (1885), file 260, doc. 10, f. 3, AHFM-FEMyA; "Justo Sierra solicita informe al conservador," file 250, docs. 4–6, ff. 215–16, AHFM-FEMyA.
25. Michel Foucault, *The Birth of the Clinic: An Archaeology of Medical Perception*, trans. A. M. Sheridan Smith (New York: Vintage, 1973).
26. Jiménez championed using the hospitals for instruction. In 1858 he published his *Lecciones de clínica médica*, a series of lectures based on the study of clinical cases. Fernando Martínez Cortés, *La medicina científica y el siglo XIX* (Mexico City: Fondo de Cultura Económica, 2003), 90–97.
27. Jiménez, *Lecciones de clínica*, quoted in Martínez Cortés, *La medicina científica*, 99, 100; Foucault, *Birth of the Clinic*, 137; Russell C. Maulitz, *Morbid Appearances: The Anatomy of Pathology in the Early Nineteenth Century* (Cambridge: Cambridge University Press, 1987).
28. In Mexico there were no workshops of anatomical models like Honoré Fragonard's (1777) at l'École de Vétérinaire d'Alfort in France, or the works of Felice Fontana (1775) in Italy. See, for example, Thomas Schnalke, *Diseases in Wax: The History of the Medical Moulage*, trans. Kathy Spatschek (Zurich: Quin-

tessence, 1995); Michel Lemire, "Representation and the Human Body: The Colored Wax Anatomic Models of the 18th and 19th Centuries in the Revival of Medical Instruction," *Surgical-Radiologic Anatomy* 14, no. 4 (1992): 283–91; Jonathan Simon, "The Theater of Anatomy: The Anatomical Preparations of Honoré Fragonard," *Eighteenth-Century Studies* 36, no. 1 (2002): 63–79; and Susan Lamb, "Model Behavior: A Material Culture Approach to the History of Anatomy Models," in *Building New Bridges: Sources, Methods and Interdisciplinary Sources*, ed. Jeff Keshen and Sylvie Perrier (Ottawa: University of Ottawa Press, 2005), 29–48.

29. Raymond Vasseur-Tramond, *Catalogue de M. Vasseur-Tramond: Successeur, naturaliste, préparateur d'anatomie* (Paris: Éditions de l'auteur, 1875).
30. Lavista, "Discurso pronunciado," viii, ix.
31. Lavista, "Informe," *Revista Quincenal de Anatomías Patológicas y Clínicas* 4 (1899): 324.
32. Didi-Huberman, *Devant le temps*, 16.
33. James Delbourgo and Staffan Müller-Wille, "Introduction: Listmania," *Isis* 4 (December 2012): 710–15.
34. "Reglamento del Museo Anatómico de esta Escuela, aprobado por la Junta Directiva 1871," file 5, doc. 488, AHFM-FEMyA.
35. In 1877, Rodríguez was replaced by José Ramírez (1852–1904), followed by Joaquín Huici from 1886 to 1905 and then Eduardo Galán, until 1912. Ramírez, "Nombramiento," file 149, docs. 14, 9, AHFM-FEMyA; "Inventario de objetos que se hallan en el Museo de la Escuela" (1886), file 151, doc. 23, AHFM-FEMyA. On Emilio Galán's succession, see the 1905 inventory, file 488, doc. 5, AHFM-FEMyA.
36. *Le Musée Dupuytren: L'Ecole de Paris et la naissance de l'Anatomie pathologique de Portal à Cruveilhier—Exposition organisée au Musée Dupuytren à la occasion du Cent Cinquantenaire de la Société Anatomique de Paris, 1826–1976* (Paris: Musée Dupuytren, 1976).
37. Juan María Rodríguez, "Inventarios: Museo de Anatomía Patológica" (1872), appendix, doc. 497, f. 19, AHFM-FEMyA.
38. Appadurai, *Social Life of Things*.
39. "Donaciones al Museo de la ENM" (1872), file 139, doc. 53, ff. 1–4, AHFM-FEMyA; Juan María Rodríguez, "Informes pedidos a varios empleados en esta Escuela: Informe del Conservador del Museo Anatómico de la Escuela de Medicina" (1873), file 140, doc. 36, ff. 1–2, AHFM-FEMyA.
40. Rodríguez, "Inventarios" (1872), f. 21.
41. Benjamin, *Arcades Project*; Baudrillard, *System of Objects*, 73–74; Appadurai, *Social Life of Things*.
42. "Donaciones al Museo de la ENM" (1872), file 139, doc. 53, ff. 1–4, AHFM-FEMyA. It would be impossible to cite all the clinical and natural history articles on the museum's pieces. See, for example, "Eufemio Méndez sends the Museo Nacional skulls and bones from the Sierra de Chihuahua, from a period prior

to the Conquest" (1874), vol. 2, doc. 34, f. 122, AHMNA; G. Becerril received "$7.750 for an Aztec skull," vol. 2, doc. 33, f. 114, AHMNA.

43. "Inventario general del Museo de Anatomía Patológica" (ca. 1884), file 145, doc. 42, ff. 18–19, AHFM-FEMyA; "Inventario de los objetos que se hallan en el Museo Anatómico de la Escuela N. de Medicina" (1886), file 151, doc. 23, AHFM-FEMyA.
44. "Informes administrativos para la compra de modelos anatómicos en cera e instrumental de cirugía para la Escuela Nacional de Medicina" (1874), file 174, doc. 1, ff. 1–5, AHFM-FEMyA.
45. A janiceps was a pair of twins conjoined at the thorax, with a single head and two faces looking in opposite directions. See Manuel F. Jiménez, "Sobre la aptitud de la raza indígena para ciertas enfermedades," *Anales de la Sociedad de Humboldt* 2 (1875): 139–41; Juan María Rodríguez, "Teratología: Estudio sobre varias monstruosidades ectromelianas, y más particularmente sobre Pedro Salinas, natural de Tejupilco (Estado de México)," *Anales de la Sociedad Humboldt* 1 (1872): 279–95; and Frida Gorbach, *El monstruo, objeto imposible: Un estudio sobre teratología mexicana, siglo XIX* (Mexico City: Universidad Autónoma Metropolitana–Xochimilco and Itaca, 2008).
46. Benjamin, *Arcades Project*, 207. The phrase "broken-down matter" translates "Gescheiterte Materie: das ist Erhebung der Ware in den Stand der Allegorie. Fetischcharakter der Ware und Allegorie (H 2,6)." Walter Benjamin, *Das Passagen-Werk*, vol. 1 of *Gesammelte Schriften*, ed. Rolf Tiedemann (Frankfurt: Suhrkamp Verlag, 1996), 274.
47. This is not an exhaustive description. I am drawing on notes from 1873 to 1900: vol. 2, doc. 11, ff. 72–82; doc. 35, ff. 123–37 (all 1876); doc. 50, ff. 169–80; vol. 3, doc. 1, ff. 1–21 (1877); doc. 3, ff. 24–35 (1877); and doc. 29, ff. 116–32 (1878), AHMNA.
48. See, for example, "Eufemio Méndez sends the Museo Nacional skulls and bones"; and G. Becerril received "$7.750 for an Aztec skull."
49. Hired as a professor of anthropology, Martínez Calleja was suspended from his position "for offenses committed," without further clarification, in April 1889; vol. 259, doc. 18, ff. 68–69, AHMNA.
50. In defining anthropology, Sánchez divided it into physiological and anatomical categories, an idea reprised by Herrera and Cícero in their 1895 *Catálogo de antropología*. Jesús Sánchez, "Historia natural médica: Relaciones entre la antropología y la medicina," *Gaceta médica de México* 35 (1898): 193–206.
51. Luis Alfonso Herrera and Ricardo E. Cícero, *Catálogo de Antropología del Museo Nacional* (Mexico City: Imprenta del Museo Nacional, 1895); Galindo y Villa, *Breve noticia histórico-descriptiva*, 15.
52. Vol. 236, f. 71, AHMNA; Herrera and Cícero, *Catálogo de Antropología*, vii. I will not elaborate on the Ethnology Wing, which exhibited photographs previously described and organized by Francisco del Paso y Troncoso for the *Catálogo de la Sección de México en la Exposición Histórico-Americana de Madrid* (1892),

and classificatory and descriptive tables of the "indigenous families," while the Physiological Anthropology Hall exhibited tables of anthropometric, respiratory and histological measurements of Mexicans.

53. Luis A. Herrera and Ricardo Cícero, "Estudios de antropología mexicana," *La naturaleza: Periódico científico de la Sociedad Mexicana de Historia Natural* 2 (1897): 463.
54. Nélia Dias, "Séries de crânes et armée de squelettes: Les collections anthropologiques en France dans la seconde moitié du XIXème siècle," *Bulletins et mémoires de la Société d'anthropologie de Paris* 1, no. 3–4 (1989): 203–30; Andrew Zimmerman, "Anthropology and the Place of Knowledge in Imperial Berlin" (PhD diss., University of California San Diego, 1998), 12–14.
55. Herrera and Cícero, *Catálogo de Antropología*, 138–43; Herrera and Cícero, "Estudios de antropología mexicana," 465.
56. Herrera and Cícero, *Catálogo de Antropología*, 129, 131, 137.
57. Herrera and Cícero, *Catálogo de Antropología*; Galindo y Villa, *Breve noticia histórico-descriptiva*, 15.
58. For another period and perspective, see Achim, *From Idols to Antiquity*, 9–11; and Miguel García, "Profesionalización de la antropología física en México: La investigación, las instituciones y la enseñanza (1887–1942)" (PhD diss., Universidad Nacional Autónoma de México, 2013), 89–96.
59. "Se comisiona a M. Urbina y a N. León empacar objetos del Herbario, aplicaciones zoológicas . . ." (1902), vol. 3, doc. 29, ff. 92–94, AHMNA.
60. "Inventario de las piezas anatómicas, muebles y enseres que he recibido del Sr. Dr. Joaquín Huici, y que contiene definitivamente el Museo Anatamo-Patológico de la Escuela Nacional de Medicina" (1905), file 250, doc. 2, AHFM-FEMyA.
61. Baudrillard, *System of Objects*, 43.

Part II

Fragments

\\ 4

The Tangled Journey of the Cross of Palenque

CHRISTINA BUENO

Sometime in the early nineteenth century, tomb raiders entered the Temple of the Cross in the Maya ruins of Palenque and dismantled an enormous monument. Composed of three rectangular panels with hieroglyphics and other figures—including a cross-like relief—this artifact is now known as the Cross of Palenque. Over six feet high and made of fragile limestone, each of the panels proved difficult to move. The center panel was torn out of the wall, carried down the temple, and abandoned at the banks of a nearby stream. The right panel was similarly ripped out, shattering into fragments left scattered about the ruins. The left panel, for some reason, remained embedded in the wall. The Cross of Palenque was destroyed.[1]

And so began the complicated story of this monument, three slabs of stone that went on to have very different fates. One of them, the shattered right panel, traveled all the way to Washington, D.C., where it graced the halls of the Smithsonian Institution for decades. Yet unlike most of the monoliths that have been vandalized and taken from Mexico throughout the centuries, the Cross of Palenque was eventually made whole again. In 1908, U.S. secretary of state Elihu Root repatriated the Smithsonian panel to Mexico to cement diplomatic relations with the country during the rule of Porfirio Díaz (1876–1911), the period known as the Porfiriato. One year later, all three slabs were reunited in the Museo Nacional de México. The unification of the Cross of Palenque came at the cost of tremendous material and logistical difficulties on the part of the Porfirian regime. Hauling around huge and heavy, delicate pieces of stone is no easy task. The Cross of Palenque's tangled journey offers a glimpse into the history of Mexico's tenacious efforts to control and display pre-Hispanic antiquities in the Museo Nacional de México. It also illustrates some of the many ways in which political and diplomatic relationships shape the history of artifacts. Antiquities are not just embedded in different strata of rock and soil; they are enmeshed in various layers of power. Tracing the workings of power is often complicated by the fact that the archival record left by artifacts like the Cross of Palenque is as fragmented and incomplete as the objects themselves.

The Porfirian Context

The unification of the Cross of Palenque in the Museo Nacional de México was part of a much larger project aimed at controlling antiquities during the Porfiriato. Under Díaz, Mexico placed guards at ruins, strengthened federal legislation to protect ancient artifacts, and created the nation's first official archaeological site at Teotihuacan in 1910. It established the General Inspectorate of Monuments in 1885, Mexico's first agency designed to protect pre-Hispanic remains. The government also gave unprecedented support to the Museo Nacional de México. It turned the institution into the nation's principal showcase of the ancient past, filling it with relics like the Cross of Palenque.

For Porfirian political and intellectual elites, antiquity was a means to assert and defend Mexico's national image following a long history of colonialism, foreign exploitation, and civil conflict. Mexico was a nation deemed inferior by the dominant Eurocentric racism of the times, a place considered so backward that its artifacts were ripe for the taking. Porfirian elites sought to counter this image and present Mexico as a nation with deep and prestigious roots. As many scholars have shown, antiquity can often serve as a source of pride, offering a postcolonial nation such as Mexico a history of autonomy before colonialism, or an "authentic past of its own."[2] This past was thought to take tangible, material form in the pre-Hispanic remains found throughout the country. Rather than referring to these as patrimony or cultural heritage, terms more commonly employed today, Mexican elites used the phrase "property of the nation." But they typically spoke about the artifacts in more poetic ways, as the nation's archives or the "mute witnesses of the past."[3]

The government set out to take control of these objects as it created an official history for the nation, one that harnessed the pre-Hispanic past to narratives of Mexico's national greatness. This was evident in *México a través de los siglos* (1887–89), the nation's first work of historical synthesis, a five-volume series that brought together different periods in the Mexican past and fused them into a single story.[4] The invention of these sorts of histories is central to the process of nation building because it endows a country's diverse population with a common culture and sense of unity. Sponsored by the federal government, *México a través de los siglos* placed antiquity at the beginning of a sweeping historical narrative that gave Mexicans a shared heritage and origin. The pre-Hispanic past had thus become essential to nation building. Composed by multiple authors, *México a través de los siglos* began with a volume on antiquity written by the historian, archaeologist, and statesman Alfredo Chavero.

Chavero's work, however, did not give all the ancient indigenous groups equal treatment. In the words of Haydeé López Hernández, it portrayed the Aztecs as "the direct ancestors of the Mexican nation."[5] Porfirian elites emphasized the Aztecs as the most important of Mexico's cultures. In this way, they forged a symbolic connection between Mexico's ancient rulers, who had been based in the modern capital, and the contemporary federal government. At the same time, other ancient cultures—especially the Maya—played important roles in building the image of Mexico that Porfirian leaders sought to convey.

Archaeological remains were not simply proof of Mexico's sophisticated past; the very act of controlling them, in the eyes of Porfirian elites, endowed Mexico with the aura of a scientific and modern nation on par with the most civilized countries of the globe. It also showed the world that Mexico had sovereignty over its territory and the objects within it. The drive to control pre-Hispanic antiquities, in other words, was inseparable from the larger process of political centralization that was occurring at the time. The Díaz regime is often thought to have created a central government more capable of exerting control over the national territory. By the end of the era, even Mexico's peripheries had been dominated by the capital, in wars against the Yaqui in the northern state of Sonora and the Maya in Yucatán. Accumulating artifacts in the Museo Nacional de México reflected this development. While Mexico's national mythology focused mainly on the Aztecs and other cultures of the central plateau, there was also a push to gather artifacts in the museum from as many ancient peoples as possible, including the Maya.

The Museo Nacional de México had a relatively small collection of Maya antiquities throughout the Porfiriato. Few Mexican archaeologists carried out work in Maya territory, which was cut off from the rest of the country by distance, dense jungle, and the Caste War, the long-standing armed conflict between Mexican forces and the Yucatec Maya. Most of the excavations in the region were done by foreigners, a situation that did not change during the age of Díaz. Mexicans, however, did seek to address the lack of Maya relics in the museum. During Chavero's brief tenure as museum director (1902–3), he demanded that the institution acquire more Maya objects: it "truly lacks a collection of Maya antiquities. I do not need to stress the importance of such a collection, since everyone is already aware of it."[6] Chavero's call for Maya artifacts came at the same time that the federal government was trying to control the contemporary Maya. He made his statement in 1902, a year after Mexican forces defeated the autonomous Maya in Yucatán, officially ending the Caste War. Violent episodes continued, however, giving the federal government a feeble grip over the region. Amassing objects like the Cross of Palenque in the nation's capital was emblematic of the Díaz regime's desire to control the realm of the Maya. The construction of the museum collection was in many ways an internal colonial project, one that appropriated artifacts from communities like the Maya.

At the same time, the ancient Maya had a reputation for being "the highest culture" of the New World.[7] Institutions in Europe and the United States sought out antiquities from what was often thought to be the most prestigious pre-Hispanic civilization. Mexicans also held the ancient Maya in high regard. Chavero, for instance, considered the Maya more sophisticated in many ways than the Aztecs, especially when it came to technological advances like the production of temples and sculpture.[8] Mexico's failure to preserve the objects of this esteemed culture was thought to reflect poorly on the nation. The fact that Maya artifacts were some of the most heavily exploited by foreigners similarly worried many Mexicans; the effort to conserve Maya objects such as the Cross of Palenque was thus entwined with elite concerns with portraying Mexico as a strong, sovereign nation.

Like many other countries, Mexico thus sought to promote archaeology and take charge of antiquities as a form of resistance to imperialism. While one can question the entire nature of the federal government's claims to ancient objects, the construction of the museum collection was, in part, aimed at countering the imperialist actions that had drained Mexico of artifacts. Filling the museum with relics was a way to both create a prestigious ancient past for the nation and stem the desecration of Mexico's pre-Hispanic remains, objects that were severed from archaeological sites and frequently taken abroad by foreigners. The Museo Nacional de México was not just a showcase of antiquity but also a space to conserve and preserve objects that often could not be retained at their place of origin. That one of these pieces, the Smithsonian panel, was actually repatriated by a foreign power, made the unification of the Cross of Palenque all the more momentous.

The return of the panel, however, was initiated by Secretary Root and took place outside any formal bilateral agreements between Mexico and the United States. Today, international and binational treaties provide for the repatriation of cultural property.[9] While there is a range of opinions about heritage politics and policies, discussions often invoke ideas about nationalism, colonialism, and the relationship between the Global North and South. Mexicans during the Porfiriato did not employ this sort of vocabulary. They spoke about the repatriation of the Smithsonian tablet as a personal gesture by Root rather than an act of restitution by a foreign power.

The Right Panel

Although much about the Cross of Palenque's history remains a mystery, we know that the first panel to leave the ruins was the one that was shattered, the tablet that went to the Smithsonian. Details about its removal from the ruins are unclear, but the artifact arrived in the United States in 1842, having been shipped by Charles Russell, the American consul in Laguna, Campeche. These were the days of John Lloyd Stephens and Frederick Catherwood, the famous explorers who traveled through Maya territory, documenting the ruins. Russell met with the explorers soon after their trip to Palenque in 1840, and it is possible that their "archaeological enthusiasm" rubbed off on him, inspiring the consul to either collect the pieces of the artifact himself or hire someone to do it.[10] According to another theory, Stephens may have influenced events in a different way.[11] Stephens wanted to create a national museum of antiquities in New York City; one of his most farfetched schemes involved shipping the pyramids of Copán, in present-day Honduras, to the United States. Stephens hired a certain "Mr. Pawling" to make plaster casts of objects from Palenque for his museum, which were supposed to be forwarded to Consul Russell. Pawling's work, however, was intercepted by the governor of Chiapas, and his casts were confiscated. Nevertheless, Pawling may have gathered the pieces of the shattered tablet around this time and shipped them to Russell, who sent them to the United States.

The Pawling incident demonstrates how local politics often worked to thwart the imperialist ambitions of men like Stephens. The American explorer lamented the loss of the casts he commissioned in his *Incidents of Travel in Central America, Chiapas, and Yucatan.* According to Stephens, a group of residents from the town of Palenque had asked the governor to put a stop to Pawling's work. In a letter to the governor, the locals complained that the casts would be used to make copies of artifacts and these copies would be sold, generating a wealth the inhabitants of Palenque would never see. They demanded that Pawling pay the town "four or five thousand dollars" for the right to make the casts, pointing out that the artifacts belonged to them: the "treasure is ours" and we "should be benefited from it."[12] Pawling did not pay the residents, spurring them to seek recourse from Governor José Diego Lara, who not only agreed with the locals, but also told them to notify him of any future visitors to the site. Keep a "watchful eye upon the strangers who visit," he said, and stop them from doing excavations or removing anything at the ruins, "however insignificant it may appear."

Mexico's ruins in the mid-nineteenth century were generally in the hands of those who lived near them. Local residents and officials as well as state governors often exerted more control over archaeological sites than the federal government. Stewardship of ruins was not systematic, consistent, nor grounded in any solid legal underpinnings; it really depended on the will of local communities and authorities. In this case, the inhabitants of the village of Palenque believed the ruins belong to them. They had an interest in overseeing the site or at least determining how it would be used. Like many communities, they were also keenly aware of the potential commercial value of ancient objects.

Mexico's federal government, on the other hand, had little power over archaeological sites, especially in far-flung areas that were remote from the nation's capital, places such as Chiapas and other states dotted with Maya ruins. Throughout the century, the government had enacted a series of laws regarding the monuments, rulings that were often contradictory. Most of these gave the federal government authority over the ruins, while others placed the sites in the hands of local authorities. A vague edict from 1840, for instance, asked "all Mexicans" to undertake excavations and "search for monuments from antiquity."[13] The federal government had yet to pass a law that definitively granted it ownership of Mexico's ancient ruins. Legislation prohibiting the exportation of artifacts, though, was a different matter. Taking pre-Hispanic objects out of Mexico had been deemed an illicit activity for some time. Federal laws banning the exportation of antiquities stretched back to the early years after independence.[14] Foreigners were either unaware of this legislation or simply ignored it. Plagued by chronic chaos and civil strife throughout most of the nineteenth century, Mexico was also too weak to effectively enforce it.

As a result, foreigners like Stephens often trekked through the sites with a sense of entitlement, taking possession of whatever they pleased. As the century progressed, they became especially enamored with artifacts of the Maya, the civilization touted as the most sophisticated of the Americas. The writings of Stephens popularized the culture and intensified this Maya frenzy, inspiring explorers and collectors. This development coincided with the rise of the modern public museum, an institution that surfaced throughout the United States and Europe, especially after the 1850s. The interest in pre-Hispanic objects was also spurred on by Americanism. A broad scholarly field, Americanism encompassed all disciplines related to the New World along with all historical periods. Most Americanists, however, specialized in the pre-Hispanic past. Britain, Germany, France, and the United States produced some of the most active Americanist scholars, as did Mexico and other Latin American nations. As their field grew, so did the hunger for Mexico's antiquities.

As scholars such as Robert Aguirre have noted, the fascination of Westerners with these artifacts reflected the "historical relations of power." Western countries used Mexican antiquities and the objects of others to fashion their national and imperial identities, to communicate their reach, their "power to possess and dispossess."[15] Contrary to what one might think, the foreigners who appropriated these objects were usually not freewheeling, independent explorers. They were men like Consul Russell and Stephens. They were part of the imperial quest for antiquities. They often worked as agents for museums and collectors, gathering artifacts while serving as government officials. Russell was a diplomat, and so was Stephens; the celebrated explorer served as special ambassador to Central America, the position that originally took him to the region. Their status as political figures gave both men authority, freedom, and financial means. It allowed them access to travel, shipping, and workers. It is most likely what put them in contact in the first place, enabling them to network and, possibly, to make plans related to the transfer of the broken tablet from Palenque to the Smithsonian.

Piecing together the tablet's early history in the Smithsonian is difficult. We know that the artifact arrived in Washington, D.C., in fragments in two separate boxes, during different months of 1842. These were first held in the National Institution for the Promotion of Science, which later became part of the Smithsonian. The institution's workers did not immediately realize that the stones in the boxes came from the same object but soon figured out that the pieces fit "exactly together."[16] The fragments were glued back together, and in 1858 the newly reconstructed tablet was transferred along with the rest of the institute's collections to the Smithsonian, where it awakened "profound interest, and not a little controversy," claimed one observer.[17] But the artifact's provenance and even its identity continued to be a mystery. The bulky, cumbersome tablet seems to have suffered "various accidents" as it was studied, manipulated, and moved around the museum. Ironically, antiquities were often further destroyed in the very institutions that were designed to preserve them. To prevent more chips and cracks, Smithsonian officials decided to set the panel in a strong frame. "Almost everyone" who visited the institution is said to have had "his attention arrested" by the "framed slab, measuring about 6 by 3 feet, and covered in low relief with characters resembling large seals."[18] The "large seals," the glyphs of the ancient Maya, were a special source of fascination (figure 4.1).

But it would take several years for the Smithsonian scientists to figure out that the piece was actually part of the Cross of Palenque, a discovery that was not made until 1868 when a worker making casts of the tablet recognized it as one of the monument's three panels from a drawing in Stephens's *Incidents of Travel.* Once the Smithsonian scientists realized the archaeological importance of the slab in their possession, they began studying it in earnest.

Working close to a century before the decipherment of Maya hieroglyphics, the Smithsonian scientists had no shortage of theories about the Cross of Palenque's meaning. In 1879, Charles Rau, the curator of the institution (1875–87), published his own study of the piece and concluded that it commemorated a sacrifice to a rain god during a drought or "a period of great suffering." But he also conceded that the artifact's meaning "may be quite

Figure 4.1 The shattered right tablet of the Cross of Palenque, glued back together and encased in a frame in the Smithsonian Institution. Charles Rau, "The Palenque Tablet in the United States National Museum, Washington, D.C.," *Smithsonian Contributions to Knowledge*, vol. 22 (Washington D.C.: Smithsonian Institution, 1879), 79. Photograph courtesy of the Newberry Library.

different." Its significance, he noted, would be revealed only when the glyphs or "characters ceased to be a mystery."[19] While Rau did not realize it at the time, his study most likely influenced the fate of another section of the Cross of Palenque, the center panel that lay abandoned at the banks of the stream near the ruins.

The Center Panel

Soon after the publication of Rau's work, Mexican officials set out to transport the center panel from Palenque to the Museo Nacional de México. The mastermind behind the move was Jesús Sánchez, a medical doctor by training and director of the Museo Nacional de México (1883–89). It is not clear when Sánchez and other Mexicans first realized that the Smithsonian had a section of the Cross of Palenque, but they may have found out through Rau's work. They were no doubt familiar with the study. Mexican archaeologists operated within a global community of scientists. They were active players in the Americanist movement and contributed to international publications and discussions. The Museo Nacional de México and the Smithsonian regularly exchanged publications. Within three years of the article's appearance, Rau's work had been translated into Spanish and printed in the *Anales del Museo Nacional de México*, the journal of the Museo Nacional de México.[20]

Like many Porfirian elites, Sánchez believed Mexico's control over its antiquities was inseparable from its national image since all sophisticated modern nations preserved the objects of their pasts. "If the cultured nations," he explained, such as "Germany, France, England, Italy, and the United States, spend large sums acquiring and studying the antiquities of Egypt, Greece, China, and Mexico, then it is only right that we give our antiquities the importance they deserve."[21] Mexico had to take charge of the objects, Sánchez seemed to be arguing, not to protect them from foreigners but because the foreign interest in them made them worthy of preservation. Ironically, the museum director was legitimizing a nationalist impulse—Mexico's desire to control its antiquities—by referring to imperialist behavior on the part of Western powers. Sánchez's writings also illustrate the intimate link between collecting artifacts in the Museo Nacional de México and concerns with Mexico's image as a scientific, modern nation. In neglecting antiquities, he wrote, Mexico risked "the condemnation of the scientific world."[22] Archaeology, it was believed, would allow the country to carve out a special place within the realm of science. Another Porfirian intellectual, the statesman Justo Sierra, made this point when he said that archaeology was the only discipline that gave "Mexico personality in the scientific world."[23]

To haul the tablet from the ruins of Palenque, Sánchez called on Mexico's Secretariat of Development. The museum often turned to federal agencies and the military to help transport heavy, cumbersome monuments. Under Díaz, the government channeled more funding and manpower to carrying out these types of procedures, making the process more systematic than it had been in the past. This change was also a product of Mexico's political stability. While the Díaz regime was a dictatorship notorious for its brutality, it put an end to the nation's many years of chaos, initiating a concerted effort to collect antiquities in the Mexican capital. Sánchez contacted secretary of development Carlos Pacheco with "instructions" on how to transport the panel, one of the "most valuable" objects of American antiquity.[24]

The plan was to bring the artifact to Mexico's Museo Nacional de México and make plaster copies for display at the New Orleans World's Fair in 1884, a proposal inseparable from nationalist concerns. World's fairs were the perfect venue for Mexico to assert its national image. Participation in them was seen as one of "the best ways of changing the widespread perception" that Mexico "was violent and uncivilized." The New Orleans World's Fair was the first time the country undertook a major effort to "postulate the ideal type of a modern Mexican nation."[25] The center panel, the largest and most ornate piece of the Cross of Palenque, would highlight the idea that Mexico had deep roots and a prestigious antiquity. The artifact would be of "considerable use to historical and archaeological studies," remarked Pacheco, who began the process of transporting it to the museum in 1881, if not earlier.[26]

The tablet had been lying near the stream at Palenque for decades, "washed by many floods of the rainy season, and covered with a thick coat of dirt and moss."[27] Stephens recorded that the panel had been extracted from the temple "many years ago" by one of "the inhabitants of the village, with the intention of carrying it to his house." Perhaps the man wanted to sell the piece or use it as a source of stone? Stephens does not say. Other locals assisted the man, but the object was hard to move "with no other instruments than the arms and hands of Indians, and poles cut from trees." Upon reaching the stream, however, the stone's removal "was arrested by an order from the government." Was it an order from the governor of Chiapas? Or a local official? Stephens does not specify. Like so many accounts about Mexico's monuments, the details in the story of this tablet are murky. It is also not clear where Stephens got his information, but his claim raises the very real possibility that the original tomb raiders who dismantled the Cross of Palenque may well have been the people of the area. This should come as no surprise, as local residents often used the ruins in various ways, much as they continue to do today. Stephens supposedly scrubbed the tablet, propped it up, and surmised that the next traveler who came across it would find it just as he left it.

The artifact seems to have been in the exact same place when the government engineers sent to retrieve it reached Palenque. The local authorities initially opposed the engineers, so the federal government asked the governor of Chiapas to intervene. The Díaz administration had recently sent a "general order" to the states instructing them to impede the extraction of relics, but this case was different, federal officials pointed out, as it was the Mexican government that was taking the panel to the Museo Nacional de México to protect it from being "lost or destroyed."[28] Unlike earlier governors of Chiapas, who took a more possessive stance toward Palenque's monuments—like the governor who confiscated Stephens's casts—Governor Miguel Utrilla agreed. Governors often did not resist the federal government's removal of monuments during the Porfiriato. In fact, they frequently complied with requests to send artifacts to the Museo Nacional de México, a willingness that shows the extent to which the regime had coopted—or outright installed—these political figures.[29] At the time, however, the Díaz political machine had yet to fully penetrate the state of Chiapas, which was still controlled by long-established caciques, or regional strongmen, like Utrilla. In any case, the governor told the local authorities to back down. The engineers returned to Palenque and hauled the slab of stone to the Mexican capital, an expensive procedure that ended up costing the federal government 1,500 pesos.[30] At some point, however, the panel suffered a terrible accident that left it completely split in half. This section of the Cross of Palenque—much like the one that went to the Smithsonian—arrived at the Museo Nacional de México in two separate boxes in February 1884.

Nevertheless, Sánchez and the rest of the museum scientists were thrilled with the new acquisition. Within days, the museum director sent off a quick memo telling the secretary of development that the institution was already "making every effort to decipher and study the hieroglyphics." Like the Smithsonian scientists, Sánchez was especially intrigued by the glyphs. He accurately guessed that the mysterious symbols would one day be deciphered and reveal "many points that are now completely dark and unknown about the history of the American continent."[31] Although they were a mystery, the glyphs were considered proof of "how high the Maya civilization had reached . . . one of the most industrious, intelligent, and hard-working tribes that used to populate our territory," wrote a later observer.[32]

The tablet fit certain notions about what constituted a pre-Hispanic masterpiece. While there were no set criteria to evaluate such artifacts, Mexicans tended to hold monumental and well-crafted objects—especially those engraved with hieroglyphs—in high esteem. Writing was considered an irrefutable marker of an advanced civilization. The Cross of Palenque had all these features. A few years after its arrival in the museum, the central tablet was moved to the Galería de Monolitos, a hall established in 1887 to display Mexico's finest archaeological pieces. Placed on a pedestal within this space, it was one of the few Maya objects in a gallery that held artifacts from all over the country—although museum scientists made sure that Aztec antiquities still dominated the room. An image by American photographer Charles Betts Waite depicts the tablet with a huge horizontal gash running through its middle. To hold the two halves together—in addition to the possible application of glue—the museum resorted to several large metal clamps (figure 4.2).

Not satisfied with just one piece of the Cross of Palenque, Sánchez sought out the two others. By the mid-1880s, then, there was a sense that all three panels belonged together. Shortly after the museum acquired the tablet from the ruins, Sánchez asked the Smithsonian to send a plaster copy of the panel in its possession, although it is not clear if his request was heeded. He also initiated a project to retrieve the last section that remained embedded in the temple. In a memo to Secretary Pacheco, Sánchez proposed the idea, emphasizing the importance of conserving the entire Cross of Palenque, an artifact admired "by all men of science."[33] Pacheco called on the new governor of Chiapas, José María Ramírez, to ship the object.

The governor answered that he was honored to help. Ramírez was a military man who had fought in Mexico's Reform War (1857–61) alongside Porfirio Díaz and was probably friendly with the dictator. Díaz was on a hiatus from the presidency at the time, during the tenure of Manuel González (1880–84), and was briefly in charge of the Mexican Commission for the New Orleans World's Fair. Perhaps Ramírez was trying to cozy up to the dictator. To move the last panel, the governor asked for 1,000 pesos to open

Figure 4.2 The center tablet of the Cross of Palenque on display in the Museo Nacional's Galería de Monolitos. Metal clamps hold together the two halves of the broken monument in this image taken by Charles Betts Waite. Photograph courtesy of the Benson Latin American Collection, LLILAS Benson Latin American Studies and Collections, the University of Texas at Austin.

a road, build bridges over streams, and pay for the cart, oxen, and Indians to transport the artifact.[34] But moving the piece without breaking it was no easy matter. The hunk of fragile stone needed to be pried out of the temple and lowered 174 feet down the length of the pyramid at a thirty-five-degree incline, a complicated procedure. Once he realized the magnitude of the task, the governor pulled out of the project. The initiative languished, leaving the lonely panel embedded in the ruins.

The Right Panel Revisited

The next piece to join the museum did not come from the ruins but from the Smithsonian, a transfer initiated by Secretary Root during the presidency of Theodore Roosevelt. The Smithsonian panel was not the first ancient artifact to be repatriated to Mexico. As Miruna Achim has detailed, in the 1820s the Mexican government managed to get England to send back some codices. During his short-lived reign as emperor of Mexico, Maximilian (1864–1867) also negotiated the return of an Aztec shield that had been taken out of the country in the sixteenth century.[35] The tablet returned by Root was the only piece that was repatriated to Mexico during the Porfiriato. Mexicans considered its initial removal from Palenque as a theft: "It was robbed by some Americans, who took it to the United States," explained one observer in 1888. This same reporter feared that the panel that remained at the ruins would also be taken by "foreigners" who were "motivated by greed, given that that stone has fabulous worth in the museums of Europe."[36]

Root visited Mexico in October 1907, in an extension of the "goodwill" tour he had taken to South America the previous year. The lawyer and statesman hoped to put a kinder face on the interventionist policies embodied by Roosevelt's corollary to the Monroe Doctrine. As one American journalist explained, Root will "go softly but will not carry a big stick."[37] In a nutshell, Root's trip was meant to quell Latin Americans' misgivings about Roosevelt's aggressive stance toward the region and promote "friendly relations" that would keep Latin America in the U.S. orbit. While on tour, Root used calculated phrases that made him appear less menacing than Roosevelt, but "underlying his every pronouncement was the fundamental policy of continued American domination."[38]

Although Root's trip to Mexico was an outgrowth of his general hemispheric policy, the secretary of state had two aims: to ensure Díaz's cooperation regarding developments in Central America, especially Nicaraguan president José Santos Zelaya's plan to reunite the Federal Republic of Central America, a unification that the United States considered a threat to its interests; and to ease recent tensions in U.S.-Mexico relations.[39] During the latter years of the Porfiriato, Díaz had become increasingly concerned with the predominance of American capital in the Mexican economy. To counterbalance this influence, he sought heavier investments from Europe, a move that irked the United States. At the same time, there was mounting anti-American sentiment in Mexico, as well as growing criticism of the Díaz regime, which many Mexicans believed had sold out the country's interests to Yankee capitalists. During Root's visit, he gave no hint of these tensions. Neither did the Díaz regime, which welcomed Root with open arms, celebrating him wherever he went.

The visit was full of pageantry, sumptuous banquets, and receptions. Root gave several speeches praising Mexico and Díaz, eulogizing him as one of the "great men of history who had brought untold blessings to his countrymen." The secretary of state paid his respects to the "Mexican people, Mexican civilization, Mexican progress, and Mexican friendship." He talked at length about the fruitfulness of U.S.-Mexican relations, stressing that Mexico was on the threshold of even greater prosperity and progress. In one of his last speeches, he claimed that the country had "joined forever the ranks of the great, orderly, self-controlled, self-governing republics of the world."[40]

Root took a day to visit Teotihuacan, the famed site that was undergoing reconstruction at the time. By this point, federal institutions and procedures for controlling Mexico's pre-Hispanic heritage were more firmly developed than ever before. The Díaz regime had superseded Mexico's patchwork of archaeological legislation with the Law of Monuments. Passed in 1897, this ruling explicitly nationalized the ruins, declaring them "property of the nation."[41] The Mexican government was in the process of expropriating its first site, the ruins of Teotihuacan. The massive undertaking involved the reconstruction of the Pyramid of the Sun carried out by Leopoldo Batres, who as the inspector of monuments was the archaeologist in charge of conserving Mexico's monuments. On October 8, Root arrived in Teotihuacan, accompanied by an entourage including his wife and daughter, U.S. ambassador David Thompson, and other Americans, as well as various Mexican political figures. Inspector Batres led a four-hour tour of the ruins and treated the group of thirty to a champagne lunch. Nearly all of Teotihuacan's structures were still covered in dirt, looking more like mountains than temples, complete with "trees and shrubs," noted one journalist.[42] Root climbed onto the Pyramid of the Sun, which was only partially uncovered at the time. The Mexican press commented on "his agility" and made several mentions of his curiosity about the ruins. Root gave every temple, statue, and piece of stone his "thorough attention."[43] The secretary of state seems to have had an interest in archaeology and antiquities. Once the tour was over, the group was whisked off to Cholula, where Root similarly marveled at the pyramids.

Root also visited Mexico's Museo Nacional de México, which had become a full-fledged center of archaeological research and conservation by the final years of the Porfiriato. He was accompanied by a group of Americans and Mexicans, including politicians and scientists. Zelia Nuttall, an honorary professor in the museum and one of the few female archaeologists at the time, acted as Root's guide, giving him "brief explanations about the principal monuments" in the Archaeology Department.[44] At the end of the tour, the institution's director Genaro García (1907–11, 1913) presented Root with handfuls of catalogs, guides, and other museum publications, along with "fifteen copies [molds?] of the most notable objects on display." Before leaving, the U.S. secretary of state and his entourage had their picture taken in front of the Piedra del Sol.

The idea to send the Smithsonian panel back to Mexico must have occurred to Root as a result of the museum tour and may even have been suggested to him by Nuttall. Justo Sierra, who was then Mexico's secretary of education, took care of all the paperwork with the Secretariat of Foreign Relations, and the Smithsonian shipped the tablet to Ambassador Thompson in Mexico City. Smithsonian documents about the move are surprisingly terse, noting simply that the transfer of "the Cross of Palenque to the Government of Mexico" took place through the U.S. State Department via the American ambassador.[45] The 1,350-pound slab, the "most brilliant page of Maya scripture," as museum director García referred to it, arrived in the Museo Nacional de México in March 1908.[46] Newspapers in Mexico celebrated the tablet's homecoming as the piece was reunited with its sister panel in the museum.

Although Porfirian elites had considered the object's initial appropriation as a theft, they did not speak about the repatriation as an act of restitution by the United States nor as a return of property from one nation or government to another. While Root's visit to Mexico had political and diplomatic aims, the repatriation occurred outside any official legal structures for the return of cultural property, a context that shaped perceptions of the event. Treaties about cultural property have given us frameworks for discussing acts of repatriation, something that did not exist during the Porfiriato. The legalistic language for speaking about these issues had simply not been formulated. Porfirian elites also did not employ nationalist rhetoric when discussing the repatriation. Perhaps they feared this discourse would have a negative impact on U.S.-Mexico relations? Instead, they were cordial and submissive. They stressed the beauty and importance of the artifact and discussed its return as a gesture of a private individual, much like a donation. They paid special tribute to Root. The U.S. secretary of state had offered to return the piece "during his recent visit," wrote one reporter, and he "fulfilled his promise."[47] In true belle époque fashion, they emphasized the genteel nature of the act. Museum director García summed up this sentiment, stating that the repatriation was a "gallant offering," a gentlemanly thing to do.[48] Americans discussed the event in similar ways. As a reporter in the United States explained, Root had shown "good will toward Mexico," and his act was "one of those small things which reveal friendly considerateness."[49] The new acquisition was placed in the Galería de Monolitos, alongside the other panel. Only one section of the Cross of Palenque was missing from the museum, still at the ruins.

The Left Panel

Retrieving this final tablet demonstrates the strength of the Mexican government's resolve to put the Cross of Palenque back together. One of the individuals behind this effort was secretary of education Justo Sierra, an avid promoter of archaeology, with a profound interest in the pre-Hispanic past. But the main protagonist was Leopoldo Batres, whose job as inspector included bringing artifacts to the museum. Batres was captivated by the Cross and its hieroglyphics. And like others before him, such as the German scholar Alexander von Humboldt, Batres saw Buddhist influences in Palenque and in Maya culture in general. Could the artifact represent the "teachings of the Buddha?" the inspector asked. "Who knows?" he concluded, adding that "everything in those monuments is a mystery."[50]

Early in 1909, Batres and Sierra set out to the jungles of Palenque to retrieve the last panel. Batres took advantage of the occasion to turn the trip into a full-scale scientific expedition. He sketched, photographed, and made molds of various monuments.[51] To carry out the hard labor, he hired local Indians. Batres did not record who they were or if they received any pay, but local people often worked for archaeologists and were motivated by wages. The Indians cleared a road to the town of Palenque and removed vegetation from the Temple of the Cross. They then undertook the difficult task of extracting the panel. Under the inspector's direction, they pried the giant slab of stone out of the chamber and lowered it down the pyramid on a ramp of bound tree trunks they had made. The operation was dangerous: two workers were killed and several others seriously injured when they were crushed by a falling tree. Once the panel reached the base of the pyramid, it was placed in a mahogany crate, shipped to the port town of Frontera, Tabasco, and then on to Veracruz, making most of the trip over water. From Veracruz, the crate traveled by train to the museum in Mexico City. The guard at Palenque accompanied the crate to Frontera, while Batres's son, Salvador, the assistant inspector of monuments, took charge of the rest of the journey.

As it neared the museum, rumors circulated that Batres had destroyed the artifact while extracting it from the ruins. Batres came to his own defense, publishing an editorial in the press refuting the accusation. Antiquities, as we have seen, commonly arrived in museums damaged and continue to do so today, even with state-of-the-art packing materials. But for Batres, the accusation was a threat to his archaeological expertise. He called on Sierra, who supported his claim that the small cracks in the top corners of the panel had been there when it was still embedded in the chamber. The issue was soon forgotten, and the expedition was considered a success. The panel Batres brought to the museum was the only one that arrived intact.

One by one, like pieces of a giant puzzle, the Cross of Palenque was reassembled after nearly a century of separation. The initial destruction of the monument had occurred at a time when Mexico had little control over pre-Hispanic antiquities. Its unification signaled a change. It marked the climax of Porfirian elites' efforts to take charge of the archaeological remains and forge a national history. To thank the Smithsonian for its repatriation, Mexico sent it a full plaster reproduction of the artifact—all three tablets—which the U.S. institution seems to have exhibited until at least the 1970s. Made whole, the Cross of Palenque was placed in its own separate space in the Museo Nacional de México, in a "small special room" that made up part of the Galería de Monolitos.[52] One of the last photos of the monument during the Porfiriato was taken just weeks before the Revolution broke out and ended the Díaz regime. In September 1910, President Díaz toured the museum in preparation for the Centenario, Mexico's centennial celebration of independence from Spain. He took his famous photograph in front of the Piedra del Sol, but he also posed with the Cross of Palenque, the massive artifact with a complicated and arduous history that, for decades, Mexicans had been determined to see whole again (figure 4.3).

Today, the three panels continue to be displayed together in the Museo Nacional de Antropología. United and intact, the monument seems to belie its history of fragmentation. On closer inspection, though, one might notice its many dents and cracks, despite all the glue and numerous attempts at concealing the object's history of destruction. Much like the process of nation building, which seeks to paper over schisms in a population, the making of patrimony similarly aims to erase an object's complicated and fragmented history. The goal is to make artifacts appear pristine and whole and as if they naturally belong to the state, obscuring their previous contexts along with the struggles involved in turning them into national property. The story of the Cross of Palenque offers us a peak behind the curtain, so to speak, to highlight

Figure 4.3 President Porfirio Díaz poses proudly in the Galería de Monolitos with the recently unified Cross of Palenque, a symbol of his regime's newfound (but weak) control over Maya territory. Photograph courtesy of INAH.

how these objects are not inherently state possessions. The Díaz regime's enormous efforts to take control of the monument were inseparable from the desire to project certain notions about Mexico's sovereignty and power.

Fittingly, the monument itself is also about power. Today, most archaeologists believe the Cross of Palenque depicts the transfer of power from Pakal the Great, Palenque's seventh-century ruler, to his son, Kan-Balam. Glyphs on the piece record the event as taking place in AD 690. The smaller figure on the left is Pakal, while Kan-Balam stands on the right. Both men flank a "cross," what is actually known as a world tree, a motif in Mesoamerican iconographies that represents a symbolic axis mundi connecting the heavens, earth, and the underworld (figure 4.4).

Notes

The author wishes to thank the editors of this volume for their insightful comments and suggestions.

1. This occurred sometime between the visits of Guillermo Dupaix and Jean Frédéric de Waldeck. When Dupaix went to Palenque in 1807, the panels were

Figure 4.4 Maya scholar Linda Schele's drawing of the Cross of Palenque, depicting the transfer of power from Pakal the Great to his son Kan-Balam. Photograph by Linda Schele © David Schele. Courtesy of the Ancient Americas at Los Angeles County Museum of Art.

still in place. When Waldeck arrived in 1832, they had been separated. See Otis Mason, "The Group of the Cross at Palenque," in *The American Art Review* (Boston: Estes and Lauriat, 1880), 217.

2. Rebecca Earle, "*Sobre Héroes y Tumbas*: National Symbols in Nineteenth-Century Spanish America," *Hispanic American Historical Review* 85, no. 3 (2005): 379. For the place of Latin America in postcolonial theory, see Mark Thurner and Andrés Guerrero, eds., *After Spanish Rule: Postcolonial Predicaments of the Americas* (Durham, N.C.: Duke University Press, 2003); and Mabel Moraña, Enrique Dussel, and Carlos A. Jáuregui, eds., *Coloniality at Large:*

Latin America and the Postcolonial Debate (Durham, N.C.: Duke University Press, 2008).

3. *El Monitor Republicano*, May 31, 1890, in Sonia Lombardo de Ruiz, *El pasado prehispánico en la cultura nacional: Memoria hemerográfica, 1877–1911*, 2 vols. (Mexico City: INAH, 1994), 1:186.
4. See Haydeé López Hernández, *En busca del alma nacional: La arqueología y la construcción del origen de la historia nacional en México (1867–1942)* (Mexico City: INAH, 2018); Mauricio Tenorio-Trillo, *Mexico at the World's Fairs: Crafting a Modern Nation* (Berkeley: University of California Press, 1996); and Enrique Florescano, *Imágenes de la patria a través de los siglos* (Mexico City: Taurus, 2005).
5. López Hernández, *En busca del alma nacional*, 98. All translations are mine.
6. Memo from museum director Chavero to the Secretariat of Education, the ministry that oversaw the museum and the Inspectorate of Monuments, December 18, 1902, caja 167, exp. 48, fol. 1, Archivo General de la Nación, Instrucción Pública y Bellas Artes (AGN, IPBA). The Díaz regime was selective about protecting Maya objects, however, as it turned a blind eye to Edward Thompson's appropriation of Maya relics. See Guillermo Palacios, "El cónsul Thompson, los bostonians y la formación de la galaxia Chichén, 1893–1904," *Historia Mexicana* 65, no. 1 (2015): 167–88.
7. Chris Hinsley, "From Shell-Heaps to Stelae: Early Anthropology at the Peabody Museum," in *Objects and Others: Essays on Museums and Material Culture*, ed. George W. Stocking Jr. (Madison: University of Wisconsin Press, 1985), 71.
8. See López Hernández, *En busca del alma nacional*, 91.
9. Mexico and the United States have a Treaty of Cooperation that provides for the return of stolen archaeological property. Mexican artifacts are also covered by the UNESCO 1970 Convention on the Means of Prohibiting and Preventing the Illicit Import, Export and Transport of Ownership of Cultural Property. What's more, Mexico's relics are protected under the nation's Federal Law for Archaeological, Artistic and Historical Zones and Monuments, which was passed in 1972.
10. Charles Rau, "The Palenque Tablet in the United States National Museum, Washington D.C.," *Smithsonian Contributions to Knowledge*, vol. 22 (Washington D.C.: Smithsonian Institution, 1879), 1.
11. This version of events is also recorded in Rau, "Palenque Tablet," 2.
12. John L. Stephens, *Incidents of Travel in Central America, Chiapas, and Yucatan* (New York: Harper, 1841), 471. The following quotations are from *Incidents*, 471–72.
13. Sonia Lombardo de Ruiz and Ruth Solís Vicarte, *Antecedentes de las leyes sobre monumentos históricos (1536–1910)* (Mexico City: INAH, 1988), 48.
14. For a summary of Mexico's early archaeological legislation, see Lombardo de Ruiz and Solís Vicarte, *Antecedentes*.
15. Robert D. Aguirre, *Informal Empire: Mexico and Central America in Victorian Culture* (Minneapolis: University of Minnesota Press, 2005), 28 and xiii.

16. Rau, "Palenque Tablet," 2.
17. Mason, "Group of the Cross," 218. For the artifact's arrival and early history in the Smithsonian, see Rau, "Palenque Tablet."
18. Mason, "Group of the Cross," 217–18.
19. Rau, "Palenque Tablet," 46.
20. See Charles Rau, "Tablero de Palenque en el Museo Nacional de México," *Anales del Museo Nacional de México* 2, no. 2 (1882): 135–37.
21. Museum report to the Secretariat of Education, March 1887, caja 165, exp. 57, fol. 3, AGN, IPBA.
22. Letter from Sánchez thanking a donor for an artifact, October 1, 1884, vol. 6, exp. 47, fol. 169, Archivo Histórico del Museo Nacional de Antropología (AHMNA).
23. Justo Sierra, *Epistolario y papeles privados*, ed. Catalina Sierra de Peimbert (Mexico City: UNAM, 1949), 48.
24. Museum work report, August 4, 1886, vol. 8, exp. 18, fol. 118, AHMNA.
25. Tenorio-Trillo, *Mexico at the World's Fairs*, 38. The museum made plaster molds of several other pieces for the New Orleans World's Fair, including the Piedra del Sol, the Chacmool of Chichén Itzá, and the stone of Tízoc.
26. Memo from the Secretariat of Development to the Secretariat of Education, August 3, 1881, caja 165, exp. 30, fol. 3, AGN, IPBA.
27. Stephens, *Incidents*, 345. The following quotations are from this same page.
28. Letter from the Secretariat of Education to the governor of Chiapas, caja 165, exp. 30, fol. 4, AGN, IPBA. For another case of local resistance to the extraction of a monument, see Rozental in this volume.
29. For an interesting look at the place of governors in the process of constructing an indigenous past during the Porfiriato, see Jaclyn Ann Sumner, "The Indigenous Governor of Tlaxcala and Acceptable Indigenousness in the Porfirian Regime," *Mexican Studies/Estudios Mexicanos* 35, no. 1 (2019): 61–87.
30. Memo from the Inspectorate of Monuments to the Secretariat of Education, June 19, 1903, caja 167 bis, exp. 56, fol. 6, AGN, IPBA.
31. Memo from museum director Sánchez intended for the Secretariat of Development, March 1, 1884, vol. 6, exp. 45, fol. 159, AHMNA. It would take a full century for Maya hieroglyphics to be deciphered; see Michael D. Coe, *Breaking the Maya Code* (New York: Thames and Hudson, 1999).
32. *El Imparcial*, March 30, 1908, in Lombardo de Ruiz, *El pasado prehispánico*, 2:425.
33. Sánchez memo intended for the Secretariat of Development, AHMNA.
34. Memo from Governor José M. Ramírez to the National Museum, June 16, 1884, vol. 6, exp. 45, fols. 165–66, AHMNA.
35. Miruna Achim, *From Idols to Antiquity: Forging the National Museum of Mexico* (Lincoln: Nebraska University Press, 2017).
36. *El Imparcial*, September 7, 1888, in Lombardo de Ruiz, *El pasado prehispánico*, 1:154.
37. *Mount Union (Pa.) Times*, October 18, 1907.

38. Jack Davis, "The Latin American Policy of Elihu Root" (PhD diss., University of Illinois, 1953), 136. Root held high-level positions in the U.S. government at a time when the country rapidly expanded its influence in Latin America, especially in the Caribbean and Central America. He served as secretary of war under presidents William McKinley and Teddy Roosevelt (1899–1904) and as secretary of state under Roosevelt (1905–9).
39. Davis, "Latin American Policy," 160.
40. Davis, "Latin American Policy," 164.
41. Lombardo de Ruiz and Solís Vicarte, *Antecedentes*, 68. For more on the Law of Monuments and the reconstruction of Teotihuacan, see Christina Bueno, *The Pursuit of Ruins: Archaeology, History, and the Making of Modern Mexico* (Albuquerque: University of New Mexico Press, 2016).
42. *El Imparcial*, October 9, 1907, in Lombardo de Ruiz, *El pasado prehispánico*, 2:388.
43. *El Imparcial*, October 9, 1907, in Lombardo de Ruiz, *El pasado prehispánico*, 2:391.
44. Vicente Morales, Manuel Caballero, and Luis D'Antin, *El señor Root en Mexico: Crónica de la visita hecha en octubre de 1907 al pueblo y al gobierno de la República mexicana, por su excelencia el Honorable señor Elihu Root, secretario de estado del gobierno de los Estados Unidos de América* (Mexico City: Impr. de arte y letras, 1908), 126.
45. Annual Reports 1886, 1898–1920, box 1, series 16, Division of Archeology, Records of the Department of Anthropology, National Museum of Natural History, National Anthropological Archives, Smithsonian Institution.
46. Memo from museum director Genaro García to the Secretariat of Education, March 28, 1908, caja 168, exp. 20, fol. 12, AGN, IPBA.
47. *El Imparcial*, March 30, 1908, in Lombardo de Ruiz, *El pasado prehispánico*, 2:425.
48. Genaro García memo to the Secretariat of Education, March 28, 1908, fol. 7, AGN, IPBA.
49. *Wichita (Kans.) Daily Eagle*, January 2, 1908.
50. Leopoldo Batres, *Las Ruinas de Palenque* (Mexico: Tipografía Económica, 1909), 2. This brief pamphlet is essentially a memo recording Batres's earlier trip to Palenque in January 1898. It can be found in caja 111, exp. 21, fol. 2, AGN, IPBA. For more on Porfirian notions about Buddhist influences in Maya culture, see López Hernández, *En busca del alma nacional*, 91–93.
51. An account of the expedition can be found in caja 111, exps. 17 and 21, AGN, IPBA.
52. Museum report, September 20, 1913, vol. 17, exp. 24, fol. 226, AHMNA.

\\ 5

Past and Present at the Museo de Historia Natural

FRIDA GORBACH

> *What we know about [animals] is an index of our power, and thus an index of what separates us from them.*
>
> —John Berger, "Why Look at Animals?"

Introduction: Object and Time

I recently revisited the Museo de Historia Natural de la Ciudad de México (commonly referred to as the Museo de Historia Natural) for the first time in many years. Located in Chapultepec Park and inaugurated in 1964, the same year that the Museo Nacional de Antropología opened its doors, the Museo de Historia Natural represents the culmination of a long effort. The official version of its history begins in 1790 with the opening of the Primer Gabinete de Historia Natural and its exhibition of plant, animal, and mineral collections from New Spain, amassed on a botanical expedition sent by Charles III. It continues in the nineteenth century with the Museo Nacional de México and its collections, comprising natural history, bits and pieces of national history, and archaeological "monoliths." The immediate forebearer of the Museo de Historia Natural was the Museo de Historia Natural del Chopo (commonly referred to as the Museo del Chopo), which exclusively exhibited nature collections for the first half of the twentieth century.

Upon returning to the Museo de Historia Natural and seeing the nine semispherical galleries that constitute its architecture, I forgot about that two-century-long history and remembered only the amazement I once felt on a school visit, when I got up close and personal with a polar bear, a dinosaur skeleton, an elephant, and a magnificent moose on view in the exhibit's dioramas. In retrospect I may have even returned to the museum in the hope of reliving something like that first childlike wonder, but once inside I got lost among the hundreds of objects scattered throughout this modern, technological, and interactive museum. It was an unsettling experience, as if my memories did not line up with the reality of what I was observing. At that point, without forgetting my sense of amazement, I decided to return to history.

This chapter is about wonder and history, the unsettling feeling provoked by the gap between the past and the present, the difference that opens up between the experience of the past and its recollection. For now, I can at least say that said gap is an invitation to take leave of the official story, since from this altered perspective the museum appears no longer as the culmination of a trajectory stretching back to the eighteenth century, but rather as the *remains* of that long history. Instead of describing a succession of episodes, then, the task at hand is to carefully retrace the steps of a slow process of dispossession, and then recount all that happened so that only five of the sixty-four thousand specimens that were once on view at the Museo del Chopo now remain. This alternative history would have to explain how it was that, of the countless collections of plants, animals, and minerals that occupied the large galleries of the Museo Nacional de México in the late nineteenth century, only five specimens survived. There is something in that lost splendor that prompts us to dig into the discrepancy between what the official history says and what the space itself actually reveals; something compels us to sever the line that would connect the eighteenth-century Gabinete de Historia Natural to today's Museo de Historia Natural. These five objects remind us that the turn of the twentieth century in Mexico entailed the disappearance of natural history as a way of knowing the world and the emergence of anthropology as a scientific field authorized by the state. At the turn of the century, we could say that nature was split off from culture, and that culture announced nature's imminent disappearance.

I first discuss those five surviving objects: the Diplodocus, the museum's biggest and most prominent piece, a replica of a dinosaur from the upper Jurassic bequeathed by the Carnegie project, which left Pittsburgh for Mexico City by train in thirty-six wooden crates in 1928, and which, after being reassembled in 1931, became the centerpiece of the Museo del Chopo for the next several decades; the Argonaut and Jellyfish, two nineteenth-century "beautiful replicas" in glass that "very realistically" recreate the delicate bodies of two sea creatures, "as if they were alive"; and lastly, the Kiwi and the Platypus, two stuffed animals, the former a "marvel of biological adaptation," and the latter, an animal that "lays eggs, has a beak and webbed feet like a duck and walks with its limbs at its sides like a lizard; if that were not enough, male platypuses have poisonous spurs on their hind feet."[1]

I treat these pieces as part of a "historical collection," as it is presented in the book that serves as the catalog of the Museo de Historia Natural, leaving aside for the moment the histories and trajectories of the five pieces.[2] I know that they were all different things at different times—historical objects, attractive or unimportant specimens, relics, bequests, emblems—but here I examine them together as a single collection whose common denominator is that they all constitute evidence of the past. That is largely why I am less interested in knowing the origin and itinerary of each piece before it made its way to the display cases at the Museo de Historia Natural, than in seeing them as arrows from the past that point right at the present. Rather than uncovering the sites through which those objects moved and looking for evidence of the places they occupied at different moments, I prefer to pose a more general question about the past in the museum. Behind it lies a question about historical time that feeds into the desire to break with the continuous line of historicism and to experiment with other ways of articulating the past to the present, specimens to their contexts, and current presences to documents of the past.

In this sense, the four sections of this chapter represent different ways of putting these objects in relation to time; that is, each one represents a particular way of reading the arrangement of the objects in the museum space. Since I am interested in the museum's temporal registers, these five visible, tangible objects in space catalyze a reflection on historical time, which does not always have a direct empirical correlate. After all, as François Hartog has asserted, "the book of history in the fullest sense of the word" both makes history and reflects on history at the same time.[3] Thus, in the first section, "Disappearance," the time in question corresponds to the absence of the archive, an archive made up not only of the objects that have survived but also of those that have disappeared or no longer exist.[4] The next section, "Dispersal," presents the five objects as dispersed in a space that swallows time, flattening it as if the present imposed itself by erasing the specificity of the past.[5] In the third section, "*Longue durée*," I take the five objects as evidence of a colonial history that is actualized in the present.[6] And in the final section, "Animalities," time emerges out of singularity and thus not only has the power to evoke in viewers the historical forces of the origin, but also confronts them with wonder, a dimension of time that collapses the distance between subject and object.[7]

Therefore, rather than tell the story of the Museo de Historia Natural, of the renovations it has undergone, or the specifics of its publics, we might say that I pay a *visit* to the museum; that is, I tour it from the standpoint of thought processes, personal impressions, and routes (to adapt a term from James Clifford), closer to ethnography or cultural studies than to historical research.[8] Although I propose four possible routes through the museum, or four different readings, in the end there is a question that connects them all, involving disappearance—of natural history, of objects, of the archive—as well as nostalgia, official history, the present day, and historical time. From the first, we can condense all of this into a single question: does the Museo de Historia Natural represent a break from the Museo del Chopo in the twentieth century or from the former Museo Nacional de México in the nineteenth, or is it more accurate to speak of a continuity that stretches back to the eighteenth century or even before, and extends to our present time?

Figure 5.1 Diplodocus, Museo de Historia Natural. Photograph by the author.

Figure 5.2 Jellyfish, Museo de Historia Natural. Photograph by the author.

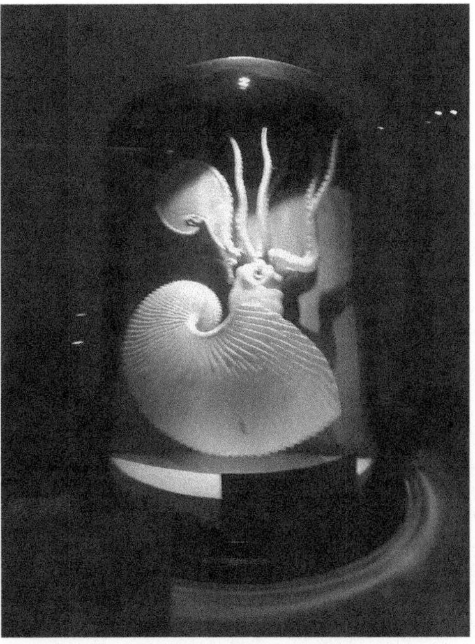

Figure 5.3 Argonaut, Museo de Historia Natural. Photograph by the author.

Figure 5.5 Kiwi, Museo de Historia Natural. Photograph by the author.

Figure 5.3 Platypus, Museo de Historia Natural. Photograph by the author.

This question ultimately relates to the persistence of "coloniality," for if natural history, as discourse and knowledge of nature, was born at the moment when the Spanish empire was taking possession of its new territories, we must ask ourselves, to what extent do we continue conceiving nature and its relationship to culture in the same way today?

One quick clarification before moving on: if I have thus far used the term "objects" to describe the Diplodocus, Jellyfish, Argonaut, Kiwi, and Platypus, they could just as well be called "pieces," "specimens," "exemplars," "artifacts" or "animals," since the appropriate label depends on the theoretical clarity available to categorize them in each discursive context (figures 5.1–5.5).

Disappearance

A good way to begin might be by presenting the archival information I found about the Diplodocus, Jellyfish, Argonaut, Kiwi, and Platypus, the five pieces that have survived over time, in order to ask first about the places from which they came and then to describe the spaces through which they moved (warehouses, galleries, means of transportation); that is, anything that would serve the purpose of gathering evidence to explain how these five pieces came to be exhibited more or less intact in the display cases of the Museo de Historia Natural. But because I am aware that the drive to reconstruct such journeys could lead me to tell a linear story, similar to the official history in which a progressive line of scientific and institutional achievements describes how a single museum has preserved the same impulse over time, and because there is not much information in this regard, I prefer to test out a different perspective.[9]

Therefore, to avoid taking any risks, I reverse the question. Instead of launching an inquiry into the objects that survived through time, I ask about the ones that are missing, whether because they were lost in transit at some point, forgotten in a warehouse, broken, or physically decayed enough to be discarded. That is, rather than formulate a question about what remains in the archive, I prefer to ask about what is missing; not about the "proofs of presence" to which the discipline generally attends in order to legitimize itself, but rather about what is no longer there.[10] For example, rather than tell the story of the Jellyfish and the Argonaut, I ask what happened to the other forty-two glass pieces from the same collection that disappeared. I want to know in the end what happened to all the stuffed animals, preserved plants, butterfly and insect collections, skeletons, stones, and monsters that used to be exhibited at the Chopo, and before that at the Museo Nacional de México.[11] What happened to all those collections that turn-of-the-century naturalists had taken such pains to gather, desiccate, classify, and exhibit?[12]

Of course, this presents me with a practical impossibility. How does one write about an archive that does not exist? By what method does one proceed? How does one construct the narrative of an archive that breaks with the three most persistent imaginaries about archives in general: their presence, totality, and temporal continuity?[13] The problem is even more serious when we recall that absence, a condition of any archive, possesses a supplement, a historical specificity that conditions it in its entirety. Although historians always have to grapple with absence, here the absence consists of deliberate acts of censorship, destruction, fires, and disappearances, all that was made to fail.[14] As Valeria Añon might ask, is the colonial archive not built atop silence and lack? Is its destiny not made of fire and ash?[15]

In any event, one possible strategy for confronting the postcolonial archive would be to compile a set of fragments detailing how time and neglect destroyed the matter held therein, consuming plants and degrading taxidermized bodies, and linger, for example, over the details of a slow organic degradation and the modalities through which matter passes as it decomposes. A different strategy would be to leave aside such chance circumstances and natural processes and instead focus on an image, using it to understand disappearance as directly related to the policies of the postcolonial state.

I thus start with an image: the one that instantly came together in my mind as I read through some archival documents. It arose from the reports that the directors of the Museo de Historia Natural del Chopo periodically sent to the government, informing it about the museum's activities and expenses; but it arose more fundamentally from a 1912 report that the museum's first director, Jesús Díaz de León, sent to the Secretariat of the Office of Public Instruction and Fine Arts. In it, Díaz de León is standing in one of the galleries of the Chopo, fighting against "the dust and light . . . that get in everywhere," destroying specimens and "sooner or later [killing] the animals' colors."[16]

In a way, that image condenses something that took place year after year at the museum. We might say that it draws a permanent "out-of-place-ness," arising from the mismatch between the museum, the building, and its own time. Year after year the academics and staff at the Chopo looked for ways to fit the collections into a building that was not designed to hold them, an ironwork building with enormous windows like the Crystal Palace in London, through which a near-blinding light continues to enter (figure 5.6).[17] I imagine the staff there hanging curtains, building fences, raising walls to keep the force of the light at bay, moving collections from one warehouse to another without knowing, for example, how to reassemble the giraffe that "fell to the floor and broke" into pieces during a 1911 earthquake, or what to do with the *megatherium* "that, being made of plaster, was destroyed forever after it had broken into pieces."[18]

The image gives an impression of Díaz de León and his colleagues hurriedly improvising under pressure, as if the Museo del Chopo had been built on the fly, as if the collections had arrived suddenly and without warning. The specimens were relegated to boxes while the building was being renovated. As they were being taken out again and put back in their cases, Díaz de León explains in his report, "it was necessary to clear all the shelves and displays, in order to move the specimens to a house that served as a warehouse, so that the museum's salon could host the Exposición Japonesa during the Centennial celebrations" in 1910.[19] One is left with the impression that no

Figure 5.6 Museo del Chopo, façade, 1910. Archivo Casasola, Fototeca Nacional. Reproduction authorized by the Instituto Nacional de Antropología e Historia.

one knew quite what to do with the natural history collections, as if a superior order had served to remind the staff at the Chopo that natural history was not a priority during the Centennial celebrations.

If I am lingering over this initial image, it is because it charts a destination. On the one hand, it shows us early twentieth-century Mexican naturalists dreaming of a museum dedicated to research, one that would have had sufficient resources to send expeditions to different parts of the country to bring back "national" specimens that could then be exhibited at the Museo de Historia Natural del Chopo. These naturalists even went so far as to plan the construction of a "large cage for birds," a botanical garden, and a zoo. On the other hand, however, those same naturalists complained repeatedly of the lack of support and government resources, such that they spent all their time engaged not in research but in installing, repairing, and conserving the damaged collections. Thus, while Díaz de León was dedicating all his energy to "really creating the Museo Nacional" and expanding its influence outward to the rest of the country, he was also helping us see that those dreams were confined to paper.[20]

We might therefore say that what functions as a historical constant is "the dust and light," that what lies at the origin of the Museo del Chopo is both a mismatch and a mistiming: the mismatch between the collections and the building, and the mistiming inscribed in a project that was being undertaken just as natural history was becoming less prominent as a way of knowing the world. I would add that, if there is a document that points directly toward the Chopo's founding, it is a 1909 government decree ordering the removal of the sixty-four thousand natural specimens from the Museo Nacional de México so that the latter could be devoted entirely to showing history, archaeology, and ethnography collections.[21] This decree effectively announced that the depository discipline of knowledge, authority, and power bestowed by the state in the twentieth century was not to be natural history with its universal ambition, but archaeology/anthropology and the question of national identity.[22]

I thus go so far as to claim that the Museo del Chopo is the product of an *expulsion*, that the ironwork building—now an inescapable point of reference in the urban landscape and in its time a representation of the country's modernization and progress—ended up housing the collections that no longer fit in the Museo Nacional de México. This expulsion is to be understood as an effect not so much of random historical conditions but of a state policy that simultaneously displays and conceals, that exhibits its archives and destroys them at the same time, destroying them while hiding that destruction.[23] The Díaz regime ambivalently promised to build a new museum dedicated to exhibiting natural history collections once natural history had lost importance; at the same time that naturalists were imagining a "national" museum, the lack of government support and economic resources was undermining its feasibility. It was an expulsion beyond different circumstances; the political slogan tended to separate nature from culture, and thus, instead of a museum whose exhibition space would display all sorts of objects—archaeological, historical, natural—as was the case at the Museo Nacional de México in the

Figure 5.7 "Stuffed animals with deformities at the Museo de Historia Natural [del Chopo]," 1938, Archivo Casasola, Fototeca Nacional. Reproduction authorized by the Instituto Nacional de Antropología e Historia.

late nineteenth century, nature was now thrown into the sphere of prehistory, a deaf, mute, immobile zone, alien to the history of humankind (figure 5.7).[24]

Dispersal

The five objects that survived the debacle seem insignificant, not only because of how little is known about them and the consequent dearth of existing interpretations, but also because they are not especially salient among the rest of the objects at the Museo de Historia Natural. Other than the catalog, there is nothing to indicate their age or provenance. Scattered in the exhibition space, they seem to have been placed at random, forming groups with other specimens and other kinds of objects, and even serving as filler for temporary exhibitions.[25]

Faced with that dispersal, anyone who might come to the museum looking for the past cannot help but be unsettled at observing the ease with which those five objects get lost among the rest, as if their incorporation within the collection as a whole were almost natural. But most unsettling, it seems to me, is the absence of the past, the sense that everything in the museum occupies the same temporal horizon, as if the passing of time had dissolved and all of history had transpired simultaneously. Even as the museum presents natural diversity, it exhibits a single time. Even the idea of evolution, appearing in many installations, text boxes, and information cards, is absorbed by the power of diversity, the slogan of the museum's most recent renovation.

Space in the museum thus seems to be superimposed on time, but that does not prevent this *spatialized* time from displaying different temporalities. For one, there are the 1960s-era dioramas, which light up every time a visitor draws near, and which once represented a great innovation in natural history museums. A realistic scene places a perfect, dramatically lit stuffed animal in the foreground, explaining it as a function of its native habitat. (We never see an old or deformed beast, as Donna Haraway has pointed out in reference to Carl Akeley's dioramas of African scenes at the American Museum of Natural History in the early twentieth century, which the dioramas at the Museo de Historia Natural emulate to a certain extent.)[26] Nearby, the exhibition presents visual installations, videos, and environmental recreations, many created during subsequent partial renovations. Crossing several galleries, the Diplodocus from the early twentieth century leans and twists to extend its full twenty-seven meters in length. Everywhere, countless stuffed animals in display cases recall the classificatory scheme of the Museo del Chopo's old cases.

There are clearly several times at the museum, then, but these different temporal registers are never submitted to the distinction between past and present (nor are visitors given any signals to indicate the different degrees of reality they are seeing). If there is a past in the Museo de Historia Natural, it has been flattened as a specific category, swallowed by a present that appears as the only intelligible dimension, but which nonetheless grinded to a halt in the 1960s.[27] It even gives the impression that the museum space itself is deliberately precluded from feeling the passage of time, as if offering us a reminder that its function is to maintain the present just as it is for as long as possible, and therefore only nature can be captured in perpetuity.[28] It is thus possible to ensure that the objects' meanings come from the present, and that the five surviving objects belong there only to the degree that they can easily be integrated into the general discourse of the Museo de Historia Natural.

But to return to the original confusion, I would have to ask once more what is really so unsettling, whether it is the homogeneity of this single temporal plane, the combination of times and sequences, the chaotic mix of the two things, or the nontime that ultimately ends up presenting nature as diverse but perpetual, plural but immutable, and inert. I do not have a clear answer, but at some point, I did feel a strong urge to hurry through the galleries once more, to take them in through a quick scanning movement and thereby make a swift exit. I also know that once I was outside, I felt another urge, not so much to "rescue" the past to give it a place in the present as to crack open that plural but homogeneous space in such a way that it would be possible to feel anew how the forces of the past still roil in that "monstrous" present.[29]

Longue durée

It suffices for the catalog of the Museo de Historia Natural to announce the presence of the Diplodocus, Jellyfish, Argonaut, Kiwi, and Platypus for these objects to exist as evidence of the past. It suffices to know that they have been exhibited in different museum settings, and that they have therefore accumulated decades' worth of dust, for their realness to be intensified. This is so much the case that, at any given moment, rather than disclosing how the present is engendered by the past, their force bursts forth, altering the homogeneity of the present.

I especially noticed that bursting forth when I had to change the kind of questions I had erstwhile been raising and formulate new ones about the temporal dividing line that determines where the past ends and the present begins. That is, the bursting forth of those five objects into the present forced me to raise a question about the present: about the relationship between past and present, about the past that the present repeats, or about the present whose independence from the past postulates a new ideological orientation toward the production of knowledge.[30]

There could be two perspectives in this regard. First, on a more obvious level, we could note a rupture between the Museo del Chopo in the first decade of the twentieth century and today's Museo de Historia Natural, given that the former emphasized classification, while the latter is more interested in the environment. Whereas the Chopo's collections were arranged in accordance with Linnaean taxonomy, the Museo de Historia Natural no longer presents a totalizing system in which stones, plants, and animals from anywhere in the world have a particular place in the universal picture—an aspiration that the Museo del Chopo shared with both the Museo Nacional de México and the Primer Gabinete de Historia Natural of the eighteenth century. Today, the Museo de Historia Natural presents nature no longer as an absence of humankind but as inhabited by Man.

In the second place, from a less obvious perspective, it is possible to perceive a historical continuity that begins in the eighteenth-century Gabinete and extends to the present. This continuity would be constituted by a single idea of nature as external to humankind, no longer tied closely to those who are a part of it, but rather the setting within which human activity takes place. Continuity is thus established through an idea of landscape that appears as the backdrop to a group of immobile objects, because even the idea of "the environment" is linked to the notion of a "setting," a term that, as Philippe Descola has argued, ultimately refers to inert matter, designed and controlled by the subject.[31] In the end, continuity is constituted by a modern conception of nature in which it appears as mute and impersonal but governed at the same time by the gaze of a subject who remains hidden beyond the frame, the only way to guarantee the representation's objectivity. The historical constant that inaugurates the eighteenth-century Gabinete resides therefore in what Descola calls the "objectification of the subjective," an operation that "creates a distance between man and the world by making the autonomy of things depend upon man; and it systematizes and stabilizes the external universe even as it confers upon the subject absolute mastery over the organization of this new conquered exteriority."[32]

This means that the physical basis of the natural history museum, the part of it that endures over time, is rooted in an operation that objectifies the subjective, for natural history claimed to be a disinterested quest for knowledge even as that quest was always tied to the history of Europe's colonial ambitions. The origin of the museum apparatus was marked by that discourse, which always tended toward possessing the object. From a *longue durée* perspective, the museum apparatus and natural history are linked to the process of colonization, as a result of which it is no longer possible to forget that eighteenth- and nineteenth-century European travelers were closely related to natural history, regardless of whether they were scientists. As Mary Louise Pratt has argued, they all participated in the new project of knowledge construction proposed by natural history. Did that discourse not represent the first act of possessing the discovered lands?[33]

Those five objects that survived through time and burst into the present can therefore be understood as the embodiment of a *longue durée* that began in the eighteenth century—or earlier still, at the moment when Columbus reached the New World and passed from amazement to nominal possession of the territory. Ever since, a single scene has been repeated in which the armor-clad conquistador is momentarily stupefied at the sight of "Indian America, a nude woman reclining in her hammock, an unnamed presence of difference, a body which awakens within a space of exotic fauna and flora," before turning that inert, passive nature into a historicized body.[34] That inaugural scene would be repeated first in the colonial apparatuses of classification and exploitation, and later in the hierarchical taxonomies of the nineteenth century and the racial classification tables of the twentieth.[35] Further, it now seems to me, the wonder I felt when confronted with the animals on one of those grade school visits can no longer be regarded as an individual, isolated emotion. From a *longue durée* vantage point, amazement has a context that responds to certain modalities of power. Surely, that child-like attitude relates to the amazement that, according to Stephen Greenblatt, the first Europeans in the New World experienced when they encountered radical difference there.[36] The emotional and intellectual response to that "first encounter," Greenblatt argues, is a component of the discourse of discovery, because amazement is by definition the instinctive recognition of difference.[37]

In this sense, the nostalgia that accompanies the historian's work—insofar as it depends on an almost compulsive desire that takes pleasure in holding on to that which has been lost or is absent, and which surely runs through this text—is also reminiscent of what Renato Rosaldo called "imperialist nostalgia," a nostalgia for possession that continues to perceive nature through the filter of classification.[38] Classifying means a way of grouping like specimens and separating them from unlike ones, so as to place them in "the rank that corresponds to them on the scale established by nature"—to cite a late nineteenth-century naturalist.[39] In other words, have we indeed detached ourselves from the initial classificatory scheme represented by natural history and its museum, which expresses the basic experience of colonial domination?

In any event, I would prefer to take the question further: has natural history succeeded in disassociating itself entirely from its imperial legacy? Has the *anthropologization* of nature through the notion of the "environment" stopped the growing march of a mute, inert, universal nature since colonization interwove the structure of knowledge with territorial exploration? We would then have to pose the question of how the present is marked by the colonial past.

Animalities

Although the meaning of the five objects comes from the present, they also bear the weight of the past, not only because they belong to the "history collection," but also because they possess a supplementary quality, a texture, as it were, that evokes in the historian the forces of the place whence they originate. It is as though something in the object resisted the passage of time, as if an aura born from the past itself had come loose, and the subject had suddenly become aware of that aura.[40]

Borrowing a turn of phrase from Frank Ankersmit, I would say that these objects constitute "protuberances of the past in the present." But the past in question lacks concrete contents, as a result of which it cannot be described beyond the concern it prompts. It is foremost a concern produced by those object specimens, a concern resulting from different factors, perhaps from a change of place, or from the effects produced by an object that does something in the museum other than what it did in its original context. For the simple movement from one domain to another, from one register to another is, in Giorgio Agamben's words, "sufficient to render it unrecognizable and disquieting": The Argonaut and Jellyfish, two glass pieces that reproduce drawings made by a "very skilled" German artist while "looking at the live animals kept in aquariums, and the descriptions and illuminated plates made by the most notable naturalists"; the Diplodocus, a full-size plaster replica of a dinosaur skeleton; the Kiwi and Platypus, animals removed from their environments, emptied from within, stuffed and eventually exhibited as specimens in the museum setting.[41]

The concern also comes from the ambiguous, borderline condition of the objects, which, precisely because they are so insignificant, represent an entire archaeology of modernity. They blur the boundary between reality and artifice, between life and death, since they engage in the ruse of naturalizing a cultural artifact: dead animals rise up as though they were alive, skeletons stand on all fours, glass pieces seem to be living creatures. If the Diplodocus confuses an animal with its corpse, the Jellyfish and Argonaut twist the limits between reality and artifice, for, as Alfonso L. Herrera affirmed in 1897, the glass with which they are fabricated makes the color, form, and "marvelous transparency" of those creatures more *real.* Because when those bodies are taken out of water "they die, turn pale, get wrinkled and deformed to such a degree that it is difficult to study them, and they present themselves to the viewer as a wrinkly, unappealing mass."[42]

But the concern prompted by those five objects also comes from their singularity, the other power that Greenblatt detects in objects, which, in addition to evoking in the spectator the historical forces whence they arise, halts him in his tracks, confronting him with another dimension of time.[43] It then happens that, in the animal's singular presence, in a state of amazement, it is no longer possible to draw sharp boundaries, to know where one ends and the other begins, what separates the observer from the observed. It is as if that sudden encounter gave rise to an impulse from somewhere beyond "meaning," beyond categories and any reflexive operation; it is like a force that arises from the past, abstracted from all externality and all rational logic. At that moment, it is no longer important to distinguish between reality and representation, and less still to go back to the origin of the animals or materials with which the artifacts were made. Thinking, for example, about all the stuffed animals at the Museo de Historia Natural, would anything change as a result of the knowledge that, owing to a lack of material and economic resources, a dog's tail had been attached to a lion, or donkey ears to a zebra, as if the museum were a sort of medieval bestiary?[44]

At the moment of amazement, the gaze pauses and the animal object—stripped of tradition, already off the museum's epistemological screen, turned into a presence untied from anything known—steals all our attention and constitutes itself as material evidence of something anterior and disappeared. At that mediation-less, context-less moment, the one who gazes is directly confronting the past. And this is not exactly the advent of an untimely memory or an involuntary act of recollection, as if the object were only "inexhaustible receptacles of memories, but rather something that happens between bodies."[45] At that moment of contact, the subject is unable to impose itself over the object.

I cannot say what exactly happens, whether it is an encounter in which mediations are suspended and the decontextualized object begins to speak for itself, or whether it is the other way around, and our experience perfectly matches what the museum apparatus has proposed, which consists in causing the spectator to be captured by the gaze of the object. After all, in a museum that exhibits a nature that has already been subjected to cultural intervention, that encounter may respond to the logic of a modern assemblage that tends to erase the boundary between nature and culture. It could be that the distance between subject and object can only collapse in that assemblage. Whatever the case may be, there is the Lion leaping at me, forever holding the gaze of the encounter (figure 5.8).[46]

Figure 5.8 Lion, Museo de Historia Natural. Photograph by the author.

Or it could be the case that both things happen at once, and that the experience emerges from the ambivalent movement between the immediate, unreflexive, sensuous, bodily encounter with the past and the apparatuses of culture: the Diplodocus indeterminately mixing life and death, the Platypus displaying the indefinition of species, and the Jellyfish and Argonaut tangling reality and representation into a snarled mess. But it could also be that that experience is accompanied by a sensation similar to the childlike amazement we feel, stretching our arms and breathing uneasily in front of something that falls outside our familiar categories and distorts our relationship to time, otherness, and nature.

Whatever the case may be, in that instantaneous encounter in which the sharpness of the boundary disappears and the animal's gaze comes to a halt, something happens between bodies, something makes us expand into each other, recognizing ourselves in the other and the other in ourselves (figure 5.9).[47] It is as if the animal installed itself in the hollow of our psyche, generating an emotional conflict within us. At that moment, nature ceases to be the external atmosphere that surrounds the solid sphere of culture, or the backdrop in front of which to place a set of rigid elements, and instead becomes something that circulates in the life of things, in the force of an "archaic" time that insinuates itself into the present.[48] At the very least, a passageway opens, pointing us toward another way of thinking about nature. At the very least, that confusion discloses another register of time and perhaps a way of relating to nature that is no longer "modern." At the very least, that instant that somehow returns us to our childhood sustains our desire to open ourselves to the world.

Figure 5.9 **Stuffed spider monkey at the Museo de Historia Natural, ca. 1910. Fototeca Nacional. Reproduction authorized by the Instituto Nacional de Antropología e Historia.**

Notes

John Berger, "Why Look at Animals?" in *Why Look at Animals?* (1977; London: Penguin, 2009), x.

1. Antonio Lazcano Araujo and Víctor Jiménez, *Museo de Historia Natural: 50 piezas emblemáticas* (Mexico City: Artes de México y el Mundo, 2014), 22, 49, 54.
2. Lazcano Araujo and Jiménez, *Museo de Historia Natural*, 54.
3. François Hartog, "Prefacio a la edición en español," in *Regímenes de historicidad: Presentismo y experiencias del tiempo*, trans. Norma Durán and Pablo Avilés (Mexico City: Universidad Iberoamericana, 2007), 13.
4. Walter Benjamin, "On the Concept of History," trans. Harry Zohn, in *Selected Writings*, vol. 4 (1938–1940), ed. Michael W. Jennings (Cambridge, Mass.: Harvard University Press, 2003), 389–400.
5. François Hartog, "¿El historiador en un mundo presentista? Una propuesta de perspectiva crítica," trans. Fernanda Núñez, in *Los historiadores y la historia para el siglo XXI: Homenaje a Eric J. Hobsbawm*, ed. Gumersindo Vera Hernández, José R. Pantoja Reyes, María Xochitl Domínguez Pérez, and Orlando Arreola Rosas (Mexico City: Escuela Nacional de Antropología e Historia, 2006), 89–110.
6. Valeria Añon and Mario Rufer, "Lo colonial como silencio, la conquista como tabú: Reflexiones en tiempo presente," *Tabula Rasa* 29 (July–December 2018): 107–31; Laura Catelli, "Lo colonial en la contemporaneidad: Imaginario, archivo, memoria," *Tabula Rasa* 29 (July–December 2018): 133–56.
7. Stephen Greenblatt, *Marvelous Possessions: The Wonder of the New World* (Chicago: University of Chicago Press, 1991); Gabriel Giorgi, *Formas comunes: Animalidad, cultura, biopolítica* (Buenos Aires: Eterna Cadencia, 2014).
8. James Clifford, *Routes: Travel and Translation in the Late Twentieth Century* (Cambridge, Mass.: Harvard University Press, 1997).
9. The first kind of history would be similar to the one told, for example, by Ana Cecilia Rodríguez de Romo about the development of the natural sciences in Mexico. In the framework of this narrative, knowledge accumulates over the course of a sequential history of the leading figures of natural history in Mexico. Recent years have seen the publication of studies addressing the history of museum objects that do not follow official histories. See, for example, Rozental in this volume. Cf. Ana Cecilia Rodríguez de Romo, "Las ciencias naturales en el México independiente: Una visión de conjunto," in *Las ciencias en México*, ed. Hugo Aréchiga and Carlos Beyer (Mexico City: Fondo de Cultura Económica, 1999), 93–128.
10. Mario Rufer, "El archivo: De la metáfora extractiva a la ruptura poscolonial," in *(In)Disciplinar la investigación: Archivo, trabajo de campo y escritura*, ed. Frida Gorbach and Mario Rufer (Mexico City: UAM and Siglo XXI, 2016), 163.
11. Rummaging through the archives to reconstruct origins and trajectories is a basic task that requires a great deal of work, particularly considering the "evidence" is scattered among different archives, for which reason one has to follow

the scarcest of clues, to struggle against what Añon calls "the excessive silences of institutions," and against all those intervals of time during which the documents do not appear. Valeria Añon, "Los usos del archivo: Reflexiones situadas sobre literatura y discurso colonial," in Gorbach and Rufer, *(In)Disciplinar la investigación*, 256.

12. It is possible that other specimens survive, some of which may be held by the Instituto de Biología. For reasons that are unclear, access to them is restricted.
13. Rufer, "El archivo," 161. There is of course a large critical bibliography on the imaginary of the archive as presence and totality. See, for example, Carolyn Hamilton, Verne Harris, Jane Taylor, Michele Pickover, Graeme Reid, and Razia Saleh, eds., *Refiguring the Archive* (Dordrecht: Kluwer Academic, 2002); and Ann Laura Stoler, "Colonial Archives and the Arts of Governance," *Archival Science* 2, no. 1–2 (2002): 87–109.
14. As Didi-Huberman has put it, the "gray" tone of the archive results not only from the time through which it has passed but also from the "ashes of everything that went up in flames around it." Georges Didi-Huberman, "L'image brûle," in *Penser par les images: Autour des travaux de Georges Didi-Huberman*, ed. Laurent Zimmerman (Paris: Cécile Defaut, 2006), 23. An example of deliberate acts to produce absence was the teratology collection that had been displayed at the Museo Nacional de México, above the archaeology pieces and next to the anthropology gallery: years after the collection was moved to the Museo de Historia Natural del Chopo, in the first decade of the twentieth century, it was taken away and, in a story of few details and many rumors, the monsters were taken to another institution, then another, and when there was nowhere left to house them, it is said, they were buried behind the wall of one of the tunnels of the university stadium, and then taken to the botanical garden at the Universidad Nacional, where a fire did away with them. Frida Gorbach, *El monstruo, objeto imposible: Un estudio sobre teratología mexicana, siglo XIX* (Mexico City: Universidad Autónoma Metropolitana–Xochimilco and Itaca, 2008).
15. Añon, "Los usos del archivo," 251.
16. Jesús Díaz de León, report to the Secretariat of the Office of Public Instruction and Fine Arts, 1912, file 152, box 8, 1914, p. 2, Archivo Histórico-Universidad Nacional Autónoma de México (AH-UNAM).
17. Carlos A. Molina, *Érase una vez un museo: Apuntes históricos para el edificio y Museo Universitario del Chopo* (Mexico City: Universidad Nacional Autónoma de México, 2014); Paloma Porraz del Amo, Armando H. Egido Villareal, Maria Teresa Germán, *Historia del Museo Universitario del Chopo* (Mexico City: Universidad Nacional Autónoma de México, 1993). On the opening of the Museo de Historia Natural in 1964, some newspapers highlighted that the building for this museum was one of the first built with the aim to which it was destined.
18. Folder 191, box 7, p. 27 (1911–1912), AH-UNAM. In reports from subsequent years, the naturalists continue to complain about the difficulties of arranging and conserving the specimens on the shelves and in the display cases.

19. Jesús Díaz de León, report to the Secretariat of the Office of Public Instruction and Fine Arts, folder 191, box 7, p. 27 (1911–1912), AH-UNAM.
20. Díaz de León's ambition was to forge a national museum of natural history. Jesús Díaz de León, report to the Secretariat of the Office of Public Instruction and Fine Arts (1911–1912), folder 191, box 7, p. 38, AH-UNAM.
21. Frida Gorbach, "El museo olvidado," in *Museo Nacional de Antropología: 50 aniversario (1825–1964)*, ed. Antonio Saborit and Carla Zarebska (Mexico City: Conaculta/INAH, 2014), 116–25. Gorbach, "Commemorate, Consecrate, Demolish: Thoughts about the Mexican Museum of Anthropology and Its History," in *Entangled Heritages: Postcolonial Perspectives on the Uses of the Past in Latin America*, ed. Olaf Kaltmeier and Mario Rufer (London: Routledge, 2017), 109–21.
22. Similarly, this happened across Latin America, where an interest in the natural landscape was replaced by an interest in humanity itself: its origin, cultures, and heritage. In this sense, Roberto González Echeverría identifies three phases in the Latin American narrative: he postulates that in the sixteenth century, the novel resulted from the legal discourse of the Spanish empire; in the nineteenth century, from natural history and its interest to name and catalog the natural features of the New World; and in the twentieth century, from anthropology, a discipline preoccupied with national identity. Roberto González Echeverría, *Myth and Archive: A Theory of Latin American Narrative* (Durham, N.C.: Duke University Press, 1998).
23. Achille Mbembe, "The Power of the Archive and Its Limits," trans. Judith Inggs, in Hamilton et al., *Refiguring the Archive*, 19–26.
24. Philippe Descola, *Beyond Nature and Culture*, trans. Janet Lloyd (Chicago: University of Chicago Press, 2013).
25. On one of my visits to the Museo de Historia Natural, the Argonaut and the Jellyfish were part of a temporary exhibit about the oceans.
26. Donna Haraway, "Teddy Bear Patriarchy: Taxidermy in the Garden of Eden, New York City, 1908–1936," *Social Text* 11 (Winter 1984–1985): 24.
27. I am referring, for example, to the board depicting the human races, which would come under scrutiny today, or the installation evoking the moon landing, an event that took place half a century ago.
28. Donald Preziosi, "Brain of the Earth's Body: Museums and the Framing of Modernity," in *Museum Studies: An Anthology of Contexts*, ed. Bettina Messias Carbonell (Malden, Mass.: Blackwell, 2004), 75–76.
29. Philippe Artières, "Dire l'actualité: Le travail de diagnostic chez Michel Foucault," in *Foucault: Le courage de la vérité*, ed. Frédéric Gros (Paris: Presses Universitaires de France, 2002), 11–34.
30. Preziosi, "Brain of the Earth's Body," 76.
31. Philippe Descola, "Beyond Nature and Culture: Forms of Attachment," trans. Janet Lloyd, *HAU: Journal of Ethnographic Theory* 2, no. 1 (2012): 459.
32. Descola, *Beyond Nature and Culture*, 59–60.

33. Mary Louise Pratt, *Imperial Eyes: Travel Writing and Transculturation*, 2nd ed. (New York: Routledge, 2008).
34. Michel De Certeau, *The Writing of History*, trans. Tom Conley (New York: Columbia University Press, 1988), xxv.
35. Christophe Giudicelli, "'Altas culturas,' antepasados legítimos y naturalistas orgánicos: La patrimonialización del pasado indígena y sus dueños (Argentina 1877–1910)," in *Nación y alteridad: Mestizos, indígenas y extranjeros en el proceso de formación nacional*, ed. Daniela Gleizer Salzman, Paula López Caballero, and Claudia Briones (Mexico City: Universidad Autónoma de México–Cuajimalpa, 2015), 244; Añon and Rufer, "Lo colonial como silencio"; Catelli, "Lo colonial en la contemporaneidad."
36. Greenblatt, *Marvelous Possessions*, 14.
37. Greenblatt, *Marvelous Possessions*, 20.
38. Renato Rosaldo, "Imperialist Nostalgia," in *Culture and Truth: The Remaking of Social Analysis* (Boston: Beacon Press, 1989), 68–87.
39. Ramón López Muñoz, "Zoología: Ligera reseña sobre la clasificación zoológica e historia de los principales naturalistas," *El Porvenir* 2 (1870): 281–82.
40. Frank Ankersmit, *Sublime Historical Experience* (Stanford, Calif.: Stanford University Press, 2005), 263–66.
41. Giorgio Agamben, *Stanzas: Word and Phantasm in Western Culture*, trans. Ronald L. Martinez (Minneapolis: University of Minnesota Press, 1993), 56–57; Alfonso L. Herrera, *Catálogo de las imitaciones en cristal de varios animales invertebrados del Museo Nacional* (Mexico City: Imprenta del Museo Nacional, 1897), i.
42. Herrera, *Catálogo*, i.
43. Greenblatt, *Marvelous Possessions*, 25.
44. Personal communication with the curator of the Museo de Historia Natural, May 2019.
45. Georges Didi-Huberman, *Ante el tiempo. Historia del arte y anacronismo de las imágenes* (Buenos Aires: Adriana Hidalgo Editora, 2008), 63.
46. Haraway, "Teddy Bear Patriarchy," 25.
47. Greenblatt, *Marvelous Possessions*, 25.
48. Tim Ingold, *The Life of Lines* (New York: Routledge, 2015).

6

Clues and Gazes

Indigenous Faces in the Museo Nacional de Antropología

HAYDEÉ LÓPEZ HERNÁNDEZ

A baby peers out over a tangle of fibers, eyes twinkling and toes curled up into a little ball in a cotton hammock. His head is sticking out, his hands are at either side, and he bites the edge, while the toes of his right foot are entangled in the hammock. He is gazing curiously at the photographer who captured his image in the silver halide of a black and white photograph. The enlarged print mounted on a wooden frame already shows signs of the passage of time: instead of its original black and white, it has taken on a dirty, yellowish cast. Measuring ninety centimeters on each side, it was surely hung on a wall at some point. Now, its edges cracked, it sits abandoned at the entrance of a storage area, forgotten and covered in dust. It is no longer an object worthy of being exhibited, and since it has no inventory number, it is not considered a piece of national heritage that must be conserved (figure 6.1). Nevertheless, the gaze that peers out over the cotton threads captivates me as I pass through the overstuffed passageways of the ethnographic storehouses of the Museo Nacional de Antropología—that long, labyrinthine corridor that runs beneath the archaeological exhibition halls.

The gaze in the photograph offers a clue about objects that once inhabited the museum's exhibition halls and the stories they told. My own gaze is not innocent, combing that trace for the desires of museum staff and *indigenista* scholars alike to capture and conserve the faces and realities of indigenous

Figure 6.1 Photograph on wooden frame at the doors of the ethnography storehouse at the Museo Nacional de Antropología. Photograph by author, February 2019.

peoples, even when they allow themselves to be glimpsed only between the threads of a hammock.

Clues

As I walk through the museum's labyrinthine bowels, down the hallways that adjoin the ethnography storehouses, I see several photographic enlargements on wooden frames like the one I described above, scattered about in no apparent order. Others are hung on office walls. At first the images catch my attention because they have been forgotten: they are no longer meant to be exhibited, although they had been at some point—so I am told by Valerio Paredes, my guide to this unfamiliar world. These valueless objects are to be discarded. It would seem that the whole of which they had been a part is now unimportant. This troubles me because I see them as tossing out the history of the whole along with the photographs, as well as the history of anthropology and of a community of anthropologists. My concern grows with time because those images do not match my preconceptions of the building's history, which Néstor García Canclini described critically so many years ago as showing "'pure' and unified cultural patrimony" in its ethnography halls.[1] When I look at those portraits, I see no "purity." I am unable to identify the ethnic group to which the baby in the hammock "should" belong.

The originals for the enlarged prints are kept in the Archivo Fotográfico de Etnografía (AFE). They consist of black and white and color photographs, 35mm positive prints (contact sheets) and 5 × 7 inch and 8 × 10 inch enlargements, classified by ethnic group in thick black folders: Mixtec, Mixe, Ocuiltec, Pápago, Seri, Ópata, Tarasco, Tarahumara, Chinanteco, Chatino, Cora, Cuicatec, Chontal (Oaxaca), Huastec, Huave, Maya, Lacandón, Mayo, Mazatec, Mazahua, Matlazinca, Mam, Yaqui, Zoque (Chiapas), Zapotec, Tzeltal, Tzotzil, Otomí, as well as mestizos and Nahuas from various states (Estado de México, Hidalgo, Veracruz, Morelos, Guerrero, and Puebla). The negatives in various formats for some of these images are also held at the AFE.

All together there must be several thousand samples. This may well be the largest visual ethnographic record made by the Museo Nacional de Antropología up to that point.[2] The AFE encompasses thirty-one of the country's different ethnic groups. The dates of the collection (1961–64), along with the consistency of the images' formal qualities and topics, suggest that it was produced as a single project, which may have coincided with the construction of the Museo Nacional de Antropología—as Valerio suggested to me.[3] Nevertheless, the details of its origins are unknown.[4] The gap in historical knowledge regarding this collection strikes me as revealing, especially given the conventional use of the AFE as an image bank to illustrate current exhibition projects (rather than as a historical archive used for research purposes). Inevitably, these documents have been resignified, obscuring their historicity and stripping time (and with it, agency and change) away from subjects who were photographed over six decades earlier.

Sources are constructed in the contingency of how documents interact with an observer's questions and subjectivity.[5] It is possible, therefore, to decenter our gaze, moving away from the atemporality associated with "ethnic types" to get a glimpse of some of the parameters that guided the inclusion of photography as key to anthropological fieldwork (e.g., documenting landscapes and urban scenes, housing and colonial architecture, economic activities, handicrafts, festivities and rituals, as well as physical types). In this sense, the photographs in the AFE appear to share the totalizing and ingenuous concern central to the discipline since its nineteenth-century beginnings, namely, to describe indigenous societies by creating records—in this case, visual ones.[6]

Yet the portraits (mostly of women) seem to escape this norm, confirming my initial concern given that they completely dilute the ethnic specificity of the subjects typified in each of the archive's folders.[7] Some of the photographs were taken without the subjects' awareness, either because their backs were turned or because they did not notice the furtive presence of the photographer, who happened upon them as they walked, worked, or conversed, always in motion. One woman, for example, has her back turned, her head covered in a woven shawl, serving as a visual frame as she cradles a baby who sleeps peacefully with his head on her shoulder. The tenderness and tranquility radiating from the sleeping infant is accentuated by the close-up of his face, easily grabbing the observer's attention (figure 6.2).[8]

Other photographs are characterized by complicity rather than guile. Some models face the camera, displaying their typical attire with stiff, serious expressions. Others go even further, participating actively in aesthetic compositions that evoke the dialogue that must have taken place between photographer and subject. One depicts a woman with her arms resting on a table. One hand lightly clasps the other in the unfocused foreground of the image. Her head tilts to the left and slightly downward, and her hair is down, tucked loosely behind her ears so that all the details of her face are visible: her thin, well-shaped eyebrows; her broad, straight nose; her strong cheekbones, accentuated by the slightly elevated angle of the shot; and her broad, delicate smile. Her large, bright eyes look up and to her left, directly meeting the gaze of the photographer and subsequent viewers alike. Sunlight streams dazzlingly from behind her through a window that fills the entire photograph, giving her a brilliant aura that stylizes her figure and highlights her coquettishness (figure 6.3).

Although some of the subjects portrayed do wear traditional clothing, making it possible to associate them with a particular region or culture, these elements do not always constitute the photographs' visual core. Another woman is centered in a medium-long shot, her body in a three-quarter turn and her face looking quizzically at the camera. A tangled fiber net is barely visible in her right hand. Her torso is bare, aside from three beaded necklaces of different colors and sizes; her head is covered by a long huipil that frames her figure like a halo of light. She is in the middle of a plaza. Over her left

Figure 6.2 *Untitled.* Amatenango, Chiapas. Photograph by Gertrude Duby. Tzeltal Catalog, no. 16349(63)1.36dl-416, AFE. Reproduction authorized by the Instituto Nacional de Antropología e Historia del INAH.

shoulder, past the focal plane, two men observe the scene mischievously; to her right, another walks by, seemingly unaware of the photographer. The visual center of the image lies not in any of the material elements that might speak of the Oaxacan coast, but rather in the woman's striking expression: her furrowed brow, which accentuates her deep, dark, almond-shaped eyes; her full, half-open lips, revealing her teeth; her defiant attitude, directly and openly confronting the photographer (and by extension the spectator) who dares to gaze at her from the other side of the lens (figure 6.4).

These portraits do not constitute the bulk of the photographs in the AFE's collection, but their inclusion there is important because they differ so

Figure 6.3 *Untitled*. Chinantec Catalog, no. 7283(64)6.28–242, AFE. Reproduction authorized by the Instituto Nacional de Antropología e Historia del INAH.

profoundly from the rigidity and attempted objectivity of the records from prior decades.[9] In the latter, subjects were portrayed in the nude against white or homogeneous backdrops, first from the front and again from the side so as to highlight their anatomical features, as in the anthropometric photography of the late nineteenth century.[10] Alternatively, they were depicted in "local" settings (either natural or re-created), garbed in "typical" attire and objects, as in early twentieth-century cartes de visite or in the folkloricizing photographs of Hugo Brehme, with their characteristic cloud-studded skies and compositions prominently featuring magueys, nopal cacti, charros, "nice little Indians," and handicrafts.

Figure 6.4 *Untitled.* Pinotepa, Oaxaca. Photograph by Carlos Sáenz. Mixtec Catalog II, no. 6082(64)6.37a1–1199, AFE. Reproduction authorized by the Instituto Nacional de Antropología e Historia del INAH.

The portraits in the AFE, by contrast, show an intimate proximity between photographer and subjects, as if the former had had the time and disposition to get to know the latter, to exchange a few words and seek out the right angle after having toured the local context, gotten to know its ins and outs, and untangled its labyrinths. This can be explained in part by the mid-twentieth-century rise of photojournalism, which broadened the parameters of what was worth documenting, to include everyday life, social movements, workers, students, and other actors in ordinary (as opposed to political) life. Photojournalists also experimented with different styles, lending vitality and movement to their images. In Mexico, Nacho López (1923–86), Rodrigo

Moya (b. 1934), and others pioneered this photographic movement with their reports in *Mañana* and *Hoy*, while criticizing the objectification and folkloricization of ethnographic photography.[11]

Even though we have no information about most of the photographers whose images are held in the AFE, we can easily associate them with this photographic tendency because of their style, not to mention the presence of photos by Nacho López, Alfonso Muñoz (1908–92), and Óscar Menéndez (?—?), who dedicated themselves to anthropological photography in the following years.[12] But rather than assuage my initial concern, this only caused it to grow. How are we to understand the presence of these critical exercises in the context of Mexican *indigenismo*? Could the Museo Nacional de Antropología have been part of this movement? Or did these photographs swim against the tide of anthropological discourse? Did they submit to it in the end, or was there any overlap between the two?

Analyses of these photographs in terms of aesthetics, history (i.e., in relation to the photographer and their time), or semantics (i.e., relating to the messages encoded in their composition and tonalities) do not delve deeply enough into my concerns.[13] I thus turn to intuition, a tool of the historian's trade, to view these photographs as *clues*, following their tracks back to the discipline of anthropology and to the museum, revealing the tensions and possible contradictions implied by their presence within that "monument of monuments" that turned indigenous people into the main thrust of its narrative.[14]

Indigenous Faces

The Museo Nacional de Antropología was the culmination of the construction of a new historical narrative that was first outlined in 1936, based on the desire to visualize and give value to cultural "difference," while paradoxically using indigenous faces as a symbol of national unification.[15] Years later, the architect overseeing the project, Pedro Ramírez Vázquez, recalled that the "museum's original layout focused especially on archaeology, but, from the very first conversations with the advisory board, there was also a concern to show aspects of native cultures that are still alive, to provide a broader educational panorama and to foster admiration and respect for the indigenous past."[16]

The architect's recollections may point toward a reshaping of the museographic and historical narrative of which the Museo Nacional de Antropología was the latest episode. By then, the collections belonging to the nineteenth-century museum had already been split up, first in 1909, when natural history was pulled out of the museum, then again in 1942, when the colonial history and ethnography collections were taken to a new building, the Museo Nacional de Historia.[17] Thereafter, the archaeological and ethnographic pieces that had remained in the Moneda building became the Museo Nacional de Antropología, but the place of these two collections in the museum was unbalanced from the start. The ethnographic collections lost more and more ground, occupying just one of the building's twenty-eight halls in 1956.[18] It is possible, however, that the ethnographic exhibits at the Museo Nacional de Antropología were shrinking in response to the 1951 opening of the Museo Nacional de Artes e Industrias Populares at the former Corpus Christi church.

The process of splitting up the collections resulted from the specialization and differentiation of scientific disciplines, as well as from a reconfiguration of a historical narrative, initially constructed in the nineteenth century, positing a new break in historical time and a reconfiguring of subjects and their representation in museums. By separating the three centuries of the colonial period and the first century after independence from the pre-Hispanic past and the indigenous present, the Spanish legacy was confined to an island without any bridges to the continent of the indigenous imaginary in the narrative of the Museo Nacional de Antropología. In this imaginary, the origin of the ethnographic collection was rooted in pre-Columbian time, which was only tenuously linked to a thoroughly depleted indigenous present by means of a narrative bridge spanning a four-century-wide chasm.

On the other hand, the revaluing of indigenous and popular industries, especially their being recategorized as art, was a long process that ran parallel to the debate between communities of artists, anthropologists, and educator-functionaries. The Museo Nacional de Artes e Industrias Populares proposed to turn such objects into both part of an amalgamated national heritage and, paradoxically, the only museographic representation of indigenous people once the ethnography halls had all but disappeared from the Museo Nacional de Antropología. In this sense, indigeneity was set outside the sweep of history as represented in the national museums of history and anthropology, entering instead the spaces of aesthetic valuation, as would happen shortly thereafter with colonial art at the Museo Nacional del Virreinato. In other words, with the creation of the Museo de Arte Popular, indigeneity was excluded from the study of primitive societies (i.e., anthropology) and integrated into the aesthetic realm of contemplating the highest achievements of a civilization (i.e., art), even as the notions of primitivism and purism that had erstwhile prevailed in the valuation of these peoples and their objects were not abandoned in the process.[19]

These new parameters for valuing indigeneity are understandable given that, just as this process of museographic fragmentation took place, there was a generalized revaluation of non-Western cultures and a boom in cultural anthropology on a worldwide scale.[20] There was also a desire to observe Mexico on its own terms rather than those of nineteenth-century universalism—a tendency that was also visible, for example, in a philosophy of Mexicanness that was amply supported by the midcentury regime.[21] Those years also saw the beginnings of so-called indigenism in Mexico and Latin America, when some of the most emblematic institutions and educational and governmental projects were created and consolidated, including the Proyecto Tarasco, the *México indígena* exhibition, the Escuela Nacional de Antropología e Historia, the Departamento de Asuntos Indígenas, the Instituto Nacional Indigenista, and the Instituto Indigenista Interamericano.[22]

Despite this institutional effervescence of all things indigenous, the scholarly community—and possibly the general population—did not reach a consensus about the form in which native populations were to be valued. In the mid-twentieth century, anthropologist Arturo Monzón drew on data gathered in 1942 and 1952 to argue that statistics showed a steady decline of visitors to the Museo Nacional de Antropología. This was especially the case for Mexican nationals, who preferred historical exhibitions, despite recent renovations meant "to fill the gaps left by the history collections" and to modernize its operating procedures.[23] As a result, Monzón averred that the museum's main objective should be to instill and encourage an appreciation of non-Western cultures, which have "different aesthetic, technological and moral values that are just as high as Western culture's greatest values, worthy of being placed in the respectable position they deserve within national and international life, given that the current manifestations of our own tradition are rooted in native peoples, both past and present."[24]

Monzón's inclusion of the "present time" is important. Far from being a matter of his personal opinion, it reflects a broader interest that would influence the museographic narrative at the Museo Nacional de Antropología. Indeed, his assessment probably supported calls for a new venue. In

1957, museum director Luis Aveleyra once again insisted on the need for a new building, presenting a proposal to the Secretaría de Educación Pública in which he detailed the inconveniences, inadequacies, and dangers of the building on Calle de la Moneda, endorsing the petition with signatures from thirty-four representatives of the country's main scientific and cultural institutions. The project for a new building took shape thanks largely to support from Amalia González Caballero (1898–1986), the widow of Castillo Ledón (who had been the museum's director on several occasions in decades past) and later the undersecretary of cultural affairs for the Secretaría de Educación Pública, and from the secretary of education, Jaime Torres Bodet (1902–74).[25]

Nevertheless, the initial request for a new space did not take the ethnographic exhibit into account. Both Ramírez Vázquez and Fernando Cámara (1919–2007; who was to serve as ethnology adviser) shared this recollection, as just one of several discussions that were held in those years.[26] Although Cámara was one of the first students at the Escuela Nacional de Antropología e Historia and among the founders of Mexican institutions, his training was more closely aligned with social anthropology. He was a student of Sol Tax (1907–95), doing research on highland Chiapas. He pursued graduate studies in social anthropology at the University of Chicago during two periods (1944 and 1947) and was part of the research team on the Papaloapan Commission, with Alfonso Villa Rojas (1897–1998).[27] Villa Rojas and Tax were both Robert Redfield's students and collaborators, and in Mexico, they worked toward promoting social anthropology through their research (as with the Papaloapan project) and by training new teams. The latter were to join the indigenist projects that were being headed by the Mexican community at the time, so much so that some have argued that "Redfield had a powerful influence on . . . applied anthropology and the way indigenism developed as an educational strategy."[28]

Redfield and his students thought that social anthropology should focus on processes of social and cultural change in rural and urban societies so as to shape their *acculturation* (or integration into national culture).[29] The influence of the Chicago School on Mexican anthropologists of that generation has been interpreted as a historical break that lent a scientific and international character to the Mexican tradition, which had supposedly been theoretically and methodologically limited, focusing as it did on the folkloric and museographic aspects of indigenous populations—that is, on "dead culture."[30] Recently, however, the supposed backwardness of Mexican anthropology, which was more focused on historical and geographical analyses of indigenous groups during those years, has been questioned.[31] This suggests that although there are notable differences between the two academic projects, they also had overlaps and continuities.

Before his involvement in the Museo Nacional de Antropología, Cámara was doing research and teaching, leading large-scale projects—such as Project 104 for the Organization of American States—and advancing the development of social and applied anthropology. In this regard, it is understandable that he would worry that the museum project was not taking the ethnographic collections into account. Although we do not know the specifics of the debate, nor of the tensions that must have shaped it, it is quite plausible that the museum was hotly contested by advocates for different proposals.

Starting with the first formal proposals for the project presented to Secretaría de Educación Pública authorities, there was a sense that the new Museo Nacional de Antropología should "effectively house, protect and promote the most genuine manifestations of its *rich indigenous cultural heritage, past and present*."[32] The historical (i.e., identitarian) continuity implicit in such a notion of heritage determined the designs for a sequence of exhibitions beginning in remote prehistory and culminating in the current cultural manifestations of "our indigenous peoples." Leaving the lobby, visitors would enter an introductory hall and then be guided to a Hall of Mexico's Indigenous Cultures, where they would be offered "a comparative panorama to help them contextualize Mexico's diverse aboriginal cultures in space and time. [T]his Hall . . . will constitute a true synthesis of the most decisive elements in Mexico's *indigenous history*. There, a short tour will enable visitors to take in a highly interesting, agreeable and instructive message."[33]

Visitors would then move on to the Archaeological or Ethnographic Hall, in which they would find detailed information about each culture. The aim was for the museum to be both scientifically sound and socially beneficial, rather than a simple "museum of indigenous art addressed to a learned minority who contemplates art for its own sake"—that is, like the Museo Nacional de Artes e Industrias Populares.[34] To achieve this, Cámara argued, the exhibitions should feature "inhospitable environmental" conditions. "[This] would raise awareness and interest in knowing more about the social problems that they and we must solve. It is no longer the time for Museums to show astounding, frightening or incredible things. Now is the time to exhibit what is real and unfamiliar so that it may be understood and absorbed; to identify with the situation and grasp the meaning of the problem and a sense of our own responsibility."[35]

The point was to turn indigenous peoples into one of the main thrusts of the museum's historical narrative, with clear educational and political intentions. It was therefore essential for the museum to present the country's indigenous faces in light of social problems, as a tool for raising awareness about the precarious social state of Mexico's native groups, arousing empathy for them and, at the same time, for the workings of applied anthropology.

Achieving this, however, was no easy task. Although the advisers for each ethnographic area regarded the existing collections as plentiful, MXP$233,600 was requested to carry out expeditions and acquire more ethnographic objects.[36] According to Pedro Ramírez Vázquez, 95 percent of the material exhibited resulted from those expeditions. "In keeping with the museographic criteria that we had established, it was crucial to show the ethnographic richness of our country in the real context of its production and time, and not just follow the same classification scheme of many of the world's museums, i.e., kitchen utensils, furniture, musical instruments, etc. To do this, we needed to reproduce the cultural context as a whole."[37]

Furthermore, the ethnographic expeditions carried out to obtain these materials were intended to gather more information from each region, perhaps because, even though it went unsaid, it was necessary to reconstruct the cultural context for each area. Under the general coordination of Alfonso Villa Rojas, assisted by Fernando Cámara, the members of the advising group were Wigberto Jiménez Moreno (1909–85) for Central Mexico; Roberto Weitlaner (1883–1968) for Oaxaca; Ricardo Pozas (1912–94) for Chiapas; Alfonso Villa Rojas for the southeast (Tabasco, Campeche, Yucatán); Roberto Williams (1925–2008) for the Gulf Coast; Barbro Dahlgren (1912–2002) for the west; and Fernando Cámara for the north.[38] Aside from Jiménez Moreno and Williams, all were disciples of the Chicago School.[39]

The result was a set of guidebooks for the museographic and educational teams.[40] In total 2,271 pages of "original research" were presented, a "stock of systematic information [that] had never before been compiled, constituting the basis for the first complete treatise of Mexican Ethnography."[41] This might seem like an exaggeration considering that Carlos Basauri had undertaken a similar study three decades earlier, the results of which had been published in *La población indígena de México*. Lucio Mendieta y Núñez had shortly thereafter overseen a series of research projects that after a decade culminated with the publication of *Etnografía de México*. Nevertheless, Basauri's study took place in the context of 1930s educational policies, assisted by rural teachers who collected survey data in the field, while Mendieta's had been bitterly criticized by anthropologist Juan Comas.[42] The museum's sense of pride is thus understandable, given that its Ethnography Department had never before secured enough of a budget to undertake such an ambitious research project directed by its own members.

This "treatise" could well be seen as a first attempt at synthesizing the proponents of social anthropology, even though the monographs were not entirely homogeneous. They all covered the same topics—history, geography, language, economy, agricultural technology, handicrafts, worldview (including rituals and religion), arts (music, dance, poetry, etc.), housing, and clothing—but only the monographs written by the disciples of the Chicago School focused on social and political organization, material culture, and acculturation.[43]

Interesting as a detailed analysis of the differences between the monographs may be, I limit myself here to their treatments of temporal issues. Whereas Williams, for example, proposed to present scenes from mestizo and indigenous groups' daily life, and even to devote a section on southern Tamaulipas to "cowboys in suede suits" (in the absence of ethnographic studies of indigenous groups), Barbro Dahlgren suggested that an introductory section of the Occidente Hall (in the event that it was separated from the archaeological wing) should include archaeological pieces "related to daily life, showing the continuity of material culture, which will be necessary for establishing the internal unity of the area." For the ethnographic section, he proposed presenting "the technological principles common to all ancient Mesoamerican indigenous peoples." Pozas emphasized the existence of "pre-Hispanic procedures" in some of the activities of the Chiapanec Maya, while Villa Rojas proposed that the Sureste Hall should feature the historical process they had undergone, "from the most ancient group, represented by the Lacandon Maya, to the most acculturated, found in Campeche and Yucatán. Quintana Roo occupies an intermediate position, corresponding to the colonial era."[44]

The concern with representing *pure* ethnic types, as well as their *unity* and *historical continuity* since pre-Hispanic times, dominated the project's overarching narrative to such a degree that it was decided that the ethnographic halls would follow the same organizational criteria as the archaeological ones. That is, they were to be classified by culture area, establishing "a physical relationship between the archaeological and ethnographic halls such that members of the public, if they so desire, can visit first the archaeology and then the ethnography of a single region" on a tour connecting the most distant points of the ancient past to the present.[45]

In this way, the new Museo Nacional de Antropología not only integrated the ethnography halls in an equivalent proportion to the archaeology ones but made *indigeneity* the main thrust of its narrative. What had previously occupied a modest exhibition hall on Moneda Street became the face of Mexico in the new Museo Nacional de Antropología in Chapultepec, as evidence of the fusion of past and present in the history of the nation. This transfiguration entailed more museographic space and greater narrative power, but these came at a high cost insofar as the integration of indigenous subjects to the national narrative cut off their relation to time, and with it, their historicity.

Dissonant Gazes

Representing indigenous people out of time required some tricks of the museographic trade. In August 1961, Raúl Estrada Discua delivered his budget. He solicited MXP$17,750 to take two thousand photographs that would serve as a "photographic archive of different ethnological aspects of the Mexican Republic (physical type, residence, geographical setting, etc.)."[46] The archive holds no further documentation regarding this matter, but a few years after the Museo Nacional de Antropología opened, Luis Aveleyra stated that over the course of sixty ethnographic expeditions directed by the anthropological advisers (each accompanied by a museographer, a photographer, and assistants), thousands of objects had been gathered, as well as "over 15,000 color and black and white photographs, hundreds of drawings, indigenous language and music recordings on magnetic tape, and above all, a large volume of fieldnotes and observations."[47]

It is possible that some of these photographic records are among those currently held at the AFE, the earliest images of which match the date of Discua's budget (1961), with the latest ones corresponding to the museum's opening (1964). These photographs encompass all the topics mentioned in that document, but then again, not a single photograph was taken by Discua, whose rigid, racialist style differed completely from those photographs (in which the individual subjectivities of the models are evidenced). This undermines the idea that the renowned photographer coordinated or even participated in the project.[48]

Although photography may have been understood as supplemental to the advisers' primary body of research, I have been unable to locate the "copious inestimable scientific archive" (fieldnotes, drawings, and sound recordings) described by Aveleyra.[49] From the material held at the Archivo Histórico del Museo Nacional de Antropología, it seems that the advisers did not submit reports during their research projects, aside from brief notes detailing ethnographic material acquired or requesting funding, and a few preliminary reports by Cámara's students.[50] The guidebooks they did eventually submit are finished monographs that could well have been meant for publication; that is, they are neatly composed texts from which the trials, tribulations, and minutiae of the expeditions have been omitted, such that it is no longer possible to discern the rough stages of research traveled prior to being smoothed over in a set of guidebooks.[51]

These monographs were submitted from July 1961 to late 1962, so it is possible that, rather than being a mere supplement to the research, the AFE's photographic records (dating from 1961 to 1964) had the ingenuous objective of capturing *reality* as defined by the anthropologists. In this regard, Margarita Nolasco, one of Cámara's students, recalled that they were faced with three museographic currents: one that proposed "to reflect indigenous culture," one that opted to "reinterpret and recreate it," and the "Indianist tendency of the extremists who thought that Indians themselves should decide what to exhibit, in what order, and how."[52] Although the anthropologist recalls that they ultimately opted for a "certain freedom," the museographic and educational teams carried out several trips to major museums in the United States and Europe to learn more about how to design their exhibitions.[53] Upon returning to Mexico, they proposed to put "authenticity" on display so as not "to lose their anthropological, historical and living value." Such was the case for the scenes with mannequins, for example, which were regarded as "true models" rather than reconstructions because—or so it was argued—they were actually made by indigenous people, who had ended up "directing the architects and museographers."[54]

Shortly after the museum's opening, the museographer Mario Vázquez also emphasized the importance of having documentation that captured all "aspects" of a scene and of gathering "all sorts of materials relevant to its *reconstruction*." In addition to anthropologists and museographers, then, there were sculptors, illustrators, photographers, musicologists, and filmmakers. For example, to make the diorama of a rain-petition ceremony that was still being practiced by Maya groups in Quintana Roo, it was necessary to take

> an enormous amount of photographs marking every step and every movement of the action. The anthropologists produced an exhaustive study of the ceremony, while the musicologists recorded the voices and songs accompanying the ceremony. Countless objects, flowers, leaves, soil, textiles, foodstuffs, utensils, stones, etc., were also gathered. Back in the city, the small-scale sculptural reconstruction of the scene was carried out with maximum fidelity, exactness, realism and mastery.[55]

In this connection, the photographs were considered part of the documentary record of the populations; that is, they were visual *testimonies* and *objective data* that ensured and enabled that those involved could come to know the local *reality*, and then that they could *reproduce it* in another setting with "fidelity, exactness, realism and mastery," without marking the presence of the photographers nor the mediations of the artists involved in making the dioramas and sculptures.

On the other hand, photographs were also considered *fragments of reality* in themselves; that is, *objects* or *specimens* that could be collected and taken away as a representative samples of the *reality* of which they were a part, without losing any of their meaning. As such they were part of the collections exhibited in the halls, which included dioramas, information cards, mannequins, models, display cases, sculptures, maps, mural paintings and "gigantic photographs."[56] We may not know what these halls ultimately looked like, but we do have photographic documents in which it is possible to identify some of the photographs from the AFE, "gigantic" and mounted on wooden frames, constructing a visual narrative in concert with the mannequins and other objects from the collections.[57]

The photographs were not the center of the exhibition, thanks, perhaps, to a suggestion by the exhibition designer Julio Prieto, who advised Ramírez Vázquez that such displays should never be turned into an "exhibition of pictures, but rather be subordinated to the exhibition of the pieces."[58] The photographs were a consubstantial but auxiliary part of these museographic narratives, because they functioned as *evidence* and *testimony* of the real existence of the scenes reproduced in the display cases. Behind a replica of a Huichol shrine, for example, visitors could observe photographs of the relevant ceremonies hung on a partition screen: behind mannequins pulling apart the fibers of a maguey plant, there was a photo of two indigenous men busy at the same task, while two model Huichol figures dressed up beside an atrial cross were framed by a painting and four photographs reproducing the ceremony in which they were presumably participating, as if part of a parallel narrative that would authenticate the actual occurrence of the scene represented by the mannequins.

Photographs were also a supplementary didactic resource for "contextualizing the archaeological or ethnographic pieces in the spectator's mind as part of an ordered system in which each piece would be explained and understood in terms of the community that created it."[59] Images were meant to illustrate context and to bring the pieces in the display cases to life. For example, behind Tarascan nets and other fishing gear, one could see a portrait of a man using these implements. Images of vase sellers and an elderly woman carrying baskets with a leather strap accompanied the display cases that contained pitchers, hats, baskets, and birdcages. And a photograph of a hunter backlit by a luminous sky, his arms tensed ready to fire his bow and arrow, accompanied a set of arrows in a display case (figures 6.5–6.7).

At the same time that the photographs endowed the objects in the display cases with a living context, as testaments to the scenes represented by the mannequins, their presence also served to "demonstrate" the supposed historical continuity of the populations. Alongside pre-Hispanic (Mexica, Maya, and Totonac) anthropomorphic sculptures, one display case featured frontal and close-up portraits of three men and a woman, so that the visitor could verify "the direct relationship between pre-Hispanic heritage and [the] contemporary culture and customs [of the indigenous people depicted therein], the relationship between their past and their present" (figure 6.8).[60]

One might suspect that the montage resulting from the addition of the photographs derived from aesthetic considerations on the part of the exhibition designers, but it is doubtful that the latter would have been able to impose their own vision on the ethnographers' project for the ethnographic halls. Indeed, given the ethnographers' proposals, it is more likely that this technique grew out of their own theoretical framework and their political

Figure 6.5 Purépecha Hall, Sub-Fondo Fotográfico–Museo Nacional de Antropología–Sección Museográfica-Negativos no. 3. Reproduction authorized by the Instituto Nacional de Antropología e Historia del INAH.

Figure 6.6 Otomí Ethnography 010. Fototeca–Acervo Arquitecto Pedro Ramírez Vázquez.

and ideological objectives, which prevailed over and above the evidence at their disposal. The decision was a deliberate one, and the museum's planning team was clear that "contrary to what is generally assumed, *there is very rarely a clear cultural continuity from before the conquest to the current era*."[61]

Furthermore, there was evidence showing that "the groups in each area have scattered culturally and have been influenced by mestizos to different

Figure 6.7 Oaxacan Ethnography, negative 177. Fototeca–Acervo Arquitecto Pedro Ramírez Vázquez.

Figure 6.8 Ethnography 009. Fototeca–Acervo Arquitecto Pedro Ramírez Vázquez.

degrees [such that] there is no homogeneous culture within each area, but rather a cultural mosaic." In spite of this, the decision was to "highlight the 'purest' and most representative groups in order to present them in an extensive, detailed way, and to present related groups from the same area succinctly in the same hall."[62] Thanks to the guidebooks provided by ethnographers and the constructed museographic narrative, the subjects in the photographs were turned into timeless ethnic types that were camouflaged with the traits of *their* material culture: the man readying to fire his bow was turned into a Lacandón, and the one holding the net into a Purépecha, while the old woman with the leather strap and the vase sellers were to be viewed as Otomís because that was the label that appeared on top of the display case.

This trick of the trade was needed to fill the gaps hidden by the mesh of the hammock (figure 6.1), and to overcome the individuality of the subjects in the photographs, like that of the woman in the middle of the plaza, whose energy and nudity is contained and covered by the various pieces of clothing that surround her photographic image (figure 6.9). There was an urgent need to eclipse the actors and moments of everyday life captured by the photographers' cameras and subjectivities, and instead "show the ancient civilization and its descendants up to the present, so that it can be understood and appreciated as part of our national spirit, and thus collaborate in the dignification of indigenous people and their culture."[63] It was essential to direct and train the observer's eye so that it would be capable of transmuting a subject into a representative exemplar/datum/object/testament of the totality consisting of nature (landscape) and ways of living (housing), acting (handicrafts, trades, and markets) and thinking (festivities) pertaining to the *other* (physical type)—that is, into an ideal ethnic group, even though such a group was nowhere to be found in reality as recorded by the camera's lens or the ethnographers' data.

Figure 6.9 Oaxaca Ethnography 019. Fototeca–Acervo Arquitecto Pedro Ramírez Vázquez.

Epilogue

The AFE photographs can be seen as traces of the tensions that arose in the mid-twentieth century and, in particular, as vestiges of the confluence of the critique of ethnographic photography and the efforts of applied anthropologists, spearheaded by the disciples of the Chicago School, to reinsert indigenous people into the national museographic narrative, their political and ideological goal being to make the latter's social marginalization apparent. These photographs are also clues about how the (re)insertion of indigenous faces into this national narrative involved reducing them to ideal types and obscuring their individuality and especially their historicity.

The latter aspect of these photographs' artifice was the one that ultimately had the most bearing on the narrative, as indigenous faces were made into *relics*: "remains of a magnificent past . . . worthy of veneration."[64] The ideal types constructed at the Museo Nacional de Antropología were mirrored in the objects exhibited (photographs, instruments, clothing, etc.), despite their ideologues' previous critiques of earlier experiences with folkloricized representations of these groups. As Giraudo has pointed out, the attempt to disabuse *indigenismo* of the racialist constructions of evolutionism also ended up naturalizing indigeneity, but now on the basis of cultural traits.[65] In this context, photographs continued to build "anthropology's naturalistic illusion," that is, the fantasy that reality can be captured by an external agent (a photographer or anthropologist) without it being mediated by their own subjectivity.[66]

Furthermore, indigeneity was overshadowed by the past to which it was relegated, in particular by the magnificence of the massive works of stone on the first floor. The outcome would seem to be almost inevitable: How could one overcome the appeal of a past that looks so distant, exotic, and attractive? How could one resist being beguiled by Coatlicue's serpent skirt or her necklace made out of human hands, or by the overwhelming presence of the Piedra del Sol, with its enigmatic hieroglyphics and its sheer twenty-four-ton mass? As Roger Bartra pointed out more than twenty years ago:

> Those who built the new Museo de Antropología allowed the specter of indigenismo to roam its halls in an attempt to insinuate that the spectacularity of the pre-Hispanic past was connected to the grandeur of the modern revolutionary nation State. . . . What this made apparent was the terrible

> catastrophe that devastated indigenous societies since the Spanish Conquest while leaving that process unexplained. . . . But the Museum cannot be a sort of multicultural parliament of display cases in which the different ethnic groups are all represented, and connected via imaginary staircases to the impressive archaeological spectacle on the floor below. It is necessary to rethink the relationship between ethnology and archaeology.[67]

This specter was not haunting the students of the Chicago School, nor the proponents of Mexican indigenismo, but rather two different legacies: that of nineteenth-century modernity in its ways of valuing the past, and that of the Revolution, which established a link between antiquity and the indigenous populations of today, first to explain and justify their presence, and then to revalue them. That inheritance encompasses anthropology and archaeology as scientific projects of modernity, requiring us to think about the relationship between these disciplines, and between the past and the present. How do we accept the historical fact of Spanish colonization without victimizing colonized peoples? How are we to recognize and acknowledge Spanish influences on indigenous populations when we have gone to such great lengths to value them for their difference and originality? How do we avoid idealizing a past that we feel to be both *ours* and *indigenous*? How do we abandon chauvinism and distance ourselves from what is supposedly "our pre-Hispanic heritage"? How do we make orphans of ourselves? How do we set aside this Oedipal conflict with our past? How do we escape, finally, from being beguiled by the pre-Hispanic past, by its national and indigenist illusions and its constructions of ethnic identity, to forge a different present that would not need to impose a name on the baby who gazes at us so curiously over the strings of a hammock?

Acknowledgments

I am indebted to the editors of this volume for their valuable comments and suggestions on earlier drafts. I am also grateful to Valerio Paredes for his generosity consulting the Archivo Fotográfico de Etnografía; to Aarón Hernández Carrillo (Subdirección de Etnografía–Museo Nacional de Antropología), for his help locating and reproducing figure 6.1; to Sergio Torres González (Acervo de Colecciones Etnográficas), for identifying the photographs in the halls; to Javier Ramírez Campusano and Karina García, for allowing me to consult the Archivo Arquitecto Pedro Ramírez Vázquez; and to Joel Álvarez de la Borda, for listening closely, and for his recommendations for locating photographs.

Notes

1. Néstor García Canclini, *Hybrid Cultures: Strategies for Entering and Leaving Modernity*, trans. Christopher L. Chiappari and Sylvia L. López (Minneapolis: University of Minnesota Press, 1995), 130.
2. The museum kept a collection of photographs at least as early as 1895. Alfonso L. Herrera and Ricardo E. Cícero, *Catálogo de la colección antropología del Museo Nacional*, commemorative facsimile edition compiled by Teresa Rojas Rabiela and Ignacio Gutiérrez Ruvalcaba (1895; Mexico City: INAH, 2018).
3. Not all of the photographs are accompanied by information documenting the circumstances of their production, but we can propose general dates for each set by reconstructing their sequence. The AFE also has photographs from the 1970s and 1990s that I do not discuss in this chapter.
4. A first approach to this topic is in Haydeé López Hernández, "Los indios del Museo Nacional," *Dimensión Antropológica* 76 (May–August 2019): 165–87.
5. Saurabh Dube, "El nacimiento de un archivo," in *(In)disciplinar la investigación: Archivo, trabajo de campo y escritura*, ed. Frida Gorbach and Mario Rufer (Mexico City: UAM–Siglo XXI Editores, 2016), 275–94.
6. Raymundo Mier, "La fotografía antropológica: Ubicuidad e imposibilidad de la mirada," *Cuicuilco* 5, no. 13 (May–August 1998): 53–75.
7. As interesting as it is, I do not discuss the heavy presence of women in the collection.
8. This visual composition recalls Tina Modotti's photographs *Woman with Water Jug* and *Woman Wearing a Ribbon with a Child in Her Arms*.
9. On photography's pretensions to objectivity and "externality," see Claudine Leysinger, "Exploración de personajes del Nuevo Mundo: El peculiar caso de la mirada sensible de Teobert Maler," in *El indígena en el imaginario iconográfico*, comp. Ivonne Morales (Mexico City: CDI, 2010), 71–102; and Christopher Pinney, *Photography and Anthropology* (London: Reaktion, 2011).
10. Herrera and Cícero, *Catálogo de la colección*.
11. John Mraz, *Looking for Mexico: Modern Visual Culture and National Identity* (Durham, N.C.: Duke University Press, 2009).
12. See also Gertrude Duby (1901–93), Carlos Sáenz (or Sainz?), Eduardo Ugarte, Beatriz Oliver Vega, Margarita Díaz, Cecilia Miranda, Robert Bruce, and Jorge Gómez Poncet. See John Mraz, *Nacho López, Mexican Photographer* (Minneapolis: University of Minnesota Press, 2003); "Fototeca Nacho López," Instituto Nacional de los Pueblos Indígenas, accessed January 9, 2018, http://www.inpi.gob.mx/acervos/fototeca.html; Rosa Casanova, "Desde la lente de Alfonso Muñoz," unpublished manuscript, 2002, author's possession, 2002;

and "Alfonso Muñoz, in memoriam," *El Universal*, February 23, 2001, http://archivo.eluniversal.com.mx/cultura/10469.html.

13. For the relationship between photographer and time, see analyses such as John Mraz's "graphic history," that is, taking photographs themselves as historical documents. See John Mraz, "Una historiografía crítica," *Cuicuilco* 5, no. 13 (May–August 1998): 77–92. For encoded messages, see Mier, "La fotografía antropológica."
14. Carlo Ginzburg, "Clues: Roots of an Evidential Paradigm," in *Clues, Myths, and the Historical Method*, trans. John Tedeschi and Anne C. Tedeschi (Baltimore, Md.: Johns Hopkins University Press, 1989), 87–113. The Museo Nacional de Antropología was called "monument of monuments" by Jaime Torres Bodet, secretary of education, on the occasion of its opening, and in Jaime Torres Bodet, "Palabras preliminaries," in *El Museo Nacional de Antropología: Arte, arquitectura, arqueología, etnografía*, ed. Beatrice Trueblood (Mexico City: Panorama Editorial, 1968), 9.
15. The creation of the museum was moreover a symbol of the scientific importance of anthropology in the country, and therefore, of the role of its scientific community.
16. Pedro Ramírez Vázquez, *Museo Nacional de Antropología: Gestación, proyecto y construcción* (Mexico City: INAH, 2012), 130.
17. See Gorbach's analysis in the present volume.
18. Instituto Nacional de Antropología e Historia, *Museo Nacional de Antropología: Official Guide* (Mexico City: INAH, 1956).
19. For an extensive discussion, see Haydeé López Hernández, "Arte, folklore e industria: artes populares e indigenismo en México, 1920–1946," unpublished manuscript out for review, 2020. As Peter Burke pointed out, starting in the late eighteenth century, the study of folk culture was subsumed under three basic categories: primitivism, purism, and communalism. In the Mexican case, these notions continue to permeate anthropology up to the present. See Peter Burke, *Popular Culture in Early Modern Europe* (New York: Harper and Row, 1978).
20. On changes in art and culture influencing this process of revaluation, see James Clifford, *The Predicament of Culture: Twentieth-Century Ethnography, Literature, and Art* (Cambridge, Mass.: Harvard University Press, 2002).
21. Ana Santos Ruiz, *Los hijos de los dioses: El grupo filosófico Hiperión y la filosofía de lo mexicano* (Mexico City: Bonilla Artigas Editores, 2015).
22. I borrow this characterization of indigenism from Laura Giraudo and Juan Martín-Sánchez, "Acotando el indigenismo en su historia," in *La ambivalente historia del indigenismo: Campo interamericano y trayectorias nacionales, 1940–1970*, ed. Laura Giraudo and Juan Martín-Sánchez (Lima: Instituto de Estudios Peruanos, 2011), 9–20.
23. Arturo Monzón, "Bases para incrementar el público que visita el Museo Nacional de Antropología," *Anales del Instituto Nacional de Antropología e Historia* 6, part 2 (1952): 87–131. I am grateful to Erika Fernanda García for a copy

of this material. Quotation from Carlos Vázquez Olvera, *Iker Larrauri Prado, museógrafo mexicano* (Mexico City: INAH, 2005), 69.

24. Monzón, "Bases para incrementar el público," 87.
25. Ignacio Marquina and Luis Aveleyra, "Informe general de las labores desarrolladas durante el lapso inicial del proyecto, del 1 de enero al 31 de diciembre de 1961", January 15, 1962, typescript 194, exp. 40, fs. 203–4, AHMNA.
26. Cámara is quoted in Dora Sierra, *Cien años de etnografía en el Museo* (Mexico City: INAH, 1994), 79.
27. Silvia Ortiz Echániz, "Fernando Cámara Barbachano," in *La antropología en México: Panorama histórico*, vol. 9, ed. Carlos García Mora (Mexico City: INAH, 1988), 386–400.
28. Ana Bella Pérez Castro, María Guadalupe Ochoa Ávila, and María de la Paz Soriano Pérez, "Introducción," in *Antropología sin fronteras: Robert Redfield*, ed. Ana Bella Pérez Castro, María Guadalupe Ochoa Ávila, and María de la Paz Soriano Pérez (Mexico City: UNAM, 2002), 17.
29. Redfield's study in Morelos and his work on folk culture are emblematic of this branch.
30. See, for example, Robert Kemper, "From Nationalism to Internationalism: The Development of Mexican Anthropology, 1934–1946," in *Social Contexts of American Ethnology, 1840–1984*, ed. June Helm (Washington, D.C.: American Ethnological Society, 1984), 139–56.
31. Eduardo González, "La ciencia al servicio del estado: La antropología politécnica en México (1936–1941)" (paper presented at the Congreso Internacional *Ciencias del Estado / Estados de la ciencia*, Mexico City, June 11, 2019).
32. Document without date, title, or author, typescript. Vol. 185, exp. 27, f. 199, AHMNA, emphasis mine.
33. Iker Larrauri, Jorge Angulo, Mario Vázquez, and Miguel Celorio, untitled document, June 1961, typescript, vol. 182, exp. 12, fs. 159–60, AHMNA, emphasis mine.
34. Amalia Castillo to Ignacio Marquina, January 11, 1961; Ignacio Marquina to Eusebio Dávalos, February 9, 1961, vol. 182, exp. 54, AHMNA.
35. Fernando Cámara Barbachano, "Principios y guías para el contenido de las salas de exhibición en el nuevo Museo Nacional," April 27, 1961, typescript, vol. 186, exp. 10, f. 114, AHMNA.
36. This represented a third of the requested budget (MXP$800,000). The archaeological component was evidently more onerous. Ignacio Marquina to Eusebio Dávalos, and "Estimación económica," September 22, 1961, typescript, vol. 185, exp. 26, fs. 191–97, AHMNA.
37. Ramírez Vázquez, *Museo Nacional de Antropología*, 32.
38. "Lista de las exhibiciones fundamentales del Museo Nacional de Antropología, con los respectivos asesores científicos que sean designado para cada una," undated typescript, vol. 181, exp. 19, f. 99; Luis Aveleyra to Amalia Castillo, and "Lista del personal directivo, técnico, científico y administrativo que participará

en la Planeación e Instalación del nuevo Museo Nacional, . . ." November 12, 1960. typescript, exp. 21, fs. 103–7, AHMNA.

39. Wigberto Jiménez began working at the museum in the 1930s under the tutelage of Alfonso Caso.
40. The planning was overseen by teams of ethnographic and archaeological advisers (organized by area), in coordination with the museographers and educators, responsible for building the general outlines of the halls, selecting the materials to be displayed and the order in which they were to be presented, as well as the data for information cards and texts. These teams were coordinated by an Executive Board for Planning and Installation of the Museo Nacional de Antropología, chaired by Luis Aveleyra (director of the Museo Nacional de Antropología) and Ignacio Marquina (director of the INAH). Luis Aveleyra, undated typescript, vol. 181, exp. 10, f. 34, AHMNA.
41. Document without date, title, or author, typescript, vol. 185, exp. 28, f. 202, AHMNA.
42. On Basauri and Mendieta, respectively, see Haydeé López Hernández, "El *problema indígena* en el Cardenismo: Un problema de definición," in *Temas de la antropología mexicana II*, ed. José Luis Vera Cortés, Fernando López Aguilar, Marina Anguiano Fernández, and Xabier Lizárraga Cruchaga (Mexico City: Academia Mexicana de Ciencias Antropológicas, 2014), 145–89; and Déborah Dorotinsky, "La vida de un archivo: 'México indígena' y la fotografía etnográfica de los años cuarenta en México" (PhD diss., Universidad Nacional Autónoma de México, 2003).
43. For the preliminary programs for each monograph, see vol. 181, exp. 156–73, AHMNA.
44. Preliminary programs for each monograph, vol. 181, exp. 25, fs. 161, 164, 168, 169, AHMNA.
45. Iker Larrauri, untitled typescript, December 6, 1961, vol. 185, exp. 32, fs. 236, AHMNA.
46. Estrada Discua budget, August 1961, vol. 185, exp. 24, f. 188, AHMNA.
47. Luis Aveleyra, "Investigación arqueológica," in Trueblood, *El Museo Nacional de Antropología*, 33.
48. A clear example is his work for the exhibition *México indígena*. See Dorotinsky, "La vida de un archivo."
49. Aveleyra, "Investigación arqueológica," 33.
50. The exception is a report by an expedition to the northern sierra of Puebla in July 1960, by Ramírez Vázquez, José Lameiras, and Alfonso Soto Soria, to film and make color slides and black and white plates of festivities, with support from the Museo Universitario de Ciencias y Artes–UNAM. See vol. 182, exp. 53, AHMNA. This theme coincides with the one in the Catálogo Nahuas de Puebla–AFE, carried out by Luis Berruecos and Oliver Vega in various small towns around that state. There are also reports by Cámara's students in the Archivo Histórico de Etnografía–MNA.

51. The absence of such material in the country's archives constitutes one of the most serious limitations for carrying out historical research on ethnography.
52. Margarita Nolasco Armas, "Pueblos indios," in *Museo Nacional de Antropología: Libro conmemorativo del cuarenta aniversario* (Mexico City: CONACULTA/INAH, 2004), 53.
53. Namely, the American Museum of Natural History in New York, the Natural History Museum in Chicago, the Smithsonian's Museum of History and Technology, and the Museum of the American Indian. Luis Aveleyra's official correspondence with various museums, November 1960, vol. 181, exp. 22, AHMNA.
54. Ramírez Vázquez, *Museo Nacional de Antropología*, 40 and 131. Interestingly, it was Roberto Williams (the Gulf Coast adviser) who proposed a "preliminary program" to present twelve scenes with "physical types in wax sculptures dressed in characteristic attire and posed in attitudes matching the scene being staged." See vol. 181, exp. 18, fs. 166–67, AHMNA. It seems to me that this aspect reveals one of the first attempts (despite the Museo Nacional de Antropología's centralism) at transforming museographic discourse, as Rufer has described, in favor of local memories—now common under the politics of diversity and multiculturalism—whereby nineteenth-century rhetoric about progress and modernity moved toward a "poetics of return," albeit from the standpoint of "heraldry." See Mario Rufer, "La exhibición del otro: Tradición, memoria y colonialidad en museos en México," *Antítesis* 7, no. 14 (July–December 2014): 94–120.
55. Mario Vázquez, "Museografía del nuevo Museo Nacional de Antropología," *Artes de México* 12, nos. 66–67 (1965): 43.
56. Vazquez, "Museografía del nuevo Museo," 44.
57. From the time it opened, the Museo Nacional de Antropología's visual records came second to the majesty of the archaeological collections. The photographic dossier in a special issue of the magazine *Artes de México* dedicated to the Museo Nacional de Antropología, for example, included only 5 images of the ethnography halls, compared to 104 photos from the archaeological halls. The same is true of García Canclini's critical analysis in *Hybrid Cultures*, which reproduces only one photograph from the ethnographic halls and seven from the archaeological ones. The exception here is Trueblood, *El Museo Nacional de Antropología*, which includes photographs held in the Archivo Arquitecto Pedro Ramírez Vázquez (AAPRV). See also Vázquez, "Museografía del nuevo Museo."
58. Uncataloged, Fondo documental, AAPRV.
59. Pedro Ramírez Vázquez, "El Museo hace cuarenta años," in *Museo Nacional de Antropología: Libro*, 38.
60. Ramírez Vázquez, *Museo Nacional de Antropología* (2012), 130.
61. Vol. 185, exp. 32, f. 235, AHMNA, emphasis added.
62. Vol. 185, exp. 32, f. 236, AHMNA.
63. Ignacio Bernal, "Introducción," in Trueblood, *El Museo Nacional de Antropología*, 8.

64. I borrow this insight from Mario Rufer, “La tradición como reliquia: Nación e identidad desde los estudios culturales,” in *Nación y estudios culturales: Debates desde la poscolonialidad*, ed. María del Carmen de la Peza and Mario Rufer (Mexico City: UAM–Xochimilco Editorial Itaca, 2016), 64.
65. Laura Giraudo, “El indio como categoría colonial: El gran reverso del indigenismo” (paper presented at the conference *La representación del indio a través de imágenes y textos*, Mexico City, Mexico, October 26, 2017), https://www.youtube.com/watch?v=jC20jOdg7DE&t=14139s.
66. Pinney, *Photography and Anthropology*, 147.
67. Roger Bartra, “Sonata etnográfica en no bemol,” in *Museo Nacional de Antropología: Libro*, 331–47.

\\ 7

Unsettled Objects

The Pacific Collection at the Museo Nacional de las Culturas

CARLOS MONDRAGÓN

In October 2010, a date chosen to coincide with the bicentennial independence celebrations, the Museo Nacional de las Culturas del Mundo, located on Moneda Street, in the iconic Casa de Moneda, the colonial-era Royal Mint in downtown Mexico City, reopened after a long hiatus for major renovations.[1] The centerpiece of the renewed Museo Nacional de las Culturas was the Sala del Pacífico (Pacific Hall), a novel introductory exhibition space located in the grand gallery opposite the museum's main entrance and central courtyard.[2] The intention of the Pacific Hall was to foreground some of the most significant objects from the museum's Pacific, American, and Asian collections, which represent the bulk of the museum's holdings. The backbone of these holdings is the so-called South Seas Collection, an assemblage of over six hundred artifacts from across Oceania and the Pacific Northwest, most of which were brought to the museum by Miguel Covarrubias and Daniel Rubín de la Borbolla in 1951, during a unique exchange with the Field Museum in Chicago.

What were the ideas and motives of Covarrubias as the principal agent in the assembly of this collection? What museographical and institutional factors came together to bring this unusual set of items, with roots in a distant, unfamiliar culture region, to a major Mexican museum? How can we reflect on this fragile collection, made mostly from perishable materials, among the broader assemblages of stones that characterize Mexican storerooms and exhibit halls? These are some of the guiding questions that I have taken as points of departure for the present chapter.

In the first section I intervene in the historiographical construction of Miguel Covarrubias as an artist and museum agent. This part of my text contributes to an emerging conversation regarding Covarrubias's peculiar intellectual and artistic biography and his relation to museum history and the discipline of anthropology in Mexico.[3] This discussion aims to illustrate how the criteria that led him to bring together the South Seas Collection were a result of patchworks of relations, experiences, and intellectual debates that were contingent as much as deliberate. My emphasis is therefore on his experiences and the linkages of concepts by which he arrived at a certain ethnological imaginary. Those experiences included museographical interventions, world expositions, and travel, which contributed to Covarrubias's enduring interest in the Pacific and his understanding of it as a confluence of culture regions that held the key to understanding the Mexican indigenous past. This notion of culture region was in turn laden with conceptual influences emanating from early anthropological debates about diffusion, migration, and the idea of culture as a configuration of styles. Covarrubias brought a particular emphasis on comparison and the typological ordering of visual forms to make sense of the Pacific and American puzzles. Taking these elements further, one can see how contingencies and patchworks of relations were also of special relevance to the origin and eventual displacements that brought the South Seas Collection to the center of modern Mexican museography.

In the second section I address more directly the social and material aspects of the collection, to explore those factors. I explain how the South Seas objects possess a perishable materiality that was meant to make them both dynamic and with a limited lifespan. They emanate from social and ritual spheres that are directed to practices of remembering and forgetting, which run counter to museological concerns with conservation and static exhibition. Their organic, ephemeral nature thereby stands in contrast to the solid, often monumental attributes of stone, mineral, and ceramic that dominate collections and archaeological sites across Mexico, referring us to notions of permanence and millenarian continuity that are frequently deployed as metaphors for the nation's imagined pre-Columbian origins. In this regard, the South Seas objects stand in ongoing defiance of the expectations of Covarrubias and his curatorial successors at the Museo Nacional de las Culturas.

This is not a marginal issue, given that the transpacific influences that shaped Covarrubias's collecting criteria also powerfully influenced the definition of Mesoamerican studies in the 1930s and 1940s. Covarrubias's museographical efforts were part of a broader importation of anthropological and artistic concepts developed in the Dutch East Indies (Bali, Eastern Indonesia, and the Pacific Islands) that would inform the idea of Mesoamerica as a coherent culture region. Between 1938 and 1942 Covarrubias, with several prominent scholars, would establish Mesoamerica as a "field of ethnographic study" with a "mother culture" (the Olmecs) from which successive "civilizations" originated and evolved in a progressive timeline that reached its perceived technological, social, and urban heights with the Aztec empire. Thus, the unsettled, impermanent nature of the South Seas Collection calls up questions of what "civilization" is and is not in relation to Mexican history and museography; its continuing presence stands as a useful counter to received ideas about the nation's origins and indigenous past.

The purpose of this chapter is, therefore, double: to address the intellectual and biographical events that came together to shape Covarrubias's motivations to put together a collection of South Seas items for Mexico, while also delving into the particularities and materiality of the collection itself. In the process I hope to shed new light on aspects of this collection in relation to the larger history of the Museo Nacional de Antropología, but also to the principal agent that brought it together, and to the unlikely medium in which it stands to this day.

Institutional Antecedents

During the first half of the twentieth century, comparative approaches to non-Mexican societies were scarce. Where comparison was present, it was largely confined to probing perceived traces of North American indigenous cultural borrowings in relation to specific aspects of pre-Columbian Mexico's material culture. Following the appointment, in 1933, of Alfonso Caso as head of the Department of Archaeology, History and Ethnology at the Museo Nacional de Arqueología, Historia y Etnología, the effort to establish an indigenous "mother culture" was pursued with a specifically empirical emphasis.[4] Caso increased the museum's range of archaeological field expeditions partly with the hope that increasing the volume of objective (material) evidence would allow him to establish a definitive chronological and regional scheme for Mesoamerican cultural origins and the subsequent evolution of its ancient civilizations. Importantly, the effort to increase the volume of field data went hand in hand with the need to organize and increase the existing collections at the museum on Moneda Street.

It was in this context of renewed field research and collecting that Caso and others successfully lobbied the government of Lázaro Cárdenas to undertake the radical expansion and formalization of the nation's cultural research infrastructure by founding the Instituto Nacional de Antropología e Historia (INAH) and ordering the creation of a network of national museums, across which the multifarious holdings at the Casa de Moneda could be distributed according to discrete historical periods and specific disciplinary specialties.[5]

In late December 1938 the Cárdenas government ordered the creation of the INAH and of three different national museums. The Museo Nacional del Virreinato was dedicated to the colonial history of the Viceroyalty of New Spain; by 1964, it was established in the ex-Jesuit convent of Tepotzotlan—a magnificent building located in the outer northern periphery of Mexico City.[6] In turn, the Museo Nacional de Historia was established in the Castle of Chapultepec and was largely dedicated to the postindependence processes that marked the emergence of the Mexican polity in the nineteenth and early twentieth centuries.

The winner from this reorganization was the Museo Nacional de Antropología at the Casa de Moneda, which also became the seat of INAH. This placed pre-Columbian archaeology and modern indigenous (ethnographic) studies in a privileged position in relation to the nation's new cultural research and museographical authority. Four years later, in 1943, the Escuela Nacional de Antropología e Historia (ENAH) was added to the purview of the Museo Nacional de Antropología.[7]

With the prioritization of archaeological and anthropological research at the heart of the state's nation-building narrative and cultural policymaking efforts, the stage was set for the increase of the museum's collections. This increase reflected a renewed interest in ancient borrowings and connections with North American Indian "cultures." The year 1938 also marked the first phase in a fortuitous set of events that would eventually influence the creation of the first—and to date only—discrete non-Mexican collection dedicated to North America and the Pacific at the National Museum. The principal agent in these events was Miguel Covarrubias.

Covarrubias and Pacific Arts

Miguel Covarrubias was a prominent member of the Mexican avant-garde of the 1930s and 1940s. Despite the oft-repeated claim that he was an "ethnographer," even an "anthropologist," Covarrubias was neither. He was an artist and autodidact who held no professional academic training and never professed interest in generating scholarly output from within academia. His artistic talent and intellectual enthusiasm, however, led him to collaborate with prominent archaeologists, anthropologists, and museum specialists. It was through this work that he became influential in the establishment of key concepts in Mesoamerican studies, and eventually came to contribute to the development of one of the most important collections of non-Mexican objects in a national museum.

In the following pages I turn to the principal museographical experiences that preceded and influenced Covarrubias's assembly of the collections at the Museo Nacional de las Culturas. I also scrutinize the intellectual influences and interpretations that shaped Covarrubias's work in relation to Asian, American, and Pacific arts, history, and culture. Taken together, what follows is a timeline of events but also a commentary on the principal conceptual contributions that shaped Covarrubias's criteria as both artist and museum specialist.

Early in 1938, Covarrubias was in New York, celebrating the opening of a major new exhibit at the Museum of Modern Art (MoMA). According to MoMA's own summation, *Twenty Centuries of Mexican Art* was an "unparalleled exhibition featur[ing] some 5,000 examples of ancient, colonial, folk, and modern Mexican art. It filled the entire Museum and even extended into the courtyard, where MoMA staged an open-air Mexican market with stalls selling ceramics, leather goods, and other crafts, flanked by a series of giant pre-colonial statues."[8] This enormous endeavor required more than one hundred museum staff for its assemblage, while the organizing committee was composed of an extended roster of prominent personalities, including Nelson Rockefeller and John Abbott. Its curatorship was placed under the overall authority of Alfonso Caso (founding director of INAH), but required three additional experts: Manuel Toussaint, Roberto Montenegro, and Miguel Covarrubias, the latter given the task of curating the section dedicated to modern art. The museography was put under the direction of René d'Harnoncourt, a European aristocrat and close friend of Covarrubias who had established himself as a master of museum installations and would go on to curate twelve major exhibitions for MoMA. As curator for the modern art section, Covarrubias's principal task was to bring together a large selection of paintings, objects, and images representative of the modernist and avant-garde Mexican scene, which he knew intimately.

Twenty Centuries was the first of three exhibitions that took place at MoMA and at the Metropolitan Museum of Art between 1938 and 1946, in which d'Harnoncourt would invite Covarrubias to collaborate closely with his innovative museographic activities. While there is no direct evidence about the specific ways in which both men learned from each other's talents, they clearly experienced a mutual learning process, during which Covarrubias obtained the expert knowledge on both curatorial research and specific museum collections that would prove critical to his assembly of the Pacific and North American collections for the museum at Casa de Moneda.

In June 1938, shortly after the opening of *Twenty Centuries*, Covarrubias received an unusual invitation from the organizing committee of the Golden Gate International Exposition to create a series of six large-scale mural maps representing the peoples, flora and fauna, commerce, arts, modes of transportation, and traditional architecture of the nations and societies of the Pacific Rim and Islands. The murals were to be placed at the thematic centerpoint of the exposition grounds, a structure that came to be known as Pacific House, which was situated in the middle of an artificial lake and surrounded by some of the most iconic pavilions of the fairground.

The rationale for the Golden Gate Exposition was to celebrate U.S. technical prowess—notably, the completion of the Golden Gate and San Francisco–Oakland Bay Bridges. More broadly, the aim was to promote a certain idea of empire by projecting U.S. power, commerce, and geopolitical interests across the Pacific Ocean.[9] These colonialist undertones were duly occluded and nuanced under the celebratory and nonthreatening themes of the exposition, labeled "The Pageant of the Pacific" and "Pacific Peace and Unity."[10]

Covarrubias's participation in the exposition took place over a short period, between July 1938 and the opening of the exposition in February 1939. The innovative style and complexity of content of the murals conveyed an enormous amount of information and required a significant investment in time, energy, and artistic and research assistance.[11] Notably, the murals took the form of chorographic maps, visually striking geographical representations of the Pacific Rim and Ocean that sought to cast it as a region at the center of the world map, independent from the Atlantic and the European worlds.[12] This "ocean as landscape" neatly conveyed Covarrubias's own growing interest in the representation of regional cultural borrowings and connections, in this case between the "mongoloid races" of Asia and the Americas.[13] That his interest in transpacific connections dovetailed neatly with the theme of the exposition helps explain the excitement and positive reception that his maps generated among the fair's organizers.[14]

The mural maps would prove crucial to the development of Covarrubias's concept of the Pacific as a world region characterized by connections, migrations, and diversity. The effort of comparing styles of indigenous art was further informed by Covarrubias's focus on the contrast between North American and Mexican indigenous peoples. Shortly after the 1939 exposition, Covarrubias began to assist d'Harnoncourt in relation to the curatorship of a second major exhibition at MoMA, *Indigenous Art of the Americas,* which opened in 1941. This experience cemented his determination to explore the ancient connections between early Mexican "cultures" and those of the North American indigenous peoples.

The four years following the Golden Gate Exposition were among the busiest in Covarrubias's life.[15] It was then that he carried out his most influential work in relation to Mexican archaeology and anthropology. His participation in what was to be the founding paradigm of pre-Columbian studies in Mexico, the idea of the Olmec as the "mother culture" of Mesoamerican civilizations, is worth recounting, because it positioned him at the very center of the activities at the Museo Nacional de Antropología—and thereby allowed him, between 1946 and 1949, to successfully propose and undertake the assembly of the Pacific and North American collections for the museum.

Between 1940 and 1942, Covarrubias accompanied Alfonso Caso during his now famous exploration of Monte Albán, in Oaxaca, and was also present in various important archaeological excavations in Veracruz and the Isthmus of Tehuantepec. This firsthand experience allowed him to devise an iconic chart of pre-Columbian artistic styles, which suggested an enticing evolutionary set of formal connections that purported to link the spiritual, artistic, and social development of prominent indigenous polities of pre-Columbian Mexico (i.e., Olmec-Zapotec-Maya-Toltec-Aztec). The climax of this effort was synthesized in a famous paper that Covarrubias copresented with Alfonso Caso and Wigberto Jiménez Moreno during the Second Congress of the Mexican Society for Anthropology in 1942.[16]

Covarrubias's proposal for the existence of an "Olmec style" and his contention that it was representative of the "mother culture" of ancient Mexico was readily conjoined with Paul Kirchhoff's seminal definition of "Mesoamerica" as a "field of ethnographic study"—which was also presented during the 1942 congress.[17] These two concepts profoundly influenced the conviction in a millenarian "Mesoamerican cosmology," with shared religious, technological, and artistic traits, which successive indigenous "civilizations" inherited and took to ever greater heights of social evolution. Over the following seventy years, this model became the predominant interpretive frame for the anthropological and archaeological study of the indigenous past; it has only recently begun to be the subject of sustained critique. Importantly, it persuaded Covarrubias that ancient artistic forms, or "styles," were manifestations of a purer—because premodern—universal human spirituality.

From early in his career, Covarrubias expressed a romantic primitivism in which a premodern form of human spirit was ideally made manifest through aesthetic forms. He believed this universal form of "primitive" spirituality (which he conflated with style) was most clearly visible in indigenous folklore. Consequently, Covarrubias directed his gaze and the selection and organization of objects, styles, and art forms in his museography toward configurations of form and style within and across culture regions. This became a core notion behind his motivation to represent Asia, the Pacific, and the Americas as a macroregional ensemble of multiple stylistic, ritual, and social borrowings and relations. It has also led to the widespread perception that Covarrubias was a diffusionist in the tradition of nineteenth-century social evolutionism. It is worth unpacking both his principal contribution to the concept of Mesoamerica and the nuanced nature of his diffusionist vision.

Covarrubias's most notable contribution to the definition of Mesoamerica was the argument—backed by compelling graphic representations of the unity of Mesoamerican art styles—that pre-Columbian civilizations had evolved from an original "mother culture." This was a powerful term that Covarrubias had imported from his previous experiences documenting Balinese art and history.[18] During the first half of the twentieth century, various Euroamerican scholars and artists had come to regard Balinese society as a living remnant, or "mother culture," to the neighboring Javanese. The search for a mythical national origin, and thereby for an underlying unity of aesthetics and cultural forms representing the indigenous antecedents of the modern nation, had its roots in social evolutionism and diffusionism. Both approaches were at the center of the prominent anthropological debates in the 1920s and 1930s regarding the definition of culture.[19] It was precisely during this period that Covarrubias first acquired and began to develop his own notion of culture.

It is often remarked that Covarrubias's panoramic representations of American, Asian, and Pacific art forms as interlinked branches of an evolutionary tree betray a kind of diffusionism inspired in Tylor's idea of culture as an organic whole evolving in linear fashion.[20] This claim bears closer scrutiny. First, the nature of diffusionism and the very definition of culture both became highly contested categories during the 1920s and 1930s, the very period when Covarrubias was learning and developing his notions of culture history and indigenous arts. An examination of his chorographic mural representations of transpacific and Amerindian societies as interlinked via networks of relations, borrowings, and variations on shared aesthetic forms suggest something more subtle than linear evolutionary frames. His emphasis on form and visual contrast remind us that Covarrubias's diffusionism was tempered by a strong interest in comparativism: how best to represent culture regions in terms of shared patterns of thought and formal (visual) expression was one of the key questions that motivated his work. Indeed, his consideration toward configurations and types of style seems to have been closer to Ruth Benedict's definition of culture as a "totality whose elements were interconnected, integrated, and patterned" rather than to earlier preoccupations with social evolution and the history of progress.[21]

Covarrubias was attracted to culture history as a process of borrowings and migrations of cultural forms and aesthetic styles. While he held on to essentialist ideas about culture as a corpus of knowledge and expression that was transmitted from one ancient indigenous "civilization" to another, he was especially interested in simultaneity, in representing comparison graphically through panoramic overviews. It was this interleaving of stylistic sensitivity with an idea of simultaneous cultural connections across macroregional spaces that informed Covarrubias's particular diffusionist interests. The motivation to privilege typologies of style over evolutionary timelines or even cultural specificities was proper to his engagement with the artistic and visual, and it would eventually take precedence in Covarrubias's selection criteria during the assembly of the Pacific and North American collection for the Museo Nacional de las Culturas.

In 1943, Daniel Rubín de la Borbolla, a close colleague of Alfonso Caso, was appointed to be the first director of the ENAH.[22] Rubín de la Borbolla was also a close friend of Covarrubias and soon invited him to teach the subjects of pre-Hispanic art and museum curatorship at ENAH. Consequently, Covarrubias was able to impart his ideas about Olmec origins, stylistic evolution, and religious Mesoamerican archetypes to several generations of students who would become prominent members of the Mexican anthropology and archaeology community during the second half of the twentieth century. Perhaps without realizing, he thereby cemented his influence on the paradigm of Mesoamerica as originally outlined by Caso, Wigberto Jiménez, and Kirchhoff. In turn, his most important intervention in the history of Mexican museum collections was about to mature and take shape.

That same year Covarrubias again took part in the preparation of an important New York exhibition, this time at the Metropolitan Museum of Art. It was titled *Arts of the South Seas* and would prove to become the defining influence in Covarrubias's drive to assemble a Pacific collection for Mexico. In preparation for *Arts of the South Seas,* Covarrubias had an opportunity to explore the Pacific collections of several prominent museums in the United States, including the Field Museum in Chicago.

Arts of the South Seas brought together more than four hundred objects from across the Pacific Islands and opened to critical acclaim in January 1946. The introduction to the catalog stated: "There is good reason for dealing with this region as a unit since each of its component cultural areas has marked affinities with one or more of the others, so that together they constitute a network of related cultures . . . ; a representative collection of the arts of the South Seas reveals the existence of a number of basic trends that often extend through many cultural areas and sometimes even cross regional borders."[23]

This description reflects Covarrubias's ideas about regional networks of style and form. More important, Covarrubias was given an uncommon opportunity to visit the storage rooms of the Field Museum, in Chicago, as part of the curatorial selection of objects that the Met would take out on loan for the *South Seas* exhibition. It was here that Covarrubias obtained his first personal overview and physical proximity to many of the Pacific Islands' objects that he had only previously been able to observe behind glass cases or in print during his preparation of the mural maps for the 1939 exposition.

The South Seas Collection

The same year in which *Arts of the South Seas* opened to the public, in 1946, Rubín de la Borbolla was director of the Museo Nacional de Antropología. Covarrubias, armed with his previous artistic, museographic, and curatorial experiences, approached Rubín with the idea of creating a coherent Pacific and North American collection for the museum. This was to be effected through an exchange with the Field Museum, which held large numbers of items from those two regions and had an ongoing interest in acquiring pre-Columbian objects. In March 1948 the two men visited the Field Museum and obtained a positive response.[24] The selection of items and the legal and logistical details of the exchange took shape rapidly, and a final listing was mutually agreed upon in early 1949. It included 1,126 pre-Columbian objects from the Museo Nacional de Antropología and 650 objects from the Field Museum.[25] Of the 650 objects from the Field, 437 were related to North American indigenous contexts, while only 214 were from the Pacific Islands. The final packing lists, transportation, and mutual delivery of the collections were completed in the winter of 1951–52.

The 214 objects from Oceania, as singled out by Covarrubias, came exclusively from the large chains of island groups that make up the Melanesian arc, in the Western Pacific. This is to be expected, given that most of the interest, valuation, commoditization, and subsequent collecting efforts relating to Pacific artifacts by major international museums, collecting expeditions, and clearing houses took place in the Western Pacific during the second half of the nineteenth century. Thus, the spread of items in the South Seas Collection adequately mirrors the geographical distribution of collecting "hotspots" proper to the half century between 1870 to 1930, when most mass museum collections took shape.[26] On an intraregional scale, the distribution of the South Seas artifacts collected by Covarrubias is concentrated around the principal maritime and coastal areas of Papua New Guinea.

In descending numerical order, these include the Sepik River (41 items), the islands of New Ireland (27 items), Manus (23 items), and New Britain (13 items) in the Bismarck Sea; the Papuan Gulf (9 items); the Massim region (9 items from the Normanby and Trobriand Islands); and the Huon Gulf (8 items). Lesser numbers of items originated in the Port Moresby area (6 items), Dutch West Papua (1 item), and Bougainville (2 items). In the Solomons, the greatest number of objects was gathered in and around

Guadalcanal (20 items), with a very wide, if numerically small, representation coming from across the rest of the main islands in the chain (14 items altogether). Finally, there was Vanuatu (15 items), Kanaky / New Caledonia (6 items), and Aotearoa / New Zealand (9 items).[27] Notably, there were no Polynesian or Micronesian objects in the original exchange between the Field Museum and the Museo Nacional de Antropología.[28]

The basic information regarding exchange (significant dates, itemized packing lists, relevant institutional and political actors) has been laid out elsewhere.[29] Nonetheless, the singular materialities, the original contexts in which the Pacific collection objects emerged, and the subsequent processes, transactions, and layered resignifications that they have experienced have yet to be the subject of sustained analysis.[30] Such analysis is especially relevant to unpacking the significance of their presence within the larger Mexican museum milieu. The limits of this chapter do not allow for a detailed study, but it is possible to offer some comments on relevant items, on their surprising shared cultural significance with the rest of the collection, and on the contexts in which they were originally manufactured. The purpose of this commentary is not only to shed light on previously unremarked aspects about the original cultural contexts of the South Seas objects, but to employ that as a useful analytic contrast with the criteria that brought them to Mexico, as well as their continuing unsettled status within the Museo Nacional de las Culturas.

Rather than focus on individual items, I would point to broader sets and types of objects from the original Covarrubias listing. This mirrors Covarrubias's pursuit of typologies of form and style. Here, however, I seek to highlight types based on shared regional Oceanic values and rationales of manufacture and deployment. My objective is to recover some of the local principles by which these objects took shape, and to point to shared rationales and values that can become points of entry for future in-depth comparison and analysis. Moreover, I would argue that the principles by which these objects originally took shape are intimately woven into their materiality and presence, continuing to linger long after their original function has faded. This is germane to my claim that the objects possess a certain "unsettled" property that allowed them—by their presence and materiality—to defy the criteria and expectations by which Covarrubias brought them together.

Thus, this is not an attempt at digging up obscure cultural exotica: it is a necessary corrective to the rationale by which these objects were collected, which followed early anthropology's "view of artefacts as self-sufficient scientific specimens."[31] It is a way of recovering their contexts and values of production, which were systematically erased and forgotten in the course of taking these items into the world of international museums. Consider, for instance, that a large majority of the objects in the South Seas Collection at the Museo Nacional de las Culturas were crafted to give body and tangible presence to spirits or life forces of various kinds. As I and others have argued elsewhere, these objects are the bodies of persons, forces, and presences, and while they may have been ritually deployed, destroyed, and/or exorcised by their local producers, their forms are still extant. Even though they are no longer quite what they were at the outset, they are and will continue to be present as part of an ongoing living layering of relations and significations lodged in their forms. This stands at odds with some of the basic ideas behind collecting, storing, exhibiting, and preserving that motivated Covarrubias and his contemporaries, insofar as they held objects to be inert and stable—especially so in the context of a Mesoamerican museum culture invested in the solid unchanging qualities of stone and ceramic. By taking a deep ethnographic dive into the values and surprising human, environmental, physical, and spiritual factors that came together in the emergence of some of these perishable ritual objects, the following paragraphs are making the case for the fact that materiality matters.[32]

The largest sets of items—in terms of type and provenance—in the original 1951 collection are those hailing from across the Bismarck Sea. Especially notable are those associated with New Ireland *malanggan*, as well as Baining and Sulka spirit objects from New Britain. These astonishing "masks" and colorful effigies are present in most major museum collections, given the high visual impact that they were and continue to be seen to carry, which are part of the perceived mystery and exoticism of the ritual contexts to which they refer the museum visitor. It is not surprising that Covarrubias should have singled out objects from maritime Papua New Guinea, among which the most numerous are the so-called *malanggan* artifacts from New Ireland (figure 7.1).

Here it is worth recalling Susanne Küchler's admonition regarding the term *malanggan*: a "generic name, . . . which [has] come to epitomize the dilemma facing art in a disciplinary context that is riddled by the legacy of semiotics. . . . Long misunderstood, *malanggan* have confounded all attempts at iconographic and contextual analysis."[33] The multisemic quality of the term is replicated in many of the nearly thirty local languages of New Ireland, in which *malanggan* can mean "likeness" but also "to carve, or inscribe." With

Figure 7.1 *Malanggan.* MNC: 10–29731. Museo Nacional de las Culturas de México. Reproduction authorized by the Instituto Nacional de Antropología e Historia.

this in mind, one might observe that *malanggan* refers to an astonishingly diverse, always innovative, array of funerary effigies from New Ireland, which were and continue to be produced in secrecy, displayed in highly dramatic rituals of revelation, and immediately afterward "killed," that is, destroyed or permanently disposed of—for example, through their sale to foreign collectors—to free the life force of recently deceased persons in order that they not remain in the vicinity of the community of the living.

The majority of *malanggan*-related objects are sculpted out of large single pieces of a special kind of driftwood (derived from the tree *Alstonia scholaris,* known most commonly as *sebah* in several local languages) that is borne in on seasonal monsoon tides. *Sebah* are soft and ideal for carving from their long exposure to seawater, but their times of arrival and collection are referenced in relation to a broader set of seasonal calendrical acts and transformations proper to the New Ireland people and environment. Thus, from the outset they are part of larger holistic socioenvironmental phenomena. The working of *sebah* is a process that expert New Ireland carvers refer to as "transforming" the wood into "skin" (*tak*), which will envelop and give form to an astonishing multiple body. This body is in turn surrounded by a fretwork made up of other, enveloping bodies that remind us that we are all relational beings. The fretwork evokes aspects of the life of the deceased, of the wefts of relations, engagements, and exchanges that defined them and their circumambient spaces: fish, pigs, flying foxes, birds, and seashells are common motifs. In turn, the most common colors that highlight the texture of *malanggan* are red, black, and white—colors associated with ancestral spirits and the world of the dead.

This composite form becomes the material embodiment, via the tangible evocation of life force, of a recently deceased person. Although each effigy is by necessity unique, there are a small number of general types of *malanggan*, two of which are present in the South Seas Collection at the Museo Nacional de las Culturas.[34] One is a *tatanua* (pronounced "tantanua"), mistakenly described as a "mask" since its accession to the Museo Nacional de las Culturas, which takes the form of a highly textured head with a large split headdress, presenting a striking, symmetrical dimorphism: its right and left lobes are made of very different textures and materials.[35] The other effigy I have in mind is smaller and simpler but no less complex (figure 7.2). Its label describes it as a "*malanggan* ceremonial mouthpiece."[36]

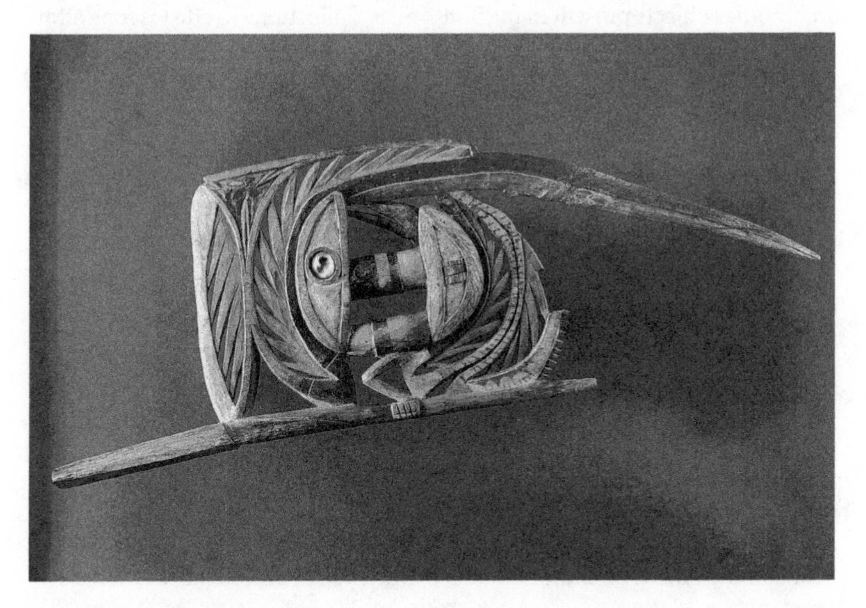

Figure 7.2 Ceremonial mouthpiece. MNC: 10-29734. Museo Nacional de las Culturas de México. Reproduction authorized by the Instituto Nacional de Antropología e Historia.

In simple terms, the rationale behind *malanggan* is to give shape to the life force of the deceased in order to recall it, display it, and then "finish" it, thus liberating the spirit permanently from the world of the living and its weft of relations.[37] Unlike their other famous cousins, the Kula valuables of the Trobriands (of which there is one exemplar, a *mwali* shell armband, in the holdings at the Museo Nacional de las Culturas, which can be paired with a *kaidibu* ritual dance paddle), *malanggan* are not made to be circulated, accumulating prestige through exchange, but to be destroyed.

> In Melanesia, as exemplified by *malanggan*, the commemorative work for the dead feeds on a memory of which amnesia is the necessary and paradoxical complement. The process of remembering that is incised in the work of mourning is thus at the same time a systematic forgetting of the dead, a process of un-stitching of the tightly woven relations of which the deceased person was so much a part. In New Ireland, one must know how to forget in order to know how to remember.[38]

This work of forgetting is present across Island Melanesia and extends to many other objects present in the South Seas Collection. To cite just one additional example, the work of evoking and forgetting is a key aspect of the spirit objects from South Malakula, Vanuatu, present in the South Seas Collection. These objects emerge within a ritual complex often known as *temes*. Like *malanggan, temes* is a multisemic term and does not simply stand as a generic label for specific objects or rituals. The *temes* cycle in South Malakula is internally diverse and complex, manifesting across at least eight distinct language communities in that area alone, but it is only a variation of broader regional funerary practices across north-central Vanuatu that, like *malanggan*, shed light on ways of revealing and concealing, remembering and forgetting.[39]

A further group of objects in the South Seas Collection that reiterates the complicated, still largely overlooked and misunderstood, relations that come into play between the living and the dead are the shields and "masks" (again, an unfortunate misnomer) from the Papuan Gulf. These items are generically referred to as *gope*, but like *malanggan* and *temes*, they emerge from nuanced and complex fields of embodiments, deployments, and social relations.

Contrast the critical importance of forgetting, first, with the preoccupation with preservation and restoration that occupy a significant proportion of the activities and resources in most international museums, including the Museo Nacional de Antropología and the broader INAH network of national museums. But also contrast the acts of erasure of spirit objects with the predominant nation-building narrative of the Museo Nacional de Antropología regarding "millenarian indigenous culture" and the perceived endurance and solidity of stone, as metaphors for the antiquity and continuity of the nation.

To finalize, it is worth emphasizing how the history of the South Seas Collection emerges from an unexpected network of social relations and processes that extends to the present.[40] These relations radiate out along unlikely paths, linking Covarrubias, the Museo Nacional de Antropología, and INAH to major figures in world anthropology, such as Bronislaw Malinowski, Franz Boas, Ruth Benedict, and even Margaret Mead.[41] The South Seas Collection is also the product of linkages that lead back to flagship American institutions, philanthropists, and museums. Its origins lie in the extraordinary collecting endeavor of A. B. Lewis in early twentieth-century German New Guinea, and thence to a multitude of colonial and indigenous actors who came together to create, distribute, and set in motion the social lives of this transcontinental set of Oceanic artifacts and beings.

Conclusion

In 1964, most Mexican ethnographic and pre-Columbian holdings of the National Museum were relocated to their new home in the current monumental building that houses the Museo Nacional de Antropología, in Chapultepec. The old museum's seat at the Casa de Moneda was converted into the Museo Nacional de las Culturas del Mundo. This institution intended to establish a rationale for the continuing storage and exhibition of the multifarious non-Mexican collections that had been left behind. In reality, the lack of government interest in items that did not neatly fit into narratives of national belonging translated into a chronic lack of funding, such that the Museo Nacional de las Culturas could hardly aspire to become little more than a curatorial storehouse for peculiar exotica. The best that could be done with some of its holdings was to exhibit them from time to time, for visiting groups of students, as useful visual exemplars of some of the classic European and Mediterranean cultures (Greek, Roman, Near Eastern) present in the standardized, uncritical, and Eurocentric narratives about universal history that made up the state's primary and secondary school syllabus.

During the second half of the twentieth century, the Museo Nacional de las Culturas thus became a repository for an ad hoc jumble of artifacts that variously made their way into its storerooms from across a patchwork of places in North America, South America, Central America, Asia, Africa, the Mediterranean, Oceania, even the Arctic.[42] To make matters worse, many of the items collected after 1965 consisted mostly of unwanted diplomatic gifts that the Mexican government "donated" to the museum. For almost sixty years after their accession, the Pacific and North American collections were stored away, a few of their constituent objects exhibited in the two cramped exhibit halls, within the same glass cases, that were originally curated by Covarrubias in 1954.[43]

The Pacific Hall at the Museo Nacional de las Culturas was unveiled in 2010. It was cocurated by me and my colleague Oscar Aguirre. Following the mission statement of the museum to offer exhibits that extend and support primary and secondary teaching subjects, we decided to put together a didactic museography that communicated the vast geographical spread and diversity of the material cultures of the Pacific Rim and Islands. Our intent was to make Oceania knowable to a larger Mexican public by making the best possible selection of objects, which necessarily depended on some of the significant components of the South Seas Collection. An important part of this effort went into turning the ample multistoried backdrop offered by the Pacific Gallery into a space whose distribution imitated that of the cultural geography of the Pacific Rim and Islands. In the middle of the gallery, we placed iconic Pacific Islands artifacts from the South Seas Collection. Surrounding this central area, from left to right, Global South to North, and East to West, we displayed items from the Museo Nacional de las Culturas's storerooms that represented Australia, Indonesia, China, Japan, the Arctic, North America, Middle America, and South America. The hall attempted to immerse the visitor in the Pacific Rim and Islands as a three-dimensional mosaic of overlapping, interconnected spheres of creativity, difference, and historicity, each represented by various archetypal objects.

At the center of the gallery, we placed a large interactive digital map of Covarrubias's *Pacific Arts* mural of from the 1939 exhibition. This was our attempt at recovering the idea of the transpacific, with its typologies and networks of relations, that originally informed the assembly of the South Seas Collection. To this end, we presented two large panels with critical explanations about the advantages and prejudices that defined Covarrubias's vision. We also added a contemporary informed set of comments and analysis regarding the physical environments, geographies, and diversities present in the hall. Color-coded labels emphasized socioenvironmental and cultural contexts, while the labels on each item sought to offer as much information as possible about its accession date, its provenance, and its overall logic as a piece of the Pacific puzzle.

The intention had been to offer a novel museography, attentive to multiple levels of interpretation. But our critical museographical content did not go down well with the career museum staff that had long supervised the Museo Nacional de las Culturas during its years of funding drought and official neglect. During President Felipe Calderón's administration (2006–12), the authorities at INAH had had a personal interest in reviving and rehabilitating the figure of Covarrubias, and this created expectations of increased funding and internal promotions. As specialists in the Asia-Pacific, our presence as external curators generated tensions and suspicions, which, in the end, led to the disassembly of the Pacific Hall in 2014. The South Seas Collection and its extraordinary objects were again confined to the storerooms, there to continue defying national museographical and educational narratives and curatorial interventions for the foreseeable future.

Notes

I would like to acknowledge Anne Müller for her revisions to the final version of this chapter.

1. The Casa de Moneda was originally built in the eighteenth century as the seat of the Royal Mint of the Viceroyalty of New Spain. Since the nineteenth century it has been the seat of the Museo Nacional de México. In 1912, after the collection of natural history was displaced, the museum was renamed the Museo Nacional de Arqueología, Historia y Etnología. By 1939, the museum was renamed again, to reflect new displacements, as the Museo Nacional de Antropología. In 1939, the Casa de Moneda also became the headquarters of the newly constituted Instituto Nacional de Antropología e Historia (INAH), and since 1964, it has been the seat of the Museo Nacional de las Culturas. It is located behind the National Palace and consequently occupies a place in the historic and administrative center of Mexico City and of the nation.
2. This gallery was formerly known as the Galería de Monolitos, and a part of its inception and history are covered in the introduction to this volume. See also Achim and Bueno in this volume.
3. Nancy Lutkehaus, "Miguel Covarrubias and the Pageant of the Pacific: The Golden Gate International Exposition and the Idea of the Transpacific, 1939–1940," in *Transpacific Studies: Framing an Emerging Field*, ed. Janet Hoskins

and Viet Thanh Nguyen (Honolulu: University of Hawai'i Press, 2014), 109–33; Haydeé López Hernández, *En busca del alma nacional: La arqueología y la construcción del origen de la historia nacional en México (1867–1942)* (Mexico City: INAH, 2018).

4. The emphasis on establishing facts in the field was a new chapter in a longer history of "cabinet" and "field" relations in archaeological research and commentary, which had been unfolding throughout the nineteenth and early twentieth centuries. See Mechthild Rutsch, *Entre el campo y el gabinete: Nacionales y extranjeros en la profesionalización de la antropología mexicana* (Mexico City: INAH, 2007). Regarding the search for the "mother culture" of the nation's indigenous past, see López Hernández, *En busca del alma nacional.*
5. Haydée López Hernández, "Entre la interdisciplina y el indigenismo: Antecedentes y creación del INAH," *Antropología: Revista interdisciplinaria del INAH* 1, no. 1 (2017): 6–22.
6. Tomás Pérez Viejo had observed that this seemed symptomatic of the government's desire to place the Spanish colonial past within a marginal, bracketed space and time that effectively decoupled the three centuries of Spanish colonial rule from the preceding pre-Hispanic indigenous past and the later independent and revolutionary periods. Tomás Pérez Viejo, "Historia, antropología y arte: Tres sujetos, dos pasados y una sola nación verdadera," *Revista de Indias* 74, no. 254 (2012): 254.
7. There was a political message underpinning the spatial and institutional separation of history from anthropology and archaeology. The government's focus was on "confining the colonial past to an island, an accident of historical time which had no roots; while the pre-Columbian origins of the nation, and the ethnographic present, *the dead Indian and the live Indian*, archaeology and anthropology, were to be fused in order to restore the perceived natural order of [the nation's] temporality and history." López Hernández, "Entre la interdisciplina," 13, my translation, emphasis added.
8. "Twenty Centuries of Mexican Art," MoMA website, accessed October 19, 2019, https://www.moma.org/calendar/exhibitions/2985. See also Michelle Elligott, *René d'Harnoncourt and the Art of Installation* (New York: Museum of Modern Art, 2018).
9. See Robert W. Rydell, *All the World's a Fair: Visions of Empire at the American International Expositions, 1876–1916* (Chicago: University of Chicago Press, 1984); and Andrew M. Shanken, *Into the Void Pacific: Building the 1939 San Francisco World's Fair* (Berkeley: University of California Press, 2014).
10. Nancy Lutkehaus has lucidly explored how the exposition constituted a "specific type of cultural formation . . . identified as characteristic of the late nineteenth- and early twentieth-century West," and convincingly argues that it played a key role in the idea of the transpacific. See Lutkehaus, "Miguel Covarrubias," 114.
11. By far the most informative, critical study of these extraordinary works is the recent book by Mónica Ramírez Bernal, *El océano como paisaje/Pageant of*

the Pacific: La serie de mapas murales de Miguel Covarrubias (Mexico City: UNAM, 2018). See also Miguel Covarrubias, *Esplendor del Pacífico* (1940; Mexico City: CONCACULTA, 2006).

12. As Mónica Ramírez has explained, from the early planning stages of the exposition, there was a concern with representing the Pacific as a region "unto itself," with civilizations, histories, and peoples whose unfolding developed independently from Europe and the Atlantic world (Ramírez Bernal, *El océano*, 40).
13. The idea of representing ethnic diversity through "race" was directly informed by Alfred Kroeber's classificatory models and maps. Ramírez Bernal, *El océano*, 63–67.
14. Covarrubias received much of his information about racial and artistic borrowings from three expert members of the Committee of the Pacific Area, namely Alfred Kroeber, Carl Ortwin Sauer, and Walter Goldschmidt, all three from the University of California at Berkeley. The committee itself was formed in 1937 specifically to oversee the organization of the exposition and included several distinguished personalities, including Ray Lyman Wilbur (Stanford), Phillip M. Youtz (former director of the Brooklyn Museum and then president of the American Federation of Arts), and René d'Harnoncourt (Museum of Modern Art). Ramírez Bernal, *El océano*, 25–36.
15. A detailed account of Covarrubias's intense calendar of engagements and commitments can be pieced together through his meticulously detailed biography by Adriana Williams, *Covarrubias*, trans. by Julio Colón (Mexico City: Fondo de Cultura Económica, 1999).
16. Miguel Covarrubias, "Origen y desarrollo del estilo artístico 'olmeca,'" in *Mayas y Olmecas: Segunda Reunión de Mesa Redonda sobre problemas antropológicos de México y Centro América, Tuxtla Gutiérrez, Chiapas*, ed. Sociedad Mexicana de Antropología (Mexico City: Talleres de la Editorial Stylo, 1942), 46.
17. The term "region of ethnographic study" was in turn inspired from the structuralist Dutch school of anthropology's characterization of Eastern Indonesia as an *ethnologisch studieveld*. See Jan Petrus Benjamin de Josselin de Jong, "The Malay Archipelago as a Field of Ethnological Study," in *Structural Anthropology in the Netherlands: A Reader*, ed. Patrick Edward de Josselin de Jong, Koninklijk Instituut voor Taal-, Land- en Volkenkunde, Translation Series 17 (The Hague: M. Nijhoff, 1977), 166–82; also Jesús Jáuregui, "La región cultural del Gran Nayar como 'campo de estudio etnológico,'" *Diario de Campo*, no. 28 (2008): 124–50.
18. Miguel Covarrubias, *Island of Bali* (1937; Singapore: Periplus, 1973); Adrian Vickers, *Bali: A Paradise Created* (Singapore: Periplus, 2012), 162–84.
19. The search for origins more broadly went back at least a century and was quite widespread in the Americanist social sciences: "At this time there was the general belief that every group, all cultural traits, could be traced back to single sources: through the mediums of diffusion, migration, and evolution." In the early twentieth century, this search was extended toward the Pacific, as "there

was a general assumption that the evidence from North America would provide the overall schema for evidence in the Pacific." In view of this, it is not difficult to imagine that Covarrubias, in his proximity to anthropological and archaeological studies, should have picked up elements of this search in his transpacific engagements. Both quotations taken from Chris Gosden and Chantal Knowles, *Collecting Colonialism: Material Culture and Colonial Change* (Oxford: Berg, 2001), 77.

20. Edward B. Tylor, *Primitive Culture: Researches into the Development of Mythology, Philosophy, Religion, Art, and Custom*, vol. 1 (1871; New York: Brentano's, 1958), 1.
21. Covarrubias's proximity to Benedict, Margaret Mead, and other prominent Boasians lends support to this claim. See Ruth Benedict, "Earthly Paradise (Review: *The Island of Bali*, by Miguel Covarrubias and Rose Covarrubias)," *New Republic*, December 8, 1937, 139. Also, Vickers, *Bali*; and Thomas C. Patterson, *A Social History of Anthropology in the United States* (Oxford: Berg, 2001), 79.
22. Rubín de la Borbolla was another of the very first generation of professionally trained social scientists in the emerging field of anthropology in Mexico. As with Gamio, Caso, Covarrubias, and others, he came from a well-to-do family and studied abroad (Switzerland, in his case). His accession to director of ENAH was the direct antecedent to his becoming the first director of the Museo Nacional de Antropología in 1946. See Johanna Faulhaber, "Origen y formación de la Escuela Nacional de Antropología," in *Daniel Rubín de la Borbolla (1907–1990): Testimonios y fuentes*, vol. 2, ed. Bertha Abraham Jalil (Mexico City: UNAM, 1996), 13–20.
23. Ralph Linton and Paul S. Wingert, *Arts of the South Seas* (New York: Simon and Schuster, 1946), 7 and 10.
24. Donald Collier, "My Life with Exhibits at the Field Museum, 1941–1976," in "Curators, Collections, and Contexts: Anthropology at the Field Museum, 1893–2002," ed. Stephen E. Nash and Gary M. Feinman, new series, *Fieldiana* 36 (2003): 199–219.
25. Most of the pre-Columbian items took the form of small ceramic figurines, pots, bowls, and fragments of potsherds. Further details in Collier, "My Life with Exhibits," 208–9; and Anahí Luna, "Oceanía en México: El intercambio entre el Museo Field de Chicago y el Museo Nacional de Antropología (1948–1951)" (master's thesis, Universidad Nacional Autónoma de México, 2015), 51–63.
26. Michael O'Hanlon and Robert L. Welsch, eds., *Hunting the Gatherers: Ethnographic Collectors, Agents and Agency in Melanesia, 1870s–1930s* (Oxford: Berghahn, 2000).
27. Memo No. 1376, Field Museum. This fifteen-page document offers the itemized packing list that includes all the objects cited in the main text as well as a substantial number of objects proper to First Nations communities from the

Pacific Northwest and indigenous groups from the West Coast, United States. A facsimile of this memo, as well as a set of didactic color-coded maps, is presented in Luna, "Oceanía en México," annexes 1 and 2, 77–111.

28. In the 1960s, the Museo Nacional de las Culturas made two distinct efforts to acquire additional objects from the Western Pacific and from the hitherto unrepresented regions of Polynesia and Micronesia. The most significant of these acquisitions was carried out in 1966–67 with a private collector, Morton D. May, from Saint Louis, Missouri, who sold thirty objects to the Museo Nacional de las Culturas, most of which originated in the Sepik region of Papua New Guinea. A further acquisition was carried out with the Carter family, private collectors residing in Cuernavaca, Mexico, in 1975; it is from this last lot that the few Polynesian and Micronesian objects appear in the Museo Nacional de las Culturas's accession documents.
29. See especially Marisa Peiró, "Asia-Pacífico en la obra del artista mexicano Miguel Covarrubias (1904–1957)" (PhD diss., University of Zaragoza, 2018); Collier, "My Life with Exhibits"; and Luna, "Oceanía en México."
30. An important exception, which is presented in the form of a plethora of short itemized descriptions, are the numerous comments to select items in the photographic section of the *Moana* exhibition catalogue. The amount of specialist research, as well as updated information, that went into the research for labels in the *Moana* exhibit was exceptional and continues to be equal to the highest-quality Pacific Islands' exhibition catalogs currently available. Yet, the quality content of these descriptions has yet to be equaled by a specific analysis of the materiality of the broader South Seas Collection at the Museo Nacional de las Culturas.
31. O'Hanlon and Welsch, *Hunting the Gatherers*, 2.
32. I have previously offered a longer discussion about these problems in Carlos Mondragón, "Encarnando a los espíritus en Melanesia: La innovación como mecanismo de continuidad en el norte de Vanuatu," in *Ritos de Paso: Arqueología y antropología de las religiones*, vol. 3, ed. Patricia Fournier, Carlos Mondragón, and Walburga Wiesheu (Mexico City: INAH, 2009), 121–49.
33. Susanne Küchler, *Malanggan: Art, Memory and Sacrifice* (Oxford: Berg, 2002), 1.
34. It is also necessary to remember that some of these types are in turn mounted on larger frames, sometimes taking the shape of house poles, sometimes of model dugout canoes, sometimes of large single-piece "friezes," which are hung over a house façade or a larger structure at the moment of their ritual revelation.
35. Museo Nacional de las Culturas, catalog number 10–29730.
36. Museo Nacional de las Culturas, catalog number 10–29734. This item was acquired by the Field Museum from J. F. K. Umlauff, a prominent Hamburg clearing house, which became a key broker for the millions of ethnographic artifacts that flowed from Melanesia to Europe and the Americas starting in the 1870s. The original collector and context for its transaction remains unknown,

as do the provenance of millions of other objects that made their way through clearing houses.

37. The information in this paragraph is taken from various parts of Susanne Küchler's outstanding ethnography of *malanggan*. See Küchler, *Malanggan*.
38. Küchler, *Malanggan*, 4–5.
39. See Carlos Mondragón, "Ocultamiento y revelación en un cosmos specular: Incertidumbre, materialidad y el mundo de los espíritus en las Islas Torres, Vanuatu," in *Mostrar y ocultar en el arte y en los rituales: Perspectivas comparativas*, ed. Johannes Neurath and Guilhem Olivier (Mexico City: UNAM, 2017), 403–5; Carlos Mondragón, "Concealment, Revelation and Cosmological Dualism: Visibility, Materiality and the Spiritscape of the Torres Islands, Vanuatu," *Cahiers d'anthropologie sociale* 1, no. 11 (2015): 38–50; and Mondragón, "Encarnando a los espíritus en Melanesia."
40. I follow here the idea of *chaînes opératoires*, elaborated on by Gosden and Knowles, *Collecting Colonialism*, following André Leroi-Gourhan, *Evolution et techniques: L'homme et la matière* (Paris: Albin Michel, 1943) and Leroi-Gourhan, *Evolution et techniques: milieu et techniques* (Paris: Albin Michel, 1945).
41. Adrian Vickers has presented compelling evidence about the likely editorial intervention of Margaret Mead in Covarrubias's Bali monograph, whose final structure Covarrubias adopted for his subsequent book on Southern Mexico. Adrian Vickers, "Word and Image in Miguel Covarrubias's *Island of Bali*," *Anales del Instituto de Investigaciones Estéticas* 42, no. 116 (2020): 53–76.
42. The largest semicoherent set of objects at the Museo Nacional de las Culturas is the so-called Americas collection, which at last count (in 2011) seems to have encompassed 6,359 items from across the continent. Other groupings from Asia, Africa, and Oceania are much smaller, numbering in the few hundreds or less. See Gerardo Pérez Taber and José Luis Pérez Flores, "El Museo Nacional de las Culturas: Ventana hacia el continente americano en México," *Quaderni di Thule XII, Atti del XXXIV Convegno Internazionale di Americanistica* (2012): 402, for the data on the American collections.
43. I was still able to visit these two rooms, located in a second-floor corner of the museum, as late as 2008. Although a few labels and items had been changed, the overall layout remained the same as the one established in 1954. These halls were taken down shortly thereafter, as a result of the renovations that gave rise to the Pacific Hall.

Part III
Disturbances

\\ 8

Tehuantepec on Display

Tlalocs, Theodolites, Fishing Traps, and the Cultures of Collecting in the Mid-Nineteenth Century

MIRUNA ACHIM

In March 1842, President Antonio López de Santa Anna granted Mexican empresario José de Garay y Garay rights to build a canal through the Tehuantepec Isthmus, and by late May, a group of engineers and marine officers, led by engineer Cayetano Moro, set off for Tehuantepec to evaluate the feasibility of the project and capitalize on its immense financial promise.[1] The survey commission produced maps, geological studies, information on geographical positions and altitudes, and descriptions of the climate, natural productions, and inhabitants of the region, which Moro collected in a book, the *Survey of the Isthmus of Tehuantepec* (1844). Besides data, the commission collected objects—most notably, minerals, as well as several antiquities from the island of Manopostiac, off the southern shores of the isthmus, which were deposited in the museum in 1843.[2] Two hollow ceramic figures attracted some degree of attention in the periodical press.

The earliest illustrations and descriptions of these ceramics appeared in 1844, in the *Museo mexicano*. The anonymous author finds the objects to be mostly incomprehensible and strives to guess their meanings and uses from what he knows of other cultures (figure 8.1):

> What can we say of this masked figure [on the left], lacking hands and feet? We have seen large collections of these figures, commonly called idols . . . but never anything that resembles [this] figure, so horribly adorned with animal

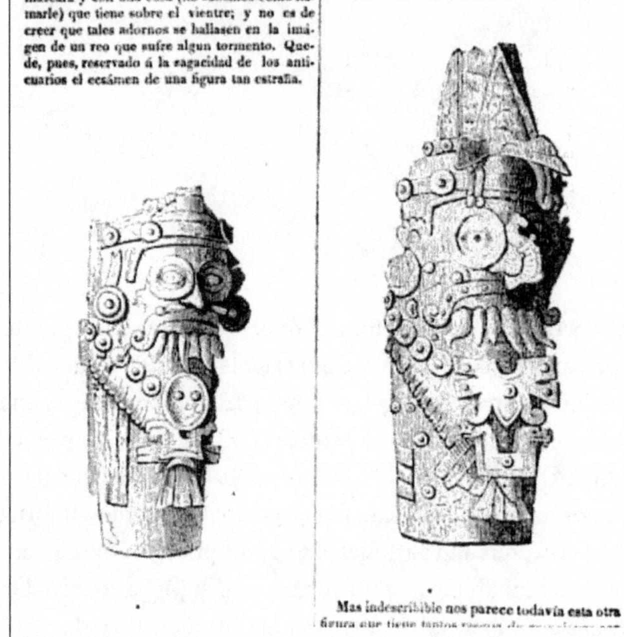

130 EL MUSEO MEXICANO.—Tomo III.

roz, y que representan los diferentes suplicios de que se usa en aquel antiguo imperio. Nuestra conjetura nos parecia mas verisímil al ver la actitud suplicante de las manos, y esas arrugas del rostro en las que veiamos la espresion del dolor y de un acerbo sufrimiento. Pero esta conjetura se desvanece cuando se observa que hay algo de adornos en ese *no sé qué* que la figura referida lleva en la cabeza; y es probable que estos adornos no se hallarian jamas en un instrumento de suplicio. Tambien hemos observado que esta figura está adornada con un collar, con una especie de zarcillos, con una máscara y con una cosa (no sabemos cómo llamarle) que tiene sobre el vientre; y no es de creer que tales adornos se hallasen en la imágen de un reo que sufre algun tormento. Quede, pues, reservado á la sagacidad de los anticuarios el ecsámen de una figura tan estraña.

sentan animales; pero nada habíamos hallado semejante á la figura que ahora tenemos á la vista, tan horriblemente adornada con esa dentadura de animal que la hace tan estraña. Se notará que está recargada de adornos, cubierta con una especie de gorro ó casco indefinible, con máscara, y á primera vista, parece que tiene tambien unos espejuelos ó antiparras. El adorno que pasa la nariz, se parece algo á los que usan los habitantes de la Australasia. El collar y el medallon que tiene al cuello, y los demas adornos, hacen creer que este raro busto representa un dios ó un grande personage.

Mas indescribible nos parece todavía esta otra figura que tiene tantas

Figure 8.1 Antiquities from Manopostiac. *Museo Mexicano* 3 (1844): 136, Biblioteca Nacional de Antropología e Historia, Mexico City. Reproduction authorized by the Instituto Nacional de Antropología e Historia.

teeth, which makes it look so strange. It is festooned with ornament and wears a kind of undefinable hat or helmet, a mask, and apparently, eyeglasses or an eye mask. The accessory which pierces its nose looks like something used by the inhabitants of Australasia. Even stranger is the other figure, which resembles the first one, [except] for a kind of crest, which makes it look so deformed. The most remarkable thing about it is the adornment on its head, which, truly, looks like some kind of mitre. Is it possible that this is the bust of a masked priest?[3]

As the above description suggests, before pre-Hispanic antiquities became the objects of an archaeological science and, later, of a nationalist narrative, many appeared horrible, deformed, monstrous, strange, and mostly incomprehensible to their viewers. It was precisely by putting them into circulation, by means of descriptions and images such as these published in the *Museo mexicano,* that the objects of Mexico's past achieved visibility—drawing the attention of scholars, collectors, and speculators and promoting the production and exchange of information about them—and became a familiar category of study and collecting.[4]

By the early twentieth century, Nicolás León, then in charge of the ethnology section at the Museo Nacional de México, included the two Manopostiac antiquities in his catalog of ninety-one Huave antiquities in the museum. The catalog is prefaced by a history of the Huaves from their settlement in the southern isthmus in pre-Hispanic times till the twentieth century and comes with an anthropometric study of the Huave "race" by U.S. anthropologist Frederick Starr.[5] The entries corresponding to the Manopostiac antiquities, cataloged as n. 90 and n. 91, give their height (one *vara,* that is, one yard) and describe them as "beautiful ceramic statues, hollow on the inside and of meticulous manufacture." Though León includes them in a collection of Huave antiquities, he suggests that the statues were upper parts of urns in the Mixteco-Zapotec tradition; it is unclear if he intends to imply that they were made by Mixtecs or Zapotecs—the ethnic groups present in the isthmus at the arrival of the Huaves—or by Huaves working in that tradition. León also includes studies of the objects by leading historians Alfredo Chavero and Francisco del Paso y Troncoso, who identify the two figures as Tlaloc, on the basis of lightning motifs and the "goggles" associated with rain deities.[6] Two decades later, Enrique Juan Palacios—archaeologist at the Museo Nacional de Arqueología, Antropología e Historia—reinforces the association of the statues with Tlaloc and identifies their material as "very special whitish-yellowish clay, with big fragments of quartz, typical of the sands in the region." He also further throws their origins into doubt: "One refuses to believe they are of Huave manufacture, unless the members of this indigenous family, of lamentable aspect, have degenerated more than any other aboriginal group."[7]

Today, the ceramics stand in two glass cases in the Sala de las Culturas de Oaxaca of the Museo Nacional de Antropología, surrounded by other objects from the region, yet still somehow isolated from them (figure 8.2). They appear lonely, uneasy with their own size, where the surrounding showcases hold much smaller things, petrified into the eternal present of their display, seeming to be either far withdrawn into themselves or, alternately, gawking down at the perplexed visitor. The label—one for both objects—does little to put the viewer or the statues at ease: it identifies them as representations of Ñuhu Savy, the Mixtec god of rain and thunder, based on iconographic attributes, principally their goggles and the serpent and wave motifs that decorate one of them. The identification, as Martha Carmona, the curator of gallery, explains, is supported by the striking similarities between these objects and representations of the thunder god in the Mixtec codices, such as the Codex Vindobonensis.[8] The label in the museum makes no mention of their provenance, giving only a general reference to the isthmus; just as vague is their dating: "Postclásico 900–1521 d.c." There is no mention of their possible relation to the Huaves. The museum's website is

Figure 8.2 Dios Ñuhu Savy, Sala Culturas de Oaxaca, Museo Nacional de Antropología. Archivo Digital de las Colecciones del Museo Nacional de Antropología. INAH-CANON. Reproduction authorized by the Instituto Nacional de Antropología e Historia.

even less detailed: it features only one of the two figures, with its photograph and catalog number: 16.0–00060.

This condensed account of how the two hollow ceramics from Manopostiac became objects under glass at the Museo Nacional de Antropología offers a glimpse into the processes by which idols were made into antiquities. As they were transformed, over a century and a half, from undefinable and grotesque things into the beautiful objects of national patrimony, pre-Hispanic objects acquired a place in the museum, an inventory number, a provenance associated not so much with the place where they were found but with a major pre-Hispanic culture, and iconographic identification, in line with the pantheon of deities—Tlaloc, Ñuhu Savy—that articulate a common Mesoamerican identity. In this account, archaeological sciences recover antiquities' supposedly intrinsic meanings and claim them as matters of fact and as increasingly objective proofs of Mexico's ancient past. In turn, the history of Mexican archaeology has told the history of the collection at the Museo Nacional de Antropología mostly as one of the smooth unfolding and unveiling of a national essence. Yet, the process by which pre-Hispanic antiquities become stabilized as metonyms of the nation's past is also a process of loss, entailing the erasure of all kinds of "superfluous" knowledge about the practices, gestures, obstacles, contradictions, and premises that made it possible to ferry things across geographical, conceptual, and linguistic spaces and regimes of use, to put them on display in their permanent state-of-the-art at the museum.

This chapter opens a breach in the more teleological narratives that have told the museum's history and that of its objects: first, by pausing a fast-paced narrative at a specific moment, to reconstruct the collection of the two ceramic figurines from Manopostiac in 1843, as a case study illustrative of nineteenth-century collecting; second, by introducing into this study things and people usually left out of archaeological histories and displays—boats, horses, scientific instruments, wood samples, plants, books, *tepalcates* (ceramic fragments), fishing traps, shrimp, waves, wind, engineers, indigenous guides, investors, and bureaucrats, among others. I envision this chapter as a proposal of sorts for a series of display cases, each of them bringing together things whose uses and meanings were entangled at different moments and in different places with those of the two Manopostiac antiquities. Specifically, I try to imagine two such kinds of sites, with their sets of practices and their material, social, and discursive densities: the southern isthmus, where the "idols" were used by local peoples and collected by surveyors from the capital; and the centers of calculation—on the move across the isthmus, in Mexico City, and in London—where scientists and investors resignified the idols and other objects collected in Tehuantepec as elements in new narratives of progress and modernity.

My objective is not to construct a seamless narrative; I bring together objects and fragments of objects and stories as a way of exploring the premises, dissonances, and contradictions that shaped collecting in mid-nineteenth-century Mexico, to make visible the regimens of exclusion and inclusion that determined what kinds of things were worth gathering in the museum and to inquire into the contested uses with which these things were invested by different actors. How some uses came to prevail over others is key to understanding what kind of museum was being built and how it came to be. Ultimately, what drives this essay is not exclusively antiquarian curiosity: indeed, exposing the conceptual and ideological buttresses that fix and sustain things as objects of collections is a way of reminding ourselves that things can be made public again, that is, available to a multiplicity of uses and viewpoints.[9]

The Night of the Broken Idols

After an arduous journey from Mexico City, the Tehuantepec survey commissioners arrived at the southern tip of the isthmus on May 28, 1842.[10] For some months, they took up residence in San Mateo del Mar, one of the four Huave villages that articulate a complex landscape of riverbeds, lagoons, and sand bars on the Pacific coast (figure 8.3). These were treacherous waters, as Hernán Cortés had found out when he launched an expedition to the Californias from here, only to have one of his two brigs smashed against the rocks.[11] The wreck was likely on the surveyors' minds as they sought to establish safe passage through the lagoons to the entrance of the projected canal. They spent some months in these regions, carrying out careful measurements of all kinds, recorded by engineer Cayetano Moro in the *Survey of the Isthmus of Tehuantepec.*

To determine elevations, they took as reference point the top of the island of Manopostiac, which rises two hundred meters in the middle of the Divenamar lagoon, and sought the help of the villagers of San Mateo to cross the lagoon and set up signals on the island. The villagers refused to help and gave in only after receiving unspecified threats. Once they delivered the surveyors

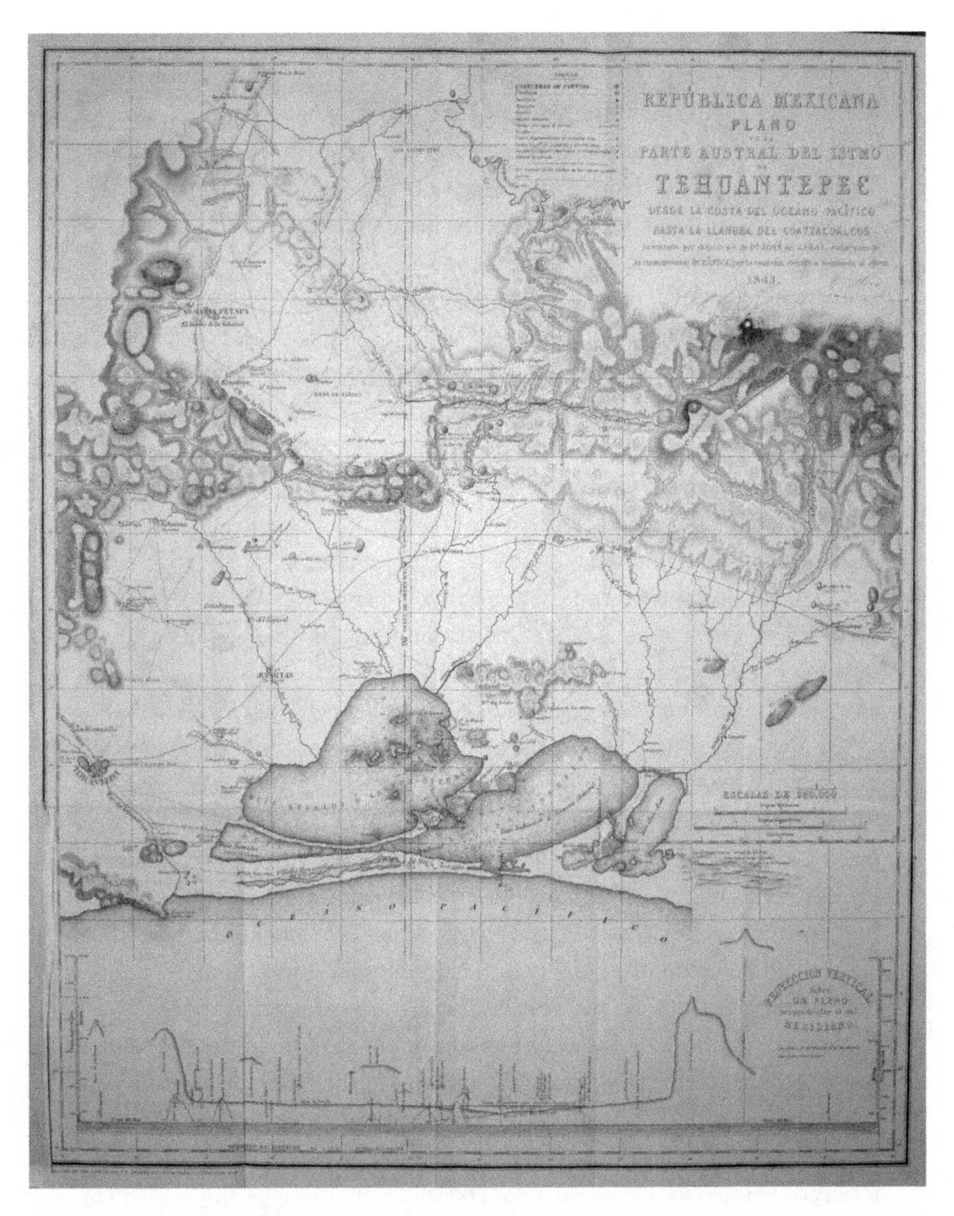

Figure 8.3 Map of the southern isthmus. In Moro, *Survey of the Isthmus of Tehuantepec* (London: Ackermann, 1844). Biblioteca Nacional de Antropología e Historia, Mexico City. Reproduction authorized by the Instituto Nacional de Antropología e Historia.

across the lagoon in their precarious boats—which, Moro is surprised to notice, lacked oars—the villagers could not be persuaded to venture onto the island to help set up the signals. The engineers hiked uphill alone and, after completing their work, returned with two clay "idols" and an incense burner, which they had found in a cave. The Huave boatmen acted surprised by the removal of the "idols," but, Moro insists, their surprise was feigned, and they astutely refused to answer questions about the objects. When the boats finally returned to San Mateo, news of the displaced objects was met with despondency among the villagers, who went as far as to "steal . . . one of the idols." The item was recovered soon after, Moro writes reassuringly and, one might add, without even as much as a touch of irony.

Some days later, after "one of the strong winds that reign on the coast of Tehuantepec" blew down one of the signals, the surveyors returned to Manopostiac. This time they carried out a more detailed inspection of the place, expecting to find more antiquities. They were rewarded with the two hollow ceramic figurines now in the Museo Nacional de Antropología, two cross-legged clay figures, and two small ceramic recipients—the latter judged by the commissioners to be of modern manufacture. Candle wax and a withered plant were found near the cache of objects, which makes me think they were being used ritually at the time of the survey. When the boats made their way back to the village that night, the wind picked up; as a result, some of the antiquities were smashed to pieces so small that the objects could not be fitted back together. The two hollow ceramic figurines survived the boat trip.

Moro ends his account of the episode with a description of the island of Manopostiac, as he tries to explain why it could have served as a depository for idols, even before the Huaves settled in the southern isthmus, centuries before the arrival of the Spaniards.[12] Alluding to a manuscript the surveyors had collected during their stay in the isthmus, Moro recounts that Cosijopi, the king of the Zapotecs, offered a "solemn sacrifice to their greatest idol, called the Heart of the Kingdom, which was placed on the island."[13] Is Moro suggesting that the "idols" were of Zapotec manufacture and that the Huaves repurposed them for their own uses? Did this hint of a suggestion—taken up by archaeologists into the twentieth century—serve to justify the removal of the idols, given that the Huaves were not their rightful owners? In any case, the island seems to have held an important place in the cultural, mythical, and religious geography of various peoples that crossed paths with each other in the southern isthmus. For the Zapotecs, it was the Enchanted

Hill—the meaning of Manopostiac in Zapotec. For Moro, the reason for the island's religious and mythological relevance was geological. Of volcanic origin, it is composed of slabs of green syenite rocks that contract and expand and clash against each other, producing metallic sounds, which the Huaves compare with the tolling of church bells.[14] The Huaves, Moro goes on to explain, held Manopostiac to have special powers, and they ventured there, crossing the turbulent lagoon in their "imperfect canoes," to pray to their ancient gods and ask for rain for their "miserable harvests." They did so with the tacit permission and indolence of the local Catholic priest, who encouraged these practices instead of extirpating them. In Moro's account, then, the displacement of the "idols" from the cave on the island of Manopostiac to the museum in Mexico City would come to mean a passage of sorts from darkness to light, from secrecy to openness, from superstition to reason, from abandon to care and conservation.

Not all the objects collected on the island made it into the museum. Some, as we saw, were smashed beyond recognition during the stormy night crossing. This episode is not exceptional; stories of collecting in the nineteenth century often include references to objects shattered in the process, sometimes intentionally. Especially stirring is the account of the removal of antiquities from the ruins of Metlaltoyuca, in Puebla, in the context of another survey commission, some twenty years later, when their Totonac carriers threatened to whip and hurt the objects because they allowed themselves to be carried away. As one Totonac man supposedly berated an idol, "You are a bad god because you let yourself be taken away; I will ask the other gods to come with the entire village to whip you. In the meantime, take this coin, so you will not harm us."[15] It is difficult to know whether reports such as this, by scientists from the capital, can be taken at face value, but to the extent that they can, they reveal the types of affective economies at stake in the translation of an object from one place to the other.

Other times, things shatter "accidentally," as was the case with some of the objects collected on Manopostiac island. One of the most glaringly unapologetic blind spots at the center of Moro's story is the destruction of the very objects that were being removed to ensure their safekeeping. There is little acknowledgment that antiquities such as those broken on the isthmus's southern shore had been kept safe for hundreds of years on the tops of mountains, in caves, or in burial offerings. It made little sense for the surveyors to burden their loads—already heavy with more complete idols and with geological and botanical samples—with the smithereens of objects beyond recognition; so they left the broken pieces behind, to be washed away by the morning tide. Can we imagine ourselves today lovingly gathering those shards to put together a museum display that would include the idols broken in the process of their collection next to the hollow ceramic statues from Manopostiac? Such a display would stand as a reminder that destruction awaits all the objects in a museum—not just total or partial material destruction, which is the fate of all things, but a more profound form of ontological shattering: bringing a thing into a collection smashes it beyond recognition by imposing on it exclusive meanings and a new logic of use. Whatever powers or affects they might have held for the Huaves, once removed from the isthmus and brought into the museum, objects of cult, ritual, or everyday life are transfigured into the objects of an archaeological science: cleaned of wax remains and of the withered plants that had stuck to them, they are drawn, described, interpreted, circulated, displayed, and compared with other objects. The "idols" of Manopostiac become antiquities in the Museo Nacional de México.

Wastelands and Resources

Cayetano Moro produced the *Survey of the Isthmus of Tehuantepec* after the commission returned to Mexico City. Moro's *Survey* was published in London in 1844, by Ackermann and Company, one of the most prestigious and prolific editors of books on Latin America at the time. The *Survey* is an unveiled attempt at publicizing the advantages of building a canal through the isthmus; 188 pages long, it is a hybrid text, seeking to provide prospective investors with information of all kinds. It comes with an annex of transcriptions of official documents—government decrees that granted empresario Garay y Garay sole proprietorship of "wastelands" up to thirty miles on both sides of the canal, placed three hundred convicts to work on the canal under his direction, and granted him exclusive privileges to execute the project, collect tolls for the following fifty years, and settle colonies on both sides of the canal.[16] The most extensive section of the *Survey* presents geological and topographical studies of the region, designed to underscore the feasibility of an eighty-kilometer passageway, which would connect the lagoons on the Pacific shores of the isthmus to the Coatzacoalcos River, via a system of rivers (specifically the Ostuta and the Chicapa) and trenches, and from there, taking advantage of the course of the Coatzacoalcos, into the Gulf of Mexico. The proposal for the canal includes financial projections, which look to the Caledonian canal in Scotland, built at the beginning of the nineteenth century. The final estimate for the Mexican canal, in French francs, came to 85 million, taking into account such variables as the number of locks and the cost to open trenches through soils very different from those crossed by the Scottish canal, while keeping in mind "what is actually paid in Mexico and the United States for similar work in soils analogous to that of the isthmus."[17] The canal through the isthmus would be cheaper than the Caledonian canal, estimates Moro, partly because the land on both sides of the Mexican canal is mostly "wastelands," and partly because where property claims did exist, land could be bought cheaply, at least a lot more cheaply than in Scotland. Drawing on units of measurement used in different places—such as French francs, kilometers, cost of labor in the United States, and cost of land in Scotland—Moro translates the construction of the canal into a language of exchange commensurable with that of international speculators and investors.

The canal is not just cheap and easy to execute. A passageway between one ocean and another, it cuts through fabulously rich lands, and Moro dedicates a substantial part of the *Survey* to unveiling the isthmus's hidden treasures—its climate, natural productions, and inhabitants—before the would-be prospectors' eager eyes. He praises the fertility of its soil, the mildness and health of its climate—"precisely in those localities where the assistance of European workmen would be required" (the implication here being that Europeans wilted in the elsewhere hot and humid climate of the tropics)—and the density and fitness of its local population, especially in the southern regions, where people were most needed "for the purpose of cutting a canal."[18] The canal would improve on that fitness, Moro hints throughout: besides a marvel of engineering, it would be a work of social engineering, which would transform an unskilled population into an effective labor force. Among the local peoples, Moro singles out the Zapotecs, whom he considers to be "superior to any other republic [of *indios*]: intelligent, industrious, docile, and joyous . . . as a result of mixing Zapotecs with the European race."[19] Zapotec soldiers had helped the surveyors with some of the measurements, and Moro could vouch for their "wonderful degree of intelligence . . . ; in a very short time, [they] became as proficient as could be wished."[20]

The other ethnic groups in the southern isthmus give Moro fewer grounds for optimism. He finds the Mixes, toward the sierras, to be "degraded and ignorant" and "notorious idolaters." Still, they are "given to agriculture" and cultivate plantains, maize, beans, and sugarcane, so, Moro hopes, they would become field hands in the foreign colonies established once the canal was under way.[21] As for the Huaves, Moro describes them as "well-formed and robust, but so grossly ignorant as to differ little from a savage tribe." One needs no further proof of their savagery than their "habitual . . . state of almost complete nudity." Unlike the Mixes, the Huaves do not practice agriculture, which, according to nineteenth-century social science, meant they had not yet mastered the most basic steps in the civilizing process. "Their industry," writes Moro, "consists of little else than fishing and even this they can only do by means of sweepnets; with the produce of their fisheries, they carry on extensive trade, although, not possessing proper vessels to venture into deep water, and being ignorant of the use of the oar, they can only frequent those spots which from their shallowness offer little dangers, such as marshes, and the margins of lakes and the sea."[22] One only wonders what role the Huaves would play in the human economy of the future canal, but there is a sense that better technology might improve their lot, for instance, by making it possible for them to carry on fishing on a larger scale.

When describing Tehuantepec's natural wealth, Moro's account has a lot in common with the wonder-eyed natural histories of the sixteenth and seventeenth centuries that bore testimony to the fabled riches of the New World. Like those earlier writers, Moro finds himself overwhelmed, at odds with language, as he tries to collect in words what he sees: "it is impossible to describe with effect the luxuriance of the vegetation," "the luxuriance and majestic appearance of the forests . . . are beyond description," "[the forests] exhibit a truly monstrous vegetation, of which ocular inspection alone can give an adequate idea," he exclaims again and again.[23] He resorts to hyperbole when nothing else would do, so references to natural "luxuriance," "exuberance," "monstrousness," and "astonishing beauty" punctuate the text, line after line, page after page. Among Tehuantepec's "treasures of incalculable value," Moro lists "iron of excellent quality" in the southern subsoil, and gypsum, petroleum, and coal in the north.[24] Fauna includes a "truly astonishing variety and quantity of fish, as well as a considerable number of tortoises of various kinds." The southern coasts boast "valuable tortoise shell, pearl, and coral in abundance."[25]

Moro's highest praise is for the region's plants, especially its precious woods and medicinal plants: "On approaching the sierra, the vegetation is more vigorous and the brazil-wood becomes very common. The *granadillo*, the mahogany tree, the *colpachi*, the bark of which is a well-known febrifuge, and the dragon-tree begin to make their appearance as well as many other shrubs unknown to me that yield resins and balsams, to which the natives ascribe the most marvellous virtues."[26] He concludes that the forests "abound with the finest and most precious woods, which without hyperbole, might supply the whole of Europe."[27] Fruit species, like vine, plantain, and *Theobroma cacao*, also "luxuriate here," as do more ordinary species of trees, like pines, suitable for construction; during colonial times, Moro reminds the reader, the Spanish government made extensive use of pine from this region to build masts.[28] Besides supporting an abundance of endemic plants, the soil and climate of the isthmus prove favorable to imported species, such as indigo and sugarcane, while "those tracks of land which are protected from the winds produce cotton of superior quality."[29]

The isthmus is ripe with the promise of wealth. But natural or demographic abundance is nothing if not put to "proper use." As Moro insists throughout, "the first impression produced in the minds of those who visit [these lands] is the immense advantages which a prudent speculator might derive from the proper use of their rich produce."[30] The way he sees it in 1842, however, the riches of the isthmus—its people, plants, animals, and subsoil—lie unrealized, "in a waste and unproductive inertness."[31] It is relevant to remember here that the lands granted to Garay y Garay on both sides of the projected canal are referred to as "wastelands," *terrenos baldíos* in Spanish. The possibility that these lands were neither "wasted" nor "barren" but were probably being worked collectively by local peoples made little or no sense to the government or to the survey commissioners, just as it seemed preposterous that cacao or mahogany trees were not being exploited massively or that antiquities would remain hidden in a cave. To become meaningful under the logic of use of the nineteenth-century state, lands, trees, minerals, people, and antiquities would have to be reconfigured and reclaimed economically, socially, politically, and scientifically as resources.[32] The survey of the isthmus is a first moment in this process of reconfiguration and, ultimately, an instrument of state making, allowing for the state to exercise action at a distance, by reaching—through infrastructure, experts, bureaucrats, and colonists—into an otherwise remote region, to explore, inventory, organize, manage, exploit, and speculate with Tehuantepec's riches.

Theodolites

To survey is to look a certain way, to examine, to record, with the purposes of constructing a plan, a map, or a description. A survey is both a modus operandi and the result of that modus operandi. The survey of the isthmus of Tehuantepec, Moro would have us persuaded, is achieved by looking through precision instruments and is the sum of the measurements carried out with those instruments. It is not arbitrary, therefore, that Moro begins his *Survey* with a list of the instruments, complete with the names of their makers, whose international reputation for reliability stands as a guarantee of the reliability of the survey itself. He writes:

> We arrived at Tehuantepec on the 28th of May and proceeded immediately to examine the state of the instruments which were to be used:
>
> 1. A theodolite beautifully constructed by Mr. W Cary of London, but with only one telescope, and of small size, its diameter being only 0,127 meters.
> 2. A sextant of Gambey of 0,20 in radius.
> 3. Two ditto of Chevalier, of 0,15 in ditto.
> 4. Another of Cary's, of 0,13 in ditto.
> 5. A good level with telescope, of unknown make.
> 6. Two barometers by Cary.
> 7. Two pocket chronometers, one by Roskel (no. 171) and the other by French.[33]

Many of the instruments had suffered some damage during the journey from Mexico City—the vertical axis of the theodolite had been bent; the barometers had filled up with air—and the commission had to spend some time fixing them.[34] To make matters worse, by the time the commissioners arrived in the isthmus, the rainy seasons had started, and cloudy skies made it difficult to perform the astronomical observations necessary to determine latitudes and longitudes. Even more troublesome was the "dense flickering vapour [which] hid from view the objects which served as guides, whilst the refractions, especially the lateral ones, produced the most strange illusions."[35]

As readers, we delve into the *Survey* and forget about the mirages and distortions on which it is built; the survey operates on the conceit that "fugitive landscapes"—overspilling nature and watery illusions—can be fixed as abstract numbers and as standardized annotations.[36] Geography is stabilized into homogeneous astronomical tables of longitudes and latitudes for specific sites; the rugged topography of the isthmus is rendered as a list of altitudes, obtained through triangulations and barometric measurements; villages appear as population statistics, which count both people and domestic animals (mules, horses, ox, and cattle); the diversity of soils and subsoils is organized as inventories of minerals and as differentiated costs of excavation. Like the hidden "idols" of Manopostiac, the dormant assets of the isthmus are transformed by the survey: translated into the standardized language of universal rationality, they are made visible and intelligible and are made available for new forms of use.

There is nothing exceptional about the fact that the Tehuantepec survey commission collected antiquities side by side with charts, maps, inventories, rock and wood samples, and plants. After all, throughout the nineteenth century, antiquities arrived at the museum in Mexico City in the wake of larger enterprises, whose explicit mission was not archaeological or antiquarian. Nor were such practices of collecting specific to Mexico; they were common for museum objects collected worldwide. Still, that someone like Moro took the time to collect, care for, and transport fragile ceramics, and then to write about them, when there were much more pressing issues to worry about—such as the welfare of his delicate instruments—should not be taken for granted. It speaks to a growing interest in Mexican antiquities in the mid-nineteenth century. At the same time, collecting antiquities and producing knowledge about the natural riches are embedded in the same logic of resource making that is at the heart of the survey of Tehuantepec.

Moro's anecdote about the removal of the Manopostiac "idols" makes a strong case for the advantages of building a canal, envisioned as it was to turn waste into profit. For Moro, taking away "idols" is a prelude to usurping "wastelands"; both forms of seizure are justified by his insistence that local populations, like the Huaves, do not know how to make right use of lands or antiquities and, in fact, are not even considered to be their rightful owners. Untilled lands, unexploited natural riches, and the worship of hidden "idols" are incriminating proofs: measuring the distance between the Huaves and the modern nation that was being forged, they function as an index of superstition, ignorance, irrationality, and savagery. Seizing their "idols" would be a way to improve on the Huaves' uncivilized condition, to make them a little bit more modern. By reverse logic, while the Huaves are made part of the nation's present, once placed in the museum in Mexico City, the Manopostiac "idols" become antiquities, meaning they are relegated to a remote past—even though it had been obvious that they were still in use when the commissioners had trekked up the island.

The Museo Nacional de México functions, like the canal, as a technology for imagining and shaping the nation. The canal promises the nation a profitable future. The museum endows it with a past. The logic of resource making—that is, the logic of colonial appropriation of lands, trees, and harvests, under the guise of moral and material improvement—also operates in the transformation of idols into antiquities. It is not common, nowadays, to imagine a museum display where natural history specimens share space with the idols of the ancient past. Such objects, one would object, belong to very different regimens of collecting, study, and display, indeed, to different museums. Still, let us suspend disbelief and bring them together again, for the sake of testing the limits of their ontological and epistemic separation and of teasing out the lessons they held for nineteenth-century collectors and that they might still hold for us today. Let us assemble then, in the same display case, the hollow ceramic statues from Manopostiac; wood samples, fruit, rocks, and photographs of the isthmus's local population; as well as the instruments and technologies—theodolites, maps, inventories, and charts, for instance—that operated their transformation of untapped riches into national resources. Together, they make manifest the ways in which collecting is intimately implicated in the construction of new forms of expertise, predicated, as Timothy Mitchell has suggested, on the elaboration and exploitation of difference and exclusion, and on the delineation of boundaries between nature and technology, between past and present, between objects and their value.[37] At stake is a binary rhetoric, of the kind used by the Tehuantepec commissioners and evoked again and again in the literature of modernization, which hinges on the distinction between the cultivated and the uncultivated, broadly defined: unexplored riches versus natural resources; inert "wastelands" versus agricultural fields; superstition versus reason; backward, isolated Indians versus scientific experts who speak the language of numbers and profits and socialize around common interests in antiquarianism and ethnology. Ultimately, these distinctions are held in place by an incontestable faith in Western science—as defined by its relation with material progress and by its use of scientific instruments—which justifies the rejection of all alternate forms of use and knowledge about things and becomes a precondition for possession.

Fishing Traps

So far, to imagine new possibilities for displaying the two Manopostiac antiquities, I have chosen objects that were associated, directly or indirectly, with their removal and with their arrival in the museum in 1843. All these objects are present, in some context or other, in the reports of the survey commission, and they uphold but also unwittingly question the premises and methods of nineteenth-century science. Other objects that belonged to the Huaves, however, did not make it into the museum or into the texts of the commission. It is possible they might not have been seen by the surveyors, maybe because they were nowhere in sight at the time the commission visited the isthmus or maybe because the surveyors did not know what to make of them. These objects might have contradicted the survey narrative or might have been of little use to it. Such is the case with the Huaves' fishing devices, about which Francisco de Burgoa, a seventeenth-century Dominican chronicler, wrote with great wonder and admiration:

> The Huaves have one thing worthy of extreme admiration for the ingenuity of its design: shrimp fishing, which takes place year after year in the village of San Francisco. . . . When with the rigor of autumn, with the northern winds, the cold season starts and waters begin to rise, and . . . the currents of this lagoon also swell, until they reach the village houses, here, in the sand, [the Huaves] assemble the structures for trapping these crawling water creatures. Using many straight reeds, each about a vara long, they build extensive fences, fixing them into the ground and leaving a large enough entrance, through which the shrimp come in, riding in with the water. After passing through the "door," the shrimp separate into many "streets," each of them with a variety of turns, like those of a snail, [built] with so much genius and art, that I confess, it took me a long time to understand how they work. Once inside, the shrimp, driven by the current, enter those canals, swimming while the current lasts; but when the water ebbs, draining out among the reeds, it leaves behind these little fishes, stuck in the sand, and

they cannot return because of the loops and windings through which they came in. This happens at night and when the sun goes up, it warms them up and kills them. This fishing lasts during the month of November.[38]

Burgoa's detailed description of the traps highlights the technical expertise of the Huaves. Where, by the mid-nineteenth century, the survey commissioners see lack and absence—precarious boats that lacked oars and inefficient fishing and product distribution—the seventeenth-century chronicler sees design, dexterity, genius, art. Burgoa goes on to explain that the Huaves had little choice but to perfect their fishing skills: as latecomers to a contested geography of conflicting imperial claims, which pitted the Mexicas against the Zapotecs, the Huaves carved out a place to live in the southernmost tip of the isthmus, where the salt waters of the Pacific meet the sweet waters of the lagoons. This did not mean, as one would imagine, that the Huaves were relegated to a backwater in any sense; they occupied a strategic site on the densely transited Mexica salt route.[39] It did mean, however, that they "lacked that principal form of sustenance, maize," writes Burgoa, so "necessity forced them to find it in the lagoons, which abound in fish."[40] Fish, then, became the Huaves' main food source, and they exchanged it for corn and other agricultural products; the *Relaciones geográficas* of the sixteenth century show them exporting fish and shrimp, and they continued to do so at the time of the 1842 isthmus survey, as documented by Moro.[41] Still, despite witnessing firsthand the Huaves' extensive trade in maritime products, it is their "miserable harvests," that is, the absence of agriculture, that the surveyors take as an index for placing the Huaves on the scale of civilization: based on this evidence, the commission decides they are a savage and backward tribe. This criterion for classification persisted into the twentieth century, when maize-based agriculture was used to define the confines of Mesoamerica. Only recently have scholars proposed less rigid definitions, to suggest the existence of "complementary economies," making room for a group such as the Huaves, who "developed a littoral culture, specialized in the use and appropriation of water resources," and carried on exchanges with surrounding agriculturalist cultures.[42]

For the Huaves, then, history meant a very particular kind of watery landscape and a specialized way of inhabiting it. The very name "Huave," of Zapotec origin, derogatory in meaning and translating as "putrefied by humidity," makes reference to a way of living with water.[43] Nowadays, the Huaves call themselves Ikoots, "people of the sea," which describes both geography and a way of being-in-the-world, dictated by the sea and by a people's need to adapt to and use advantageously what is a continuously changing landscape, where the confines between land and water, brackish and sweet, fluctuate wildly with the tide. Writing in the middle of the nineteenth century, the French traveler and antiquarian Charles Etienne Brasseur de Bourbourg described this confluence of elements in the following terms: "In various places, to the north of the superior lagoon, as around the salt flats of Juchitan Yavizendi, to the east of the lagoon of Waxlan-Diac, there is no shore properly speaking; the tide, pent up by storms, frequently floods the surrounding planes, where the wetlands are impregnated with salt and covered with aquatic plants, which grow between shrubs; the plain itself advances into the sea, at a slight inclination . . . and one cannot know for sure where the land begins or where the sea ends."[44]

Brasseur's description of the southern isthmus is a far cry from the cartographic certainties captured on the maps and in the reports of the survey commission only some years before Brasseur visited the region. Even after we account for broken instruments and the optical illusions that frustrated the surveyors, what do the contours on the map refer to? They seem arbitrary if not referenced in real time: the time of the morning or afternoon tides, as well as the time of seasonal cycles, which produce further fluctuation in the relation between land and water. As recent ethnographic work has shown, the Huaves divide the year into three seasons: a rainy season between May and September; a cool and dry season, dominated by the northern winds, from October to February; and a hot and dry season, dominated by the southern winds, between February and May. The beginning of each season is marked by special days on the liturgical calendar: the day of the virgin of Candelaria in February, Corpus Christi in May; in the case of the village of San Mateo, the dry and cool season is preceded by the celebrations of the patron saint, Mateo, on September 16. These festivities often combine elements from Catholic rites with beliefs, traditions, and practices built around natural elements—such as thunder, lightning, specific sites, and local fauna.[45]

During their stay in San Mateo, the commissioners sought to explain the presence of "idols" on the Manopostiac island as a failure or indifference on the part of the Catholic church to curtail the superstitious beliefs of the Huaves. Painting the image of a passive, downtrodden, and savage people, who contented themselves with very little, Moro went as far as to conjecture that the Huaves returned to the island each time they needed to pray for rain for their "miserable harvests." Harvesting, however, did not seem to have concerned the Huaves much. The arrival of the rains, on the other hand, did matter, for their fishing. Is it possible that the Manopostiac antiquities, broadly identified with rain and lightning, could have been at the center of rituals associated with the Huaves' most important produce, fish? Could we then imagine placing antiquities next to fishing implements, such as boats, or the traps described by Burgoa, or the elaborate nets described by anthropologists in the twentieth century? This juxtaposition contests nineteenth-century oppositions between superstition and science, man and nature, past and present, which have been reified in a museum that stakes itself on the separation between archaeology (the past), on the bottom floor, and ethnology (the present), on the top floor. Far from a signal of Huave passivity or isolation from the dynamism of modernity, as the surveyors saw the "idols" on the island, these objects were powerful tools in a people's struggle for adaptation to a very special landscape. Like their fishing traps and nets, they activated a specialized economy, which still depends on skilled knowledge of when the waters should come in and when they should recede and of the specific combinations of salt, sand, and rain that will ensure survival and prosperity.

Conclusions

This chapter is a proposal for bringing together a diversity of objects—antiquities, minerals, plants, scientific instruments, maps, and fishing implements, among others—in the same exhibit spaces. If at the beginning of the nineteenth century, it would not have been farfetched to imagine these objects together in the space of the same cabinet or museum, by the end of the nineteenth century, this became harder and harder to imagine. Nowadays, such an assemblage is not very probable, although some museums have explored the advantages of exhibiting objects by relating them to wider practices and discourses.[46] For the most part, though, antiquities, minerals, plants, theodolites, maps, and fishing traps are the objects of separate disciplines, stabilized by separate sets of norms, their meanings fixed by specific practices and methods. Hence, the question: what do we gain from imagining an exhibit that insists on placing these objects next to each other?

Ideally, this experiment would show that, while archaeology, anthropology, botany, astronomy, mineralogy, and geography have kept, for the larger part of the twentieth century, their objects apart from each other, the collection, study, and display of these objects are built on premises shared by all these different disciplines: the opposition between expert and lay knowledge, subject and object, man and nature, resource and waste, conservation and destruction, art and artifact. Many of these premises are still operational today in most museums, even as they are slowly beginning to erode.[47] Yet, exposing the fact that all museum objects have been constructed by contingent logics of use and meaning should not lead us to take a relativist stance and assume they have all been created or constructed equally. They have not. Some objects matter more than others, and by exploring how they came to be—by what combination of political, cultural, and ideological factors they were shaped—we understand why and how they matter. Why were the Huave "idols" placed in the museum in 1843 while their fishing traps were not? What use does a nineteenth-century museum have for either? What political, racial, and cultural asymmetries are exposed when maps and charts are presented side by side with oral testimony about the features and local uses of land? What separates the measuring and observation rituals of nineteenth-century surveyors, as represented by sextants and telescopes, on the one hand, from the detailed knowledge of tides and seasons by the Huaves, as incarnated in seasonal rituals and religious celebrations? How do theodolites and fishing traps question and reinforce each other's ontological stability as tools for knowing and using the world? As they interact, objects are made and unmade, and the history of the museum is the history of successive moments of creation and destruction of particular objects.

Finally, it might be relevant to ask ourselves if experiments in putting together disparate objects such as the one I attempted here have any bearing, not just on how we understand the past, but also on how we intervene in the present. In recent years, the lands of the Ikoots are again the object of intrusion by engineers and economists from the "outside" world. Tehuantepec, famed for its strong winds, is now being harnessed to produce renewable eolic energy. Some of the arguments in favor of installing wind turbines hearken back to the logic used to promote a canal there in the nineteenth century: resources are free for the taking, and it would be a waste not to do so; isolated communities will be more closely connected to the market economy. The project has been met with skepticism and distrust and has provoked serious rifts between villages that chose to install turbines (in Santa María del Mar) and those that did not (in San Mateo del Mar). Opponents have argued that eolic energy interferes with currents and energy flows in the ocean, affecting fishing, and, more pointedly, that the production of eolic energy depends on the individuation of communal land, perpetuating social and economic asymmetries.[48] As I write, in June 2020, tensions have escalated, resulting in the massacre of seventeen villagers in San Mateo del Mar.[49] What assemblage of objects could make visible the destruction underlying this new project of modernity and make it possible to hear contending arguments on the project? What role would the past play in this assemblage? Would such an assemblage find a place in the museum?

Notes

1. This was one of many projects that explored possibilities for connecting the Atlantic and the Pacific across the isthmus, the first of which dates to Hernán Cortés, who sought a "natural" passage in the Tehuantepec region. For a brief overview of these different projects both before and after independence, see Cayetano Moro, *Survey of the Isthmus of Tehuantepec* (London: Ackermann, 1844), 5–14. The isthmus was eventually connected by rail.
2. This toponymic is also spelled as Monopostiac or Monapostiac; I have chosen the spelling Manopostiac because this is the one used in the nineteenth-century literature that forms the basis of this chapter.
3. Anonymous, "Antigüedades zapotecas," *Museo Mexicano* 3 (1844): 135. All translations in this chapter are mine.
4. For different perspectives on the importance of images and descriptions as technologies for knowledge making, see Serge Lewillon, "Archaeological Illustrations: A New Development in 19th Century Science," *Antiquity* 76, no. 291 (2002): 223–34; and Stephanie Moser, "Making Expert Knowledge through the Image: Antiquarian Images in Early Modern Scientific Illustration," *Isis* 105, no. 1 (2014): 58–99.
5. The Huaves call themselves Ikoots in Huave language, or *mareños*, "people of the sea." Throughout most of this chapter, especially when recounting events in the nineteenth century, I employ the term Huave, which is the one used in the literatures I engage here.
6. Nicolás León, *Catálogo de la colección de antigüedades huavis del estado de Oaxaca existente en el Museo N. de México* (Mexico City: Imprenta del Museo Nacional, 1903), 52–54.
7. Enrique Juan Palacios, *En los confines de la selva lacandona* (Mexico City: Talleres Gráficos de la Nación, 1928), 11. Although the twentieth century has seen various ethnographic works on the Huaves, I have been unable to find

new substantial studies on the antiquities themselves. For a brief reference to the Manopostiac antiquities in a larger study of nineteenth-century archaeology, see Adam Sellen, "Giving Shape to the Past: Pre-Columbia in Nineteenth-Century Mexican Journals," *Boletim do Museu Paraense Emilio Goeldi: Ciências Humanas* 12, no. 2 (2017): 359–75.

8. Personal communication, February 2019. For further scholarship on the codex, with particular emphasis on the iconographic and mythological elements, see Ferdinand Anders, Maarten Jansen, and Gabina Aurora Pérez Jiménez, *Origen e historia de los reyes mixtecos: Libro explicativo del llamado Códice Vindobonensis* (Mexico: Fondo de Cultura Económica, 1992).
9. Bruno Latour, "From Realpolitik to Dingpolitik: An Introduction to Making Things Public," in *Making Things Public: Atmosphere of Democracy*, ed. Bruno Latour and Peter Weibel (Cambridge, Mass.: MIT Press, 2005), 6.
10. Moro, *Survey*, 15. The following description of the commissioners' activities in the southern isthmus are based on Moro's *Survey* unless otherwise noted.
11. León, *Catálogo*, 8.
12. Moro ventured the hypothesis that the Huaves were descendants of the Incas and had arrived in Tehuantepec in the course of their northern migration. The common consensus among archaeologists and ethnographers today is that the Huaves branched off from the Choles in Chiapas. See Alejandro Castaneira Yee Ben, *El Paso Mareño: La interacción huave en el Istmo Sur de Tehuantepec* (Crystal River, Fla.: FAMSI 2008), http://www.famsi.org/reports/06061es/06061esCastaneira.pdf; and Saúl Millán, *Huaves* (Mexico City: Comisión Nacional para el Desarrollo de los Pueblos Indígenas, 2003).
13. Cayetano Moro, "Noticia de las poblaciones de la parte austral del Istmo de Tehuantepec," *Ateneo Mexicano* 1 (1844): 367; Moro, *Survey*, 113. Moro gives no further details about the identity or provenance of the manuscript.
14. The bell sounds produced by the island's geology resonate with the importance of bells in Huave cultural traditions; see Elisa Ramírez Castañeda, *El fin de los montiocs* (Mexico City: INAH, 1987); and Alessandro Lupo, "El vientre que nutre y devora: Representaciones de la tierra en la cosmología de los Huaves del istmo de Tehuantepec," *Anuario: Centro de Estudios Superiores de México y Centroamérica* (2002): 357–79.
15. Ramón Almaraz, *Memoria acerca de los terrenos de Metlaltoyuca* (Mexico City: Imprenta Imperial, 1866), 19.
16. Moro, *Survey*, 155–188.
17. Moro, *Survey*, 81.
18. Moro, *Survey*, 99.
19. Moro, *Survey*, 94.
20. Moro, *Survey*, 19.
21. Moro, *Survey*, 94.
22. Moro, *Survey*, 92.
23. Moro, *Survey*, 102, 121.

24. Moro, *Survey*, 121.
25. Moro, *Survey*, 106.
26. Moro, *Survey*, 101.
27. Moro, *Survey*, 122.
28. Moro, *Survey*, 103.
29. Moro, *Survey*, 101.
30. Moro, *Survey*, 122.
31. Moro, *Survey*, 107.
32. Emma Elizabeth Ferry and Mandana Limbert, introduction to *Timely Assets: The Politics of Resources and Their Temporalities*, ed. Emma Elizabeth Ferry and Mandana Limbert (Santa Fe, N.Mex.: School for Advanced Research Press, 2008), 5.
33. A theodolite is an instrument used for surveying; it is fitted with a moveable telescope, which measures the horizontal and vertical angles between objects to position them in a plane. Moro, *Survey*, 15.
34. Moro, *Survey*, 15.
35. Moro, *Survey*, 19.
36. For cartography as a project of fixing "fugitive landscapes" on a space defined by the universal laws of science, see Raymond Craib, *Cartographic Mexico: A History of State Fixations and Fugitive Landscapes* (Durham, N.C.: Duke University Press, 2004).
37. For my description of expertise, I draw on Timothy Mitchell, *Rule of Experts: Egypt, Techno-Politics, Modernity* (Berkeley: University of California Press, 2002), 9.
38. Burgoa, cited by León, *Catálogo*, 8–9.
39. Millán, *Huaves*, 17.
40. Burgoa, cited by León, *Catálogo*, 8. Castaneira Yee Ben, *El Paso Mareño*, 43, reinforces Burgoa's observation by pointing out that the Huaves have an ample vocabulary to refer to maritime species but few words to classify corn.
41. Millán, *Huaves*, 17.
42. Castaneira Yee Ben, *El paso mareño*, 43.
43. León, *Catálogo*, 3.
44. Charles Etienne Brasseur de Bourbourg, "Coup d'oeil sur la nation et la langue des wabi," *Revue Orientale et Américaine* 5 (1861): 270.
45. See Alessandro Lupo, "La etnoastronomía de los huaves de San Mateo del Mar," in *Arqueoastronomía y etnoastronomía en Mesoamérica*, ed. Johanna Broda, Stanislaw Iwaniszweski, and Lucrecia Maupomé (Mexico City: UNAM, 1991), 219–34. See also Ramírez Castañeda, *El fin de los montiocs*, who has recorded that the Huaves also refer to themselves as "montioc," meaning "thunder" (8).
46. Such was the case with the recent exhibit *Chimalli* at the Museo Nacional de Historia in Chapultepec Park. For more on relational museums, see Chris Gosden, Frances Larson, and Alison Petch, *Knowing Things: Exploring the Collections at the Pitt Rivers Museum* (Oxford: Oxford University Press, 2008).

47. A recent temporary exhibit on the Golfo, in the Museo Nacional de Antropología, brings together objects from the permanent collection with archaeological objects in the custody of local populations, among them the famous Cascajal Block, displaying the oldest writing in Mesoamerica. The exhibit closed in May 2019, and the objects were returned to their custodians.
48. Alexander Dunlap, "The 'Solution' Is Now the 'Problem': Wind, Energy, Colonisation and the 'Genocide-Ecocide Nexus' in the Isthmus of Tehuantepec, Oaxaca," *International Journal of Human Rights* 22, no. 4 (2017): 550–73, http://dx.doi.org/10.1080/13642987.2017.1397633.
49. Luis Hernández Navarro, "La massacre de San Mateo del Mar," *La Jornada*, June 30, 2020, https://www.jornada.com.mx/2020/06/30/opinion/019a1pol.

\\ 9

Conjuring Violence Away with Culture

The Purépecha National Emblem in the Museo Nacional de Antropología

MARIO RUFER

> *From the Latin* museum, *a place dedicated to the muses. . . . Enclave where a timeless (and lifeless) history is kept: one goes there in order to lose oneself, or rather to make absence live on.*
>
> —María Negroni, *Pequeño mundo ilustrado*

One of the most difficult things to articulate about a museum, especially an ethnographic museum, is its "selection criteria."[1] Who decides when to exhibit an object that has been in storage for decades, and why? Why reactivate it for the visitor's gaze? Why make it part of a public syntax, framed by a label? Why light it in a particular way? In the specific case of the ethnographic halls of Mexico's Museo Nacional de Antropología, how do objects on display interrelate? How are we to study their relationships? Barbara Kirshenblatt-Gimblett posited a distinction between objects "in situ" versus "in context," clarifying the difference between an object's interconnections and the object *as* connection (i.e., the relationships that contextualize an object on display vis-à-vis the original milieu from which it was appropriated versus the object as a trigger of other connections, rearranged within a museum's visual regime).[2] Of course, the very notion of "context" is problematic in that it refers to an original that is always subject to erasure because of its own history. Where does a context end? What are its boundaries?

This chapter examines an object known as the Purépecha National Emblem, on display in the Sala Purépecha as part of the ethnography collection at the

Museo Nacional de Antropología. I do not consider the piece itself, that is, its technical virtues, its figural peculiarity, or its formal structure. Dating from 1829, this replica of what was then the Mexican national coat of arms was reclassified as a "featherwork handicraft" and is now displayed alongside necklaces, masks, and beads. A photograph of a basket maker is displayed beside it. What does this composition tell us about the syntax of a nation? What are the component parts of this "piece?" What anchors its meaning (e.g., the museum label), and what is foreclosed from the text, appearing only as an unsettling silence?[3]

Here I explore what displaying an object like this "connects" it to, in syntagmatic and paradigmatic terms. Syntagmatic relations enable a composition of signs to be read as a chain with a specific spatial and chronological order. (In a museum, this is the symbolic universe of its syntax: an object's components, the fragments that surround it, the elements that constitute the gallery's larger unity.) Paradigmatic, or "associative," connections, according to Saussure, are always implicit in the understanding of a sign and rarely thematized. They are defined not by the linear structure in which a sign is immersed (nearby objects, the label, the components of its signifier), but rather *by everything that the sign is not, but could be: that is, the familiarities that set it apart* but do not "belong" in that chronotope.[4] Analyses of museums privilege syntagmatic readings that assure meaning through structures that ensure the closure of the signified (gallery components, object components, labels, date of manufacture), rather than through what opens it up (to pursue less linear relationships, transversal connections, foreclosures, expulsions, or the uncanny). The sequential structure of syntagms channels our reading and *forces* meaning on us as if we were reading a sentence: one word after another "yields" the result. Paradigms formulate possible connections, the *room for alternatives* that haunts directional meaning but nevertheless remains closed off.

In attempting to read along both axes, I draw out what presenting the crest as a "picture" suggests: for example, how praising featherwork as a technique obturates a technics of war; or how insisting on an ethnographic object's link to the nation might be a way to avoid mentioning the Purépechas' legacy of resisting military, territorial, and cultural conquests, from the Mexica empire down to present-day local governments. The paradox at the heart of the Museo Nacional de Antropología is that its archaeological galleries mark the milestones of military action, violence, and sovereign power, while its ethnography galleries silence or obliterate them.[5] Hence, twisting linguistic categories somewhat, I argue that a central feature of the administration of culture in postcolonial contexts involves controlling the paradigmatic associations that an object or a sign makes possible, and closing off the latent meanings it disperses.

The central aim of this chapter is to analyze the tense relationship between culture and violence from the standpoint of a single ethnographic object. As Néstor García Canclini presciently observed, the "upper galleries" at the Museo Nacional de Antropología portray the present day of the nation's others, understood exclusively as the negation of *mestizaje*. This space is therefore reserved entirely for indigenous peoples, as if it were "obvious" that there is no need for an ethnographic museum that would recognize the contributions of black, Jewish, Chinese people, and so forth to the diversity of the nation.[6] With that in mind, what happens to the violence *of* those others, or *with* them? Can (indigenous) culture only be conceived as harmless, as unblemished beauty, as the attribute of an *already pacified* world? Is that what is on display at the museum? A living testament to extensive territorial pacification? The archaeology galleries at the Museo Nacional de Antropología focus on war, conquest, and territorial annexation, underwriting a grounding narrative that culminates in "the" central battle: the Spanish Conquest. But a radical change occurs when one heads upstairs to the ethnographic galleries. It is not just a question of trading the glory of stone for the ephemerality of textiles, necklaces, ceramics, ears of maize, mannequins and feathers. Rather, it has the potency of an interrupted history, a call to sovereignty that has somehow been closed off.

Syntagmatic Allegory: Object, Expressive Dimension and Displacement

I first took an interest in the featherwork emblem while visiting the Sala Purépecha at the Museo Nacional de Antropología with my students in 2015, precisely because of the disruption it introduced.[7] My attention was not drawn to its colors, nor its feathers, nor its differences from the more recent Mexican national coat of arms created in 1968; indeed, at the time I was unaware of such differences. I was also unaware of the prominence of pre-Hispanic featherwork as diplomatic gifts and tributes exacted after wars. I learned all that later through research. What first caught my attention were two specific points. First, whereas what I "saw" was the Mexican national coat of arms surrounded by other almost unrecognizable items, the label mentioned a "Purépecha featherwork," without any further information. At no point did it mention the words "emblem" or "coat of arms" (figure 9.1). Second, I was captivated by something I could not define, but which my training in studying museums, galleries, and artworks enabled me to perceive as a failure in syntax. "This doesn't belong here," I thought, given that the museum is so perfectly split between archaeology and ethnography, and thus expels history from its purview.

A few meters away from the Museo Nacional de Antropología, also in Chapultepec Park—a distance that highlights the short respite demanded by nature before one continues observing—the much less grandiose and less frequently visited Museo Nacional de Historia displays the remains of what is printed in time: the sequence of heroic national deeds, along with that which is demanded by the nature of such a discourse: war trophies, weapons, booty, dates, and illustrious names. All of this appears in the featherwork emblem at Museo Nacional de Antropología too. In the central oval, an eagle atop a prickly pear cactus devours the serpent; below appear the drums, quiver, cutlass, caiman, and cannon. Eight spoils of war jut out from the oval. My first thought was, therefore, "The crest *belongs* in the Museo Nacional de Historia, not here." Placed as it was in a poorly lit part of the gallery next to an enormous panel bearing the legend "Handicrafts" and a photograph of a Purépecha man sitting on a dirt floor, apparently weaving a basket, the object drew my attention even more.

But the tiny label for the piece states the following:

> FEATHERWORK
> This is an example of a pre-Hispanic handicraft that has all but disappeared. Lately, it has found refuge in urban schools. Here *we see a picture* made with feathers from hummingbirds, cardinals, geese and parrots. A craftsman named Rodríguez *seems* to have made it in 1824 to commemorate the establishment of the General Congress, a precursor to the Congress of the Union. [emphasis mine]

Where I was seeing a baroque reworking of the Mexican national coat of arms, the label spoke of a "picture," a "feather handicraft," "hummingbirds," that is, a Purépecha handicraft. The museum's website reproduces

Figure 9.1 Purépecha National Emblem, Museo Nacional de Antropología. Archivo Digital de las Colecciones del Museo Nacional de Antropología. INAH-CANON. Reproduction authorized by the Instituto Nacional de Antropología e Historia.

the emblem in its photo gallery. I consulted it on my cellphone while I was still in the gallery, curious about the piece and its relationship to the other components of the hall. The online version reads as follows:

> This piece was made using a pre-Hispanic featherwork technique, involving carefully selecting and trimming feathers. . . . It has four sections symbolizing the sky and mountains of the fatherland, the standards carried into battle during the War of Independence, weapons and military paraphernalia. . . . The central motif is the Mexican national coat of arms, surrounded by flags and items representing Chichimec warriors and the insurgent army, who joined forces to fight the War of Independence. *It was created for the First Congress of the Union.*[8]

The difference between the two statements seems to involve exactly the ambivalence that I had noticed: pre-Hispanic handicraft, or symbol of national culture? Or both? And why put this object in the Purépecha wing of the ethnographic galleries when its individual authorship is known, when (as the label notes) the culture of origin is "Mestizo" and has little to do with any kind of "traditional" Purépecha uses for featherwork, when it was expressly purchased by the Congress after a specific battle, and when its technique of manufacture was already in disuse at the time it was made? Why the trivial detail about its having "probably" been made in Pátzcuaro? Why represent a link between a pre-Hispanic community and the nascent republic through the conjunction of featherwork and the national allegory?

In the ethnography section of the museum's webpage, this object was one of very few that (prior to a recent update) referred to an event. That is, it was marked by a precise position in a temporal sequence, which is unusual in the ethnography galleries at the Museo Nacional de Antropología, since they tend to use either the ethnographic present when describing the artifacts therein (e.g., "traditional culture," "textile for domestic use") or imperfect verb forms (e.g., "these toys used to be made," "these activities used to be done").[9] The website, by contrast, referred to the formation of the modern Mexican state, the War of Independence, and the symbolic universe of the nation. Dated to 1829—rather than 1824, as the label in the gallery has it, the featherwork emblem thus is reclaimed as an early version of the national coat of arms.

It is possible to track the museum's acquisition of the piece and the latter's likely date of origin in the *Anales del Museo Nacional*. Under what circumstances did it come to the museum? The first clue appears in the 1882 catalog of the Museo Nacional's historical and archaeological collections, compiled by Gumesindo Mendoza and Jesús Sánchez. At the time, pre-Hispanic sculptures were either on the patio of the former museum building or in the "Historical museum" section within, which is where the emblem was located.[10] The object appears as number 8 in the catalog, listed as "Weapons of the Mexican Republic Surrounded by Trophies," in "imitation" of "ancient Indian mosaics."[11]

Something stands out in the "historical" section of the cataloged galleries: its militaristic dimension. There were standards, coats of arms, and weapons. Moreover, in this first catalog entry for the emblem, it is not a "pre-Hispanic handicraft," as it is now classified. Instead, we have "weapons of the Republic . . . made from feathers in *imitation*" of an "ancient" technique, which even then was already regarded as having practically disappeared and, therefore, in need of protection by the museum and the nascent nation.[12]

The Oaxacan historian Carlos María de Bustamante offers an even earlier clue about the emblem, referring to the endangered art of featherwork in his annotations to an 1829 edition of Sahagún's *Historia general de las cosas de la Nueva España*. In addition to confirming that "all these trades have gone extinct" (referring to featherwork), Bustamante mentions that on October 4 of that year, a Mexican coat of arms (*escudo*) made of feathers was presented on the balcony of the National Palace in Mexico City for the General Congress after the defeat of the royalist Isidro Barradas by Antonio López de Santa Anna and Manuel Mier y Terán in what is known as the Victory of Tampico on September 11, 1829.[13] That battle foiled yet another attempt by the Spanish crown to recover Mexico after the latter had declared its independence in 1821. One of the few present-day scholars of the emblem points out that by reading Bustamante's study, "one can claim that the making of the emblem was circumscribed by a propagandistic motive on behalf of the new republic."[14]

But for some reason, in subsequent reshufflings of the public collections, this "coat of arms" came to be called an "emblem," and ultimately ended up becoming a "featherwork handicraft." In the process, it was stripped of its historical connotations and made to represent a "picture" about a craft technique that had famously flourished in Pátzcuaro during the pre-Hispanic era but has since almost disappeared.[15] What apparently "spared" the featherwork emblem from being relegated to storage was the 2011 exhibition *El vuelo de las imágenes: Arte plumario en México y Europa*, held jointly at

Figure 9.2 Sala Purépecha, Museo Nacional de Antropología. Photograph by the author. Reproduction authorized by the Instituto Nacional de Antropología e Historia.

the Museo Nacional de Arte and the Museo Nacional de Antropología. As a result of this show, featherwork pieces were repositioned in some of the ethnography halls (figure 9.2).[16]

Here some clarifications of what I am calling the "syntagmatic axis" are in order. What universe was in dialogue with this emblem/coat of arms/imitation featherwork when it was created? Indeed, it is the only known exemplar of featherwork that refers directly to the attributes of republican symbolism. We could say that it encapsulates a pre-Hispanic *technique* that displaces its original universe of meaning to pay tribute to a *representation* of the modern nation.[17] To what, exactly, does that technique pay tribute?

The emblem's most obvious relationships are to other pieces in the same style, of which there are several, albeit not in featherwork and much less identified as ethnographic objects.[18] If we turn first to a group of similar objects recently displayed together in the exhibit *El Escudo Nacional: Flora, fauna y biodiversidad* as "antecedents of the Mexican national coat of arms," and second to numismatics, something becomes quite clear: they all deal with an allegorical universe that thematizes military victory not only over the Spanish empire, but also over a civilizing order, or rather over a specific form of "America."

Although they are sometimes taken as "exceptional items," the quiver, caiman, and arrows in the emblem derive from typical visual allegories for America starting in the mid-sixteenth century.[19] In Cesare Ripa's classic *Iconologia* (1593), for example, America is represented as a nude dark-skinned woman with messy hair, carrying a bow, arrow, and quiver. A caiman is beside her.

> The fourth and last part of the world [America] is represented almost naked, of a tawny complexion, and a fierce aspect; she has her head and other parts of the body [*le parti vergognose*] adorned with various colored feathers, according to the custom of the country. In her left hand, she holds a bow, and in the right an arrow, with a quiver full of arrows behind her. . . . The lizard which abounds in that country is of such an enormous size, and of such fierceness, that it not only devours other animals, but frequently attacks the inhabitants. One foot rests on a human head with an arrow through it, showing clearly how the inhabitants, prone to barbarism, are generally accustomed to feeding on human flesh, eating those they have defeated in war.[20]

Arrows, quiver, caiman: aside from the fierce tawny-skinned woman who occupied the center of the iconography and is replaced in this case by the oval with the eagle devouring the serpent atop a prickly pear cactus, these items are all the victorious new nation's war trophies. At the same time, the depiction of America as an Indian woman has disappeared from the universe of representations, to be replaced by items more or less in line with the French revolutionary tradition. (The Phrygian cap in the emblem alludes to that tradition.)[21]

One feature of the emblem in the Sala Purépecha puts it in an iconographic family that predates the national coat of arms, that is, the genre of the coat of arms and war trophies. The laying down of arms, the defeat of barbarian forces, the victory cap, and the replacement of the female figure of indomitable America with a national symbolism of a pre-Hispanic inflection—equally allegorical of conquest—are obvious.

It is also worth inquiring into the apparent anxiety motivating a particular erasure in the museum (as well as outside it, as we shall see): namely, the disappearance of the martial context from the universe of meaning on display, replaced by a syntax that interweaves featherwork, handicraft, and traditional skills with a platform whose function is technique rather than its expressive dimension. This inevitably stabilizes an inherited *techne* that, as an ethnic attribute, expresses consent to belonging to a larger whole, that is, the nation.

For the Centennial of the Mexican Constitution in March–May 2017, the Museo Nacional de Antropología held a show titled *El Escudo Nacional: Flora, fauna y biodiversidad,* organized by the Secretaría del Medio Ambiente y Recursos Naturales (Semarnat) and the Instituto Nacional de Antropología e Historia. The Purépecha featherwork emblem was not included. Interestingly, the exhibit's curatorial statement had two main thrusts: the national coat of arms as an expressive synthesis of the national territory's rich biodiversity and as an allegory devoid of military referents.

A pause is in order here. The exhibition website rather oxymoronically notes that explaining the origin of the national coat of arms requires understanding that

> the animal represented most frequently in Mexica sculpture is the rattlesnake, which had several symbolic connotations. . . . Its aggressiveness and its frightful venom made the reptile quite powerful in Mexica imaginaries. In some of Mexico/Tenochtitlán's foundation stories, the eagle is represented with a snake in its claw, symbolizing the suppression of an enemy or the conquest of a land.

But the same site goes on to say that

> the Mexican national coat of arms has the world's most biodiverse iconography. . . . None of its attributes conveys a sense of militarism; *on the contrary,* the symbolism behind each element evokes the legacy of our past.[22]

How would a sense of militarism be *contrary* to the legacy of the past? Why point out the military universe of conquest only to turn around and deny it expressly? In each instance, the antagonistic context is sugarcoated and displaced by the discourses of the era: the republic in the Phrygian cap, the importance of natural bounty and biodiversity for the 2017 exhibition. The day the show opened, Rafael Pacchiano, then head of the Semarnat, stated that the Mexican crest "is undoubtedly the most biologically diverse, . . . and it is quite interesting that, unlike other countries, our coat of arms lacks any arms at all." He went on to assert that analyzing the national coat of arms helps us understand "how nature determines the way we understand ourselves as a nation."[23]

Why this back and forth between nature and war, between art and trophies? If, as the entire tradition of national culture claims, the allegory of the eagle devouring the serpent stems from the Mexica tradition and was repurposed for the nation, would the "evolution" of heraldry indicate that Our Lady of Guadalupe is the sign that mediates between the pre-Hispanic tradition and national heraldry? Does that same Catholic mediation strip away the narrative of war in order to pacify the coat of arms? To ground (or uproot) those symbols and repurpose them as the unique expression of magical nature, of the land's generosity, now "scientifically proven" to have the highest biodiversity? There is an anxiousness behind hiding the language of war and replacing it with the repertoire of science and nature as attributes of modernity, and of the responsibilities of conservation.

It is true that, since the mid-nineteenth century, the national coat of arms has not featured any weaponry among its icons. But the same is true for most of the Americas.[24] Why, then, this anxiety to *pacify* an object that is by definition the symbolic expression of triumph in war? Why *return it* to nature and present the latter as a determining blueprint for the nation, in lieu of conquests, political maps, wars won by spilling blood?

Paradigmatic Allegory: Forbidden Connections

"Paradigmatic allegory" refers to connections that arise when the object in question is called on to signify based not on its "contextual" attributes, but rather on what is foreclosed or under erasure because of its intrasyntagmatic relations: that is, that which could have been connected to the object but is hidden by the system of statements, or that which is made to fail as statement (and signifier) in the museum.

If the first question that occurred to me regarding the emblem was what a national coat of arms was doing in the ethnography hall (especially in light of its having been stripped of the characteristics that give it an origin and classify it as a "handicraft"), the second question that struck me involved something that bothered me throughout the ethnography galleries: the absence of any relationship between violence and culture. Strolling through these galleries discloses practically no references to violence, no military might, no aggressive energy, no defensive attribute whatsoever that might be categorized as an ethnographic part of "indigenous culture" worthy of being exhibited.[25]

The emblem here plays a key role. To reiterate what went unsaid on the label in the gallery but appeared in the museum's online photo archive: "The central motif is the Mexican national coat of arms, surrounded by flags and items representing Chichimec warriors and the insurgent army, who joined forces to fight the War of Independence." The narrative here is about how weaving techniques condense the nation's acquisition of a tactics of war now shared by the Purépechas and the army. The object was thus inscribed explicitly in the time inaugurated by national disruption, and this is the moment when pristine culture enters time: the political time that seals all those peoples' irrevocable (and obedient) pact with the nation-state.

Pursuing this further takes us to the Museo del Ejército y de la Fuerza Aérea, which President Felipe Calderón created under the Secretaría de Defensa in 2010 as part of the celebrations of the Bicentennial of Independence—and to help legitimate his war on drug trafficking. The museum features an interactive hologram through which the military "might" of the national heroes—in the independence and revolutionary eras—becomes a "mnemonic inheritance" from Mexica warriors. In the hologram (specifically its three-dimensional optical effect, which is akin to nineteenth-century representations of phantasmagoric and spectral visions), Cuauhtémoc, the last *tlatoani* of México-Tenochtitlán, fights to organize the army and defend his people's integrity.

In the Museo Nacional de Antropología's ethnography galleries, by contrast, Indian villages are characterized by a harmless and almost always bucolic beauty. Even in the ethnographic gallery dedicated to the Maya highlands, where something obviously "had to be said" about the 1994 Zapatista uprising, a display case includes the following text: "These groups have been intervening in politics more noticeably, one of their mottos being to *defend our ethnic identity*" (emphasis mine).

While the Fourth Declaration of the Selva Lacandona (1996) made a drastic appeal to a "legitimation of ancestral forms and memories of resistance" and a "defense of the land's natural resources" (ethnicity appearing nowhere in the text), the Museo Nacional de Antropología still explains that there was "a long struggle over territory" that began among indigenous factions in the fifteenth century, *before* the conquest, which was then expanded with colonization and persists even today.[26] The museum goes on to explain that "while some [Maya] highlanders opt for negotiation, others for litigation, still others choose to take up arms, as was the case with the highlanders from La Cañada in 1994." Two lines suffice to conjure away the historical problem of Zapatismo. In turn, it is no minor point that Zapatista women are not actually portrayed but rather mimicked in a small handicraft that was—and still is—made for tourists, her balaclava barely visible beneath her straw hat.[27]

As for Purépecha culture and "its" gallery which features the emblem, the museum highlights "Tarascan [*sic*]" resistance first to the Mexica conquest and then to the Spanish.[28] The idea of this area as a "rebel" space appears in the museum as part of a past that *endowed a culture with an identity*. In the archaeological gallery dedicated to "Western peoples," we learn that "the Tarascans . . . came to Lake Pátzcuaro and mixed with the existing inhabitants. . . . The Tarascans distinguished themselves as a warrior people. They were the only people to oppose the Mexicas' territorial expansion." The process of conquering them is described as among the bloodiest and most difficult, thanks to the area's "diversity" of peoples: "It fell to the Franciscan and Augustinian friars to evangelize the area. They recognized the Indians' mastery in every trade and assigned them Christian themes according to their artisanal specialties [and] so the creative singularity of each place endures today."

At the entrance of the Sala Purépecha, where the featherwork emblem is found, a wall text specifies that "Purépecha people identify with a shared history going back to the Tarascans." After the conquest, it continues, "the Tarascans developed into and became Purépechas." It is unclear what this transformation entailed, but it seems to have involved the specific formation of basket weavers, craftspeople, and their "creative singularity."

The label "Tarascan" has derogatory connotations for the inhabitants of the Purépecha territory and is rarely used by academic anthropologists.[29] This terminological debate is entirely absent from the museum. Tarascans *transformed* into Purépechas. And after being conquered, the Purépechas continued governing themselves through "custom and belief," with the "infiltration of Spaniards and blacks" in recent centuries. The labels also refer to the loss of lands during the national period, to the "death of community," and to the fragmentation of the Purépechas into distinct groups in the period between Independence and agrarian reform.

A display case in the same gallery contains another object whose paradigmatic connections to the emblem caught my attention: the Purépecha

Figure 9.3 Purépecha flag, "Old Tradition, New Symbols." Sala Purépecha, Museo Nacional de Antropología. Photograph by the author. Reproduction authorized by the Instituto Nacional de Antropología e Historia.

flag. Off to one side and spatially unrelated to the emblem, displayed alongside masks, necklaces, and stories, there is a flag bearing the words Juchari Uinapikua, "Our Might" (figure 9.3).

The label reads: "The Purépecha flag and New Year are two symbols born as different ethnic symbols established to represent the four regions [of Purépecha territory]. . . . The fist symbolizes the Purépechas' might."[30] Beneath the flag, a text entitled "Old Tradition, New Symbols" describes the changes in the "original culture," explaining that they can be understood as products of "contact" with Mexican and international society at large. "The rise of ethnic movements around the world has helped the Purépechas' struggle for cultural recognition and for their rights to exercise it. This struggle is exemplified by a rich intellectual and artistic creativity. . . . The culture's vigor suggests that it will endure for at least several more generations."

The ambiguous notion of "ethnic movements" aside, what jumps out here is the insistence on an original matrix—a "clean text," as the Argentine poet Roberto Juarroz might put it—that has been contaminated and is now in danger, despite its legitimacy.[31] I want to emphasize that this connection—the local flag on display being tied to the "rise" of ethnic movements—supposedly focused on a demand to juridicize culture: the right to exercise it, once more corralling the signifier "culture" into the niche that the postcolonial production of identities and alterities opened as a governmental practice.[32]

It does not take detailed or exhaustive research to learn that the motive behind the creation of the Purépecha flag was not a harmless struggle for the right to culture and, further, that those "ethnic movements" primarily demand another temporality in their genealogical narrative. According to Gerardo Hernández, who studied the defeat of the *comunero* movement in Michoacán in the 1970s, the Purépecha flag was created to commemorate the conflict at Santa Fé de la Laguna in November 1979, and to advance collective actions in its aftermath. The confrontation between Purépecha *comuneros* and ranchers from the municipality of Quiroga ended with the imprisonment of twenty *comunero* leaders (including Elpidio Domínguez, who became a leader during the 1980s) and the assassination of two of them.[33]

The Comunidad Purépecha website reinforces this relationship:

> For over 450 years, the P'URHÉPECHA people have resisted invasion, exploitation, dispossession and a myriad other physical aggressions to their population, lands, forests and culture. . . . Now is the time for the Purépecha people to wake from their long slumber and discover the instruments to unite and identify with other *comuneros, jornaleros, resineros* . . . against the new forms of domination and exploitation that constantly aggrieve our communities and our entire culture in general. In homage to all those who have fallen in defense of our P'urhépecha tradition and the integrity of our communal lands . . . today our might is reborn with the ceremonial raising of our P'urhépecha flag, which now symbolizes our peoples' unity.[34]

The ceremonial raising of the Purépecha flag explains, "As the slogan for our coat of arms, we have taken the phrase that was born in the organized struggle of Santa Fe de la Laguna—JUCHARI UINAPEKUA! (Our might!)—words that encompass the entire *cultural inheritance of an undefeated people*." And the instructions for using the flag explicitly state: "Neither the colors nor the P'urhépecha flag itself may be used by any government office (official use) or any government functionary in patriotic celebrations, in their offices, or on their websites."

The flag's creation is described in the documentary *Juchari Uinhápekua! Crónica de una lucha campesina en defensa de las tierras comunales*, directed by Javier Telles in 1980 and produced at the Universidad Autónoma de Chapingo.[35] The film opens with a voiceover: "Now, as in 1910, our main demand is for land."

It is not out of place to point out that the Purépecha National Emblem "returned" to its gallery after the exhibition on pre-Hispanic feather mosaics at the same time that the Purépecha municipality of Cherán saw its greatest conflict, garnering the attention of the media, setting off an important academic debate, and revitalizing local use of the Purépecha flag as an expression of autonomy and access to communal lands.[36]

None of this information is difficult to find. The Spanish-language *Wikipedia* page, for example, cites documents and newspaper sources affirming that the creation of the Purépecha flag was tied to indigenous *comuneros'* struggle against repeated dispossessions of communal goods. Why insist on the "right to exercise culture," formulas of ancestry, reaffirmation of traditions—and above all, why do so by *exhibiting* the object in question?

The museum could well reserve the right to include it. And it does so. It would be convenient to insist that the national narrative always seeks to mend the equivocal relationship between culture and history. According to modern narratives about tradition, the latter is not necessarily characterized by its rejection or its antagonistic difference, but rather its quality as an *interchangeable sign*.[37] Tradition cannot occupy the place of the event nor of process.[38] It is a stamp. Tradition functions as a wild card within the syntagm—all the related components of a single ordering principle that is never stated (the Purépecha tradition)—without there being one sole possibility for linking them. One could split up all the elements of the Purépecha hall of the ethnography galleries and the result would be the same. Tradition commands and admits no order, precisely because what it does not admit a priori is temporality (a key attribute of the syntagm)—unless that tradition is interrupted by the very site of enunciation that makes it possible: that is, the nation-state.

The Purépecha National Emblem and the Purépecha flag, juxtaposed in the museum, play a Janus-faced role. The emblem, placed as it is next to basketry, forces any trained eye to identify the "role" of the nation, history, and politics in marking the conquest of a rebel people. (We should not forget that in this gallery, paying tribute to the eagle and serpent in the Purépecha featherwork after the battle of Tampico implies subjugating its Purépecha qualities to two juxtaposed symbolic universes, the Mexica empire and the national republic.) On the other hand, including the flag seals the state as hospitable with perennially reedited signs of tradition and the right to one's own culture.

But the other discourse, albeit mediated by the pedagogy of the syntagm, through the inescapable propaganda of the postrevolutionary state and its history, demands an incision. It sustains the notion of a *continuous violence* and at the same time imitates the discourses inherited by governmentality about culture, tradition, and ancestry, twisting them to situate them in time: "as in 1910, we are fighting for land." If the tradition function *exhibits* on the same plane as the familiar, the history function *connects* what seems to have been outside the plane of the signifiable. And that connection narrates a continuous war of conquest, an intermittent violence, a constant loss (of economic resources, lives, presence, power).

We are dealing with a play of symbols that not only "endow with identity," but that, to do so, have to seal the nation-state aporia between the modern violence that founds the law and that which conserves it.[39] A key characteristic of postcolonial governmentality is that it upholds that aporia by means of cultural discourse, with an aesthetics "by zombification," as Achille Mbembe might put it: a form from which state agency subtracts the power of an "other cultural text" (indigenous, African, etc.) to relocate it, uplift it, and at the same time domesticate it.[40] The museum indicates that the Purépecha flag is there because it symbolizes the exercise of the *right* to culture. In doing so, it emphasizes the pacification of the attribute of otherness in a juridical key: beauty, relic, display case. The tension between heritage, culture, and nation thus becomes a central question of sovereignty and domination.[41]

Closing Thoughts

Why does the museum uphold such a discomfort with the *contemporary violence of others*? Why does it need to get rid of it, make it harmless, turn it into a "picture" in a glass cabinet? Why cause the other to appear pacified on the patrimonial surface of the display case? Something fundamental is at play here: if there is, in the memory of indigenous peoples, a tactical, martial, defensive might capable of sustaining some notion of jurisdiction, it has to do with being subtracted by the sovereign will of the nation-state—something stated solely in the montage of the Museo del Ejército y la Fuerza Aérea. There it does indeed fit as an epic that habilitates, in the manner of a blessing and a destiny, the might of the regular armies.

In this way, culture is differentiated from history not just in the relationship between stasis and change, but also in the sense that, upon being clipped out of history and enunciated by these inclusive, liberal narratives, culture is established as a pacified stamp. "Culture" and "tradition" function as national lexemic fixations because they have been stripped of their capacity to interpellate, to disobey, to contradict. In the ethnography halls at the Museo Nacional de Antropología, the Indian appears no longer as heraldry in stone, but rather as an endangered relic, fragile and almost always innocent. Nothing could be more useful for dispelling the political potential of a group of people than to transform them into a list of beautiful things. As Georges Didi-Huberman suggests, we must be skeptical when peoples have been embellished by power.[42]

Notes

Epigraph: María Negroni, *Pequeño mundo ilustrado* (Buenos Aires: Caja Negra, 2012), 137.

1. Kate Sturge, *Representing Others: Translation, Ethnography and the Museum* (London: Routledge, 2007).
2. Barbara Kirshenblatt-Gimblett, "Objects of Ethnography," in *Destination Culture: Tourism, Museums, and Heritage* (Berkeley: University of California Press, 1998), 17–78.
3. Here I refer to Lacan's concept of "forclusion," whereby a signifier is excluded from the subject's symbolic universe and the signification of its historicity is "obturated," that is, sealed or filled in.
4. Ferdinand de Saussure, "Syntagmatic and Associative Relations," in *Course in General Linguistics*, ed. Charles Bally and Albert Sechehaye, trans. Wade Baskin (New York: Philosophical Library, 1959), 122–27.
5. See Rozental in this volume.
6. Néstor García Canclini, *Hybrid Cultures: Strategies for Entering and Leaving Modernity*, trans. Christopher Chiappari and Silvia L. López (Minneapolis: University of Minnesota Press, 1995), 120–32.
7. The term Puréecherio encompasses the four regions of Purépecha territory within the state of Michoacán—mountain, lake, valley, and swamp—as well as all that pertains to the Purépechas themselves, including their culture, traditions, customs, history, and vision of the future. See "Puréecherio," Museo Nacional de Antropología, accessed January 5, 2021, https://www.mna.inah.gob.mx/salas_etnografia.php?sala=14.

8. See "Aviso," Museo Nacional de Antropología, accessed April 19, 2017, http://www.mna.inah.gob.mx/index.php?option=com_sppagebuilder&view=page&id=5062; emphasis mine.
9. In Spanish, the imperfect verb form represents an action that used to happen but whose beginning and end are indeterminate.
10. The choice of order at the time was interesting: (1) objects belonging to the "immortal author" of Mexican independence, Miguel Hidalgo; (2) objects from the conquest; (3) coat of arms from Texcoco; (4–7) weapons of the heroes of independence; and (8) weapons of the Mexican Republic (including the national emblem in question). Gumesindo Mendoza and Jesús Sánchez, "Catálogo de las colecciones histórica y arqueológica del Museo Nacional de México," *Anales del Museo Nacional* 65 (1882): 455–561, https://mna.inah.gob.mx/docs/anales/65.pdf.
11. Mendoza and Sánchez, "Catálogo de las colecciones histórica," 461.
12. Herlinda Ruiz Martínez, "El arte de pintar con plumas: Resurgimiento de la técnica del mosaico en plumaria en Michoacán," *Legajos: Boletín de la Nación* 15 (January–April 2018): 85–90.
13. Bernardino de Sahagún, *Historia general de las cosas de Nueva España* (Mexico City: Alejandro Valdés, 1829), 397, cited in Montserrat A. Báez Hernández, "Arte plumaria en el siglo XIX: El Emblema Nacional, un nuevo motivo iconográfico para el México republicano," *Eviterna: Revista de arte y cultura independiente* 1 (2017): 4.
14. Montserrat A. Báez Hernández, "Arte plumaria en el siglo XIX: El Emblema Nacional, un nuevo motivo iconográfico para el México republicano," *Eviterna: Revista de arte y cultura independiente* 1 (2017): 4.
15. Ruiz Martínez, "El arte de pintar con plumas," 85–90.
16. Báez Hernández, "Arte plumaria," 8.
17. Báez Hernández discusses the seven pre-Hispanic featherworks that are currently held in Mexico's public collections, arguing that although we can regard the Chimalli (i.e., the Mexica coat of arms belonging to Moctezuma II, a diplomatic gift to Hernán Cortés, sent to Spain, and returned to Mexico in 1866 at the behest of Emperor Maximilian) as akin to the emblem (it was in a way a military "coat of arms"), its universe of meaning and its components—its colors, forms, and attributes—have no relation to the modern variety of republican politics, which the national emblem in the Purépecha gallery represents. Báez Hernández, "Arte plumaria."
18. One of these stands out. According to the Instituto Nacional de Antropología e Historia (INAH) Mediateca, an object cataloged as "Independent Coat of Arms" that is almost identical to the emblem (but not made in featherwork) was produced in Yucatán in 1827. It has the same components: eight trophies, an oval with an eagle devouring the serpent, a quiver, a caiman, kettledrums, arrows. It is missing only the Phrygian cap, a classical European element after the French Revolution. This raises a question about exhibiting these depictions

of the national coat of arms in two historically rebellious territories: Purépecha lands ever since the conquest, and the Yucatán during the constitution of the nation-state itself. The Mediateca notes, "One detail stands out: what appears to be the head of a crocodile or a lizard, perhaps a pre-Hispanic reference to the 'monster of the land.' Although the artist is unknown, the names of the authorities who commissioned the picture are recorded, all of whom had Maya surnames: Yuit, Maz, Couoh and Chan." "Escudo Independiente," Mediateca, INAH, accessed January 30, 2019, http://mediateca.inah.gob.mx/islandora_74/islandora/object/objetohistorico%3A2783. These elements are important because they reinforce the idea that in those more rebellious contexts, resistant to national union, the symbolic universe of the nation had to be constantly reinforced as a pact of sovereignty and a laying down of regional weapons in deference to the one and only sovereign army.

19. As seems to be the case in the INAH Mediateca's description of the Yucatán coat of arms from 1827. (See previous note.)
20. Cesare Ripa, *Iconology: or, A Collection of Emblematical Figures*, vol. 1, ed. George Richardson (1593; London: G. Scott, 1779), 33.
21. Báez Hernández, "Arte plumaria"; Yobenj Aucardo Chincangana Bayona, "La india de la libertad," *Estudios de filosofía práctica e historia de las ideas* 13, no. 1 (2011): 17–28.
22. Exhibition website for *El Escudo Nacional: Flora, fauna y biodiversidad*, accessed February 2, 2019, http://www.lugares.inah.gob.mx/museos-inah/exposiciones/exposicion.html?task=download&file=exposicion_guion_tematico&id=19040; emphasis mine.
23. "Exposición Escudo Nacional. Inauguración," INAH TV, March 6, 2017, 3:30 min., https://www.youtube.com/watch?v=iJd5uMJVp6k.
24. The process of regularizing the national coat of arms was erratic and reveals the difficulties of federalism. Representations of weapons continued to appear on state coinage and battle insignias long after their prohibition during the Second Empire. Curiously, weapons proliferate anew in representations of the national coat of arms during the Revolution. The coat of arms was eventually regularized in 1916 by Jorge Enciso and Álvaro Gómez. In 1968, it acquired its current form at the behest of Díaz Ordaz, who ordered the design's modification. In 2010, Felipe Calderón imposed the most recent modification to the "outline of the eagle" in the insignia. It is hard not to imagine that changes to the coat of arms are symptomatic of specific moments in Mexican history when war, weapons, and violence threatened the modern conception of the state, as if each intervention to the signs in the allegory re-marked the spoils of war, the trophies, the victors, and the vanquished.
25. Two glaring exceptions are the Sala del Gran Nayar, which includes not only a narrative about structural violence, but also a history of political resistance and recent armed revolts, and the Sala del Noroeste: Sierras, Desiertos y Valles,

which includes references to Yaqui resistance—albeit more focused on the cultural matrix of resilience—and to migration.

26. Anyone who has studied indigenous movements knows that fighting over territory is different from struggling for *land*. It is a struggle over regimes of property and usage (which is what the museum seems to avoid naming by invoking ethnic vindication and territorial concerns).
27. I thank Sandra Rozental for this insight.
28. Until recently, the terms "Tarascan" and "Purépecha" were used interchangeably in both academic and official discourse. Purépechas themselves, however, claim that they never called themselves Tarascans. Although the word does exist in the Purépecha language (meaning son-in-law or father-in-law), its use as an ethnic label was imposed either by the Mexica or the Spanish (about which there is some disagreement) *after* the conquest.
29. There is some debate about this point. The consensus is that the term Tarascan is an exonym. In ancient Purépecha it was used to indicate kinship (parent-in-law, son- or daughter-in-law), and apparently it was used among the inhabitants of the ancient Purépecha territory to designate the first Spaniards in the decade of the conquest. Nevertheless, it was never a self-ascribed term. Today the region's inhabitants dissociate themselves from it.
30. Purple for the swamp, blue for the lake, yellow for the ravine, and green for the mountain.
31. Roberto Juarroz, *Poesía vertical*, ed. Diego Sánchez Aguilar (1958; Madrid: Cátedra, 2012).
32. Rita Segato, introduction to *La nación y sus otros* (Buenos Aires: Prometeo, 2007), 15–36; Claudia Briones, "Madejas de alteridad, entramados de estados-nación: Diseños y telares de ayer y hoy en América Latina," in *Nación y alteridad: Mestizos, indígenas y extranjeros en el proceso de formación nacional*, ed. Daniela Gleizer and Paula López Caballero (Mexico City: UNAM and EyC Ediciones, 2015), 17–66.
33. Gerardo Hernández Cendejas, "El liderazgo y la ideología comunal de Elpidio Domínguez Castro en Santa Fe de la Laguna, Michoacán, 1979–1988," *Tzintzun: Revista de estudios históricos* 39 (2004): 140. The clash between two models of land use and property is not new in Michoacán and recently led to uprisings in the community of Cherán and elsewhere.
34. The website is dedicated to "community communication" and brings together Purépecha organizations from all over Michoacán. Its forums are quite active, and it organizes activities such as seminars held at the UNAM's Instituto de Investigaciones Históricas and at the Universidad Autónoma de Chapingo, as well as activist and community organizations. See "Ceremonia de toma de la bandera P'urhépecha," Purepecha, November 27, 2009, http://www.purepecha.mx/showthread.php?3348. Citing the same source to which the Museo Nacional de Antropología alludes, the *Relación de Michoacán*, the document of the

ceremonial raising of the Purépecha flag references less poetic meanings than those on the MNA label: "The center of the four aforementioned fields features an image taken from the *Relación de Michoacán* (Fragmento de la lámina no. 17), so the obsidian block must represent Curicaveri, a form of sun god which signified Great Fire, he who feeds on fire," a form that encompasses and projects the different cardinal points through four groups of arrows.

35. As of September 2019, the documentary can be streamed at "Juchari uinapekua: Lucha P'urhépecha en defensa de tierras Comunales, Santa Fe de la Laguna, Mich," Purepecha_Mx, October 26, 2011, 33:12 min., https://youtu.be/WnaNdenRL14.
36. The conflict in Cherán erupted as a result of a disavowal of the municipal and federal electoral authorities in 2011, who refused to carry out elections as a result of the generalized corruption of party representatives; drug trafficking cells that were indistinguishable from the army and were attempting to impose order; and the harassment of landowners. Cherán imposed a community police force and a semiautonomous system of political control. Jarco Amézcua Luna and Gerardo Sánchez Díaz, *Pueblos indígenas de México en el siglo XXI*, vol. 3, *P'urhépecha* (Mexico City: Comisión Nacional para el Desarrollo de los Pueblos Indígenas, 2015), 85.
37. Terence Ranger and Eric Hobsbawm, eds., *The Invention of Tradition* (Cambridge: Cambridge University Press, 1983); Saurabh Dube, "Mapping Oppositions: Enchanted Spaces and Modern Places," *Nepantla: Views from the South* 3, no. 2 (2002): 333–50; Mario Rufer, "La tradición como reliquia: Nación e identidad desde los estudios culturales," in *Nación y estudios culturales: Debates desde la poscolonialidad*, ed. María del Carmen de la Peza and Mario Rufer (Mexico City: UAM–Xochimilco Editorial Itaca, 2016), 61–90.
38. Giorgio Agamben, *Infancy and History: The Destruction of Experience*, trans. Liz Heron (London: Verso, 1993).
39. Walter Benjamin, "Critique of Violence," in *Selected Writings*, vol. 1, *1913–1926*, ed. Marcus Bullock and Michael W. Jennings, trans. Edmund Jephcott (Cambridge, Mass.: Belknap Press, 1996), 236–52.
40. Achille Mbembe, "The Aesthetics of Vulgarity," trans. Janet Roitman and Murray Last, in *On the Postcolony* (Berkeley: University of California Press, 2000), 103–5.
41. Daniel Herwitz, *Heritage, Culture, and Politics in the Postcolony* (New York: Columbia University Press, 2012).
42. Georges Didi-Huberman, *Peuples exposés, peuples figurants* (Paris: Minuit, 2012).

\\ 10

A Monolith on the Street

SANDRA ROZENTAL

Across from the gates leading to the Bosque de Chapultepec, on the sidewalk flanking Paseo de la Reforma, a pre-Hispanic monolith stands watch over Mexico City (figure 10.1). Unlike the vestiges of temples and buildings that have become urban archaeological sites, such as Tlatelolco or the Templo Mayor, and unlike objects excavated from plazas and avenues, such as the Piedra del Sol or the Coatlicue, this urban ruin was not excavated in ancient Tenochtitlan. It was through an impressive engineering feat that, in 1964, the 167-ton carved stone monolith was brought from its original location to its new Mexico City abode. Before then, it was lying in a ravine in San Miguel Coatlinchan, a town in the Municipio de Texcoco, Estado de México, some thirty miles from its current location. It had lain there for centuries, partially covered by the sediments from rivers that flowed from the Valley of Mexico's mountains and volcanoes into Lake Texcoco.

The colossal anthropomorphic figure has been on its feet for over fifty years, buttressed by steel beams and standing seven meters tall in the middle of a circular fountain. Surrounded by greenish water and shaded by the eucalyptus trees lining the museum's gardens, the sculpture watches over the city's hustle and bustle. Many now know it as the Aztec rain deity Tlaloc, although it was probably carved much prior, around 500–800 CE.[1] In view of its longevity—first as volcanic rock formed in the Pleistocene, then as

Figure 10.1 Monolith on the street, Photograph by the author, 2011.

an effigy sculpted by pre-Hispanic hands, and later as part of Coatlinchan's landscape—the sculpture has occupied its new location for a relatively brief time span. Turned into a monument at the entrance to the museum, with the words "Museo Nacional de Antropología" emblazoned on its pedestal, it functions as both a marker and a metonym of the museum and of all the objects that make up its collection. At the same time, its placement in public space, and on Reforma specifically, makes it yet another figure among a parade of statues and monuments lining the avenue as a patriotic history lesson rendered in stone and bronze.[2] It is unique, however, because it is the only one of these monuments that dates to pre-Hispanic times and because it is the sole object that, despite belonging to the museum's collection, registered with an inventory number (10–627008) and under the custodianship of the curator of the Teotihuacan Hall, is located outside the perimeter of the museum building.[3]

In this chapter, I am interested in unpacking the effects of this pre-Hispanic statue's liminal location, both inside and outside the museum, simultaneously guarded under the patrimonial mantle of the Mexican state and made accessible to all in the public space of the city. I argue that in the case of the Coatlinchan monolith, the state project initiated in the nineteenth century of "forging patria" by transferring pre-Hispanic monoliths from periphery to the capital's museums was not entirely successful.[4] Although the state justified the removal as a way of rescuing the monolith from the damages it was allegedly suffering in Coatlinchan and issued assurances that it would be placed inside the museum as the building's center of gravity, following a sequence of events that I describe below, this object ended up "on the street." There, it is exposed to the elements, to pollution, to the vibrations of urban traffic, and, more importantly, to the uses and interpretations of passersby.

The monolith's placement on the street has made it an active agent in the city's public life as a different kind of object. Its new emplacement casts doubt on the uniqueness and authenticity generally associated with ancient cultural heritage, while also making the statue available as a vehicle for political expression. The monolith became a mediator, a platform and physical medium for practices contesting the authoritarian and centralist politics of the state that in effect alienated this object from Coatlinchan in the first place. At the same time, it is being charged with and made to stand in for other kinds of forced dispossessions and displacements. The history of the monolith's relocation and its unintended fate as a public monument reveal the ways in which the Museo Nacional de Antropología itself needs to be understood as a multiple object, built from contradictions, disagreements, moments of violence, protest, and crisis. Such an understanding blurs the museum's apparent solidity and permanence as another kind of monolith made by an authoritarian and centralist state. As the trajectory of the Coatlinchan monolith shows, although the museum was conceived of as a means by which to conserve, safeguard, and protect national heritage, it was made possible through many processes of dispossession and moments of violence, which in turn led to unforeseen consequences and uses.

The Monolith's Place

In the 1880s, when it was first written about by scholars of Mexican antiquity, the monolith from Coatlinchan started a journey that culminated with its 1964 physical relocation to Chapultepec. This journey began without the stone being physically moved, thanks to widely circulating photographs, postcards, and engravings of it lying prostrate in a gully (figure 10.2).[5] These

Figure 10.2 Xicaca diosa del agua, Fototeca Nacional. Reproduction authorized by the Instituto Nacional de Antropología e Historia.

images were part of the nascent "visual economy" of all things indigenous in Mexico, furthered by the popularization of photography.[6] In both images and texts, the statue was given different names; its origin and artifices having become the objects of speculation. It was considered an enigma even for specialists who tried to make sense of its isolation from any archaeological site and who tried desperately to identify it within the pre-Hispanic pantheon and speculate over how it had ended up in the place where it was discovered.

Some argued that it was a representation of the male rain deity Tlaloc that had rolled from the mountain of the same name, where it had been carved and venerated.[7] Others contended that it was not meant to remain in Coatlinchan, but that it had merely been quarried there as a sort of workshop and was meant to eventually be moved to an important ceremonial center, probably Teotihuacan.[8] Both arguments held that the place where the stone lay was not actually "its" place, but rather arbitrary, a historical accident. Only Alfredo Chavero, one of nineteenth-century Mexico's most renowned historians, thought that the monument's final destination had always been Coatlinchan, since this location supported Mexica cosmology: the effigy represented a deity associated with "horizontal waters," therefore it was appropriate that it would be lying in a ravine where a river flowed en route to Lake Texcoco.[9]

Despite the unresolved debates over the sculpture's origin and location in pre-Hispanic times, most late nineteenth- and early twentieth-century scholars, influenced by Porfirian centralism, saw the monolith as "out of place." Specialists attributed the statue's poor state of conservation both to its exposure to the elements and to the mistreatment suffered at the hands of the region's inhabitants. They, therefore, proposed it be moved from what they considered a marginal and dangerous periphery to a more suitable place for the conservation and exhibition of heritage—the Museo Nacional de México, located geographically and culturally at the center of the country.

In the first publication to make reference to the monolith, *México a través de los siglos,* Chavero lamented the monument's location: "Unfortunately its hands have been destroyed and its face has been damaged, and it lies on its back in a gully, mistreated by the same waters of which it was once the deity."[10] In the historian's view, even though this had been its place in pre-Hispanic times, a gully with flowing water was now a risky spot for an object belonging to Mexico's pre-Hispanic legacy.

In 1882, the Museo Nacional de México commissioned a team of curators and its then draftsman, José María Velasco, to study the statue and calculate its weight and possible transport to the museum as part of its collection of Mexican monoliths.[11] The study concluded that the statue was too heavy to transport, but that a replica or plaster cast should be made instead. Shortly thereafter, Leopoldo Batres carried out the only excavation ever done in the ravine where it lay. Batres had just achieved the spectacular feat of moving another pre-Hispanic monolith, the Diosa del Agua, from Teotihuacan to the museum by making ingenious use of engineering and the railroad.[12] This move was a landmark in the process that Christina Bueno calls "forging patrimonio" during the late nineteenth century.[13] Bueno's phrasing alludes to Manuel Gamio's arguments in favor of "forging patria," framing the transfer of objects from all over Mexico to the capital as a technology of state formation.[14] Given Batres's success in transporting the Diosa del Agua, he surely had the intention of moving the Coatlinchan monolith to Mexico City. In his monograph *¿Tlaloc?*, he celebrated the work of archaeology as a state scientific discipline: "The monument had remained all but hidden until the official pickaxe came and discovered it, revealing its true shape and size."[15] And yet, the statue could not be physically moved with this "pickaxe" alone, so Batres commissioned an engineer, Guillermo Heredia, to calculate its weight and study the ravine's topography, then design ways to move it to the capital.

In another publication, engineer Luis Becerril, also lamented the sculpture's being in the ravine and suggested its relocation to the Museo Nacional de México to guarantee its conservation. He affirmed: "The truth is that those of us who study this monumental piece sympathize with it and imagine the terrible lashes it receives on the side facing the torrential flow of water, which, on its precipitous course to Lake Texcoco, carries enormous blocks of stone that, passing this idol, strike it and rob it little by little of its edges and even of whole parts like the foot and left hand, which are now missing."[16]

We do not know when the sculpture was damaged, nor whether it was truly as a result of the ravine's waters or some other kind of destruction. It is clear, however, that for the museum's scholars, the stone's exposure to the elements was not the only risk associated with its being in Coatlinchan. In 1912, the curators of the Museo Nacional de México were once again commissioned to study the possibility of moving the monolith, this time not directly to the museum, but to a public plaza somewhere in Mexico City. It was, thus, not a question merely of protecting the piece from the elements, since it would still be outdoors, but rather of protecting it from other dangers associated with its location in a distant town. The study again concluded that the monolith was too heavy to be moved and, thus, should be assigned a custodian, put on a pedestal, and surrounded by a barbed wire fence that would protect it from the populace.[17] For the curators, perhaps there was nothing to be done about the stone's location, given its enormous weight, but it could be protected from other kinds of damage, namely that inflicted by people. They never offered any details about the specific practices of the region's inhabitants, nor why they put the sculpture at risk, nor did they leave a record of whether their proposed means were ever implemented. But their anxiety hints that it was difficult for them to accept that a sculpture from ancient Mexico could continue to lie in a ravine with flowing water, so far removed from state oversight, visited by locals and curious travelers who would climb on top of it or desecrate it with graffiti.

It was only in the 1960s that moving the monolith from Coatlinchan to the new building designed *ex professo* to house Mexico's patrimony was once more considered. The architect of the new Museo Nacional de Antropología, Pedro Ramírez Vázquez, was also responsible for the statue's relocation. He maintained that the statue was to be transferred to Mexico City on the orders of then-president Adolfo López Mateos, who had come upon the monolith in his years traveling around the country. Given the statue's size and presence, López Mateos requested it be brought to the museum. Following the president's orders and echoing his nineteenth-century precursors, Ramírez Vázquez framed the move as a rescue effort. In his words, the object was "abandoned in a ravine, and the local people had left it in disrepair. The only local with any interest in the monument was a woman who stationed herself there on Sundays with a bucket of soft drinks to sell to the occasional visitor."[18] In the architect's view, the case for the monolith's relocation was grounded first on laws stipulating that archaeological monuments are the exclusive and inalienable property of the nation, and second, on the need to conserve the object in a suitable place, under the safekeeping of curators and specialists who would guarantee its conservation. Ramírez Vázquez also regarded the monolith as being put at risk by locals' practices: "The stone was all scratched up. People weren't taking care of it; they were covering it with graffiti."[19] The stone's surface was marked with etched or painted initials, doodles, and dates. In Ramírez Vázquez's view, the residents of Coatlinchan should have been thankful that the sculpture was moved to a privileged and safe place where it could be protected and appreciated by many people, Mexicans and foreigners alike.

Outside in, Inside Out

In publications about the construction of the 1964 Museo Nacional de Antropología, as well as in my conversations with Ramírez Vázquez, he maintained that placing the monolith outdoors was always part of his architectural plan.[20] The monolith's weatherproof quality was of the utmost importance in its selection. According to the architect:

> When the government decided to create the Museo Nacional de Antropología, we set out to carefully select the archaeological pieces that would be displayed as Mexico's great archaeological wealth. The idea was that a large archaeological object was necessary to express that purpose. Knowing Maya architecture in depth, we thought one of the large Maya stelae could be the expression of that heritage. We selected one from Edzná, Campeche, but even when the dimensions and quality matched what we were looking for, there was a very clear problem: the stele was made out of limestone. We

> realized that this wouldn't work, because the piece would quickly deteriorate in Mexico City's climate. Thirty advisers suggested to the committee that we look for another object made of basalt.[21]

The monolith's selection, then, was contingent on its being made of volcanic rock, a material that allowed it to be kept safely outdoors.[22]

Although the monolith was always meant to be outdoors, the original plan was not for it to be placed beyond the perimeter of the museum building, much less for it to be a public monument on the street. According to the extant documentation from the first meetings of the committee in charge of the project, it had been proposed that a large-scale archaeological object be placed at the center of the museum's architectural design. In fact, in the first plans, the building had been imagined as a series of concentric circles whose center was a rest area to which the museum's halls would lead, where visitors would be able to contemplate an ancient statue that would represent Mexico's cultural heritage.[23] This object was, therefore, initially conceived as the museum's center of gravity, functioning simultaneously as an architectural element and as a symbol of the entirety of Mexican identity contained in its many halls.

The minutes from one of the consulting board's first meetings show that the first object to be considered was the Piedra del Sol, but the board decided that it needed a more appropriate place at the center of a hall dedicated to Aztec art, which would be the climax of the museum visit.[24] A monumental Olmec head was also proposed as an option. The architect and archaeologist Ricardo de la Robina, one of the main organizers behind the museum, maintained that he had to dissuade Ramírez Vázquez from using an Olmec head because it would look like a "ping pong ball" at the center of the large modernist patio: they needed something large enough to match the scale of the building.[25]

We thus know that the Coatlinchan monolith was selected as the building's center of gravity because of its dimensions, but more importantly because of its material characteristics. The museographer in charge of the project, Mario Vázquez, and renowned set designer Julio Prieto made full-size wooden models of the museum's highlights.[26] By placing these models in their projected destinations during the construction process, curators, designers, and architects could work in tandem and thereby finish the museum on schedule. The sculpture was originally going to be raised on a platform over the pool at the center of the patio, symbolizing the basin of Lake Texcoco.[27] In the architectural design, the pool represents the centrality of the Valley of Mexico in the constitution of Mexican identity.[28] As such, the Teotihuacan-era statue from a settlement in the Central Valley supported the regime's centralist ideology, in keeping with a museographic design that privileged the cultures from the center as the common heritage of all Mexicans.[29] As shown by a photograph taken in November 1963, with the construction work already well under way and just a few months before the building's completion, the monolith's location in the original architectural design was at the center of the patio (figure 10.3). One can therefore infer that its ultimate destination outside the perimeter of the museum resulted from a rather last-minute decision made during the final months of construction.

The first documentation of the model's relocation to Reforma is a photograph held in architect Ramírez Vázquez's archive (figure 10.4). It is dated late February 1964, coinciding with the government's first attempt to extract the monolith, which was thwarted by Coatlinchan's residents, preventing the

Figure 10.3 Monolith model in the MNA courtyard. Acervo Arquitecto Pedro Ramírez Vázquez, 1964.

Figure 10.4 Monolith model on Reforma. Acervo Arquitecto Pedro Ramírez Vázquez, 1964.

engineers from meeting their original deadline.[30] On February 21, when the lowbed trailer designed for the monolith's removal reached the town, the church bells were rung, and town residents flooded into the streets. First, there was a confrontation with the trailer's driver on the road leading into town, and then town residents congregated in the area of the ravine where everything was already set up to transport the monolith. During this episode, referred to by both government agents and town residents as "the rebellion," protestors dropped the stone back to the ground by loosening the cables on which it had been suspended in a sort of steel hammock. The government responded the following morning, sending the army to intervene. For three months, while the engineers restarted their work, a curfew was set in town to avoid further confrontations. The engineer in charge of the project, Enrique del Valle Prieto, explained that after the February events, it took several months and two hydraulic jacks to lift the statue and prepare it once more for the journey.[31] The monolith's relocation was thus pushed back to mid-April, more than two months later than initially planned.

Ramírez Vázquez always denied that there was any relationship between the monolith's relocation from the center of the patio to the sidewalk along Paseo de la Reforma and the rebellion in Coatlinchan that stalled the work. He maintained that the decision to place the monolith outside the building was about "aesthetics"; the Museo Nacional de Antropología did not have an exterior façade on Reforma and needed some representative element to mark its presence from the avenue. Echoing de la Robina, he further elaborated, "We moved the model to several places, not just in the patio, and we saw that the place where it looked best was on Reforma. Inside the museum, outside the Mexica Hall, it looked like a dwarf."[32] For the architect, although the statue's original place was at the center of the patio, its dimensions ultimately justified its relocation outside the building.

By contrast, the museographer Alfonso Soto Soria, who worked on the museum during its construction, pointed out shortly before his death:

> In the patio there's a large pool and a conch shell. That's where Tlaloc was going to go, but with the sabotage and everything, Tlaloc had to be put somewhere else before the museum lobby was completed, and there was nowhere to put it. You can see that the base is cemented underneath to hold more than that conch shell! So Tlaloc was coming, but the transport had to be delayed, and the architectural work couldn't be stopped, so we made the decision to find somewhere else to put Tlaloc, outside the museum.[33]

For Soto Soria, the monolith's ideal place was where it ended up by accident, regardless of whether it had been conceived for somewhere else in the original architectural design.

> We found a place that was better, I think, than where the architect had planned to put it. Having Tlaloc as a public fountain is the museum's most important advertisement. We hadn't thought of putting anything there other than the garden and the gate surrounding the museum. Then, when we studied where else it could go, we saw that that spot was ideal. It looks good from any direction, and it's the thing that most advertises the museum. Inside, by contrast, the unfinished sculpture would have been impressive because of its size and mass, but it wouldn't have had the same meaning as Coatlicue, for example. So the place where it ended up was ideal. It was a fortunate accident.[34]

The only criticism that the museographer expressed was that the fountain's design was not as high quality as the rest of the museum. It was made hastily by the engineers, without the help of the architects and museographers who designed the rest of the museum so meticulously. So, although the sculpture's relocation was fortunate, its display on Paseo de la Reforma was ill-achieved because of timing. Soto Soria assured me that the monolith's final location on the avenue was a direct consequence of the delay caused by the Coatlinchan locals' sabotage. Thankfully, in his view, this freed it from the inappropriate place that the architect and the museographers had designated for it. For the museographer, the statue's initial location at the center of the museum was unjustified because of both the architectural design of the building and the characteristics of the monolith itself as a minor piece in the museum's collection. The unfinished monolith was only impressive because of its size, not because of its meaning or even its aesthetic. As Soto Soria added, "Besides, next to so many beautiful, well-made pre-Hispanic pieces, that clunky figure is pretty ugly."[35]

Out in the Open

The monolith from Coatlinchan is the only object in the collection of the Museo Nacional de Antropología to be found outside the building. In comparison to many of the other monuments that adorn Paseo de la Reforma, it is surprising that it is not covered in graffiti. It is separated from passersby by an aquatic barrier that hinders people from getting too close, touching it, or marking it. Nevertheless, it is exposed to the city's acid rains, to flora and fauna, and to the carbonic emissions from the thousands of cars and buses that commute past it. Although the plans for the museum had always intended for it to be outdoors, and it had been exposed to the elements in Coatlinchan, its final destination on Paseo de la Reforma exposed the monolith to new risks that affect its conservation status.

Concerned about the statue's exposure, in 1997, researchers at the Instituto Nacional de Investigadores Nucleares de la UNAM sought to repair the effects of atmospheric contamination on the ancient stone's surface. They proposed to use laser abrasion to clean the sculpture, which had been darkened by contaminating elements.[36] Their project was never carried out. Years later, however, as part of the celebrations marking the fiftieth anniversary of the museum, the Museo Nacional de Antropología itself sought to clean and stabilize the sculpture, given its exposure to the toxicity of the city.[37]

For the restoration project, which ran from 2011 to 2014, the museum's Laboratorio de Conservación focused on repairing the damages occasioned by the sculpture's street location. They concluded that it had not suffered any major damage since its relocation, aside from a change in coloration from a ruddy tone to a dark gray, almost ochre, and from the accumulation of salt deposits, sediments, and residues of biological agents brought about by its new vertical position. According to the restorer in charge of the project, Sergio González, the monolith had suffered only minimal deterioration because of its new position, which had created new spaces in which water could pool, encouraging birds and insects to nest there (figure 10.5).[38] He did not find any conservation reports on the precise state the object was in while it was in situ, nor from when it entered the museum's collections in 1964. Nevertheless, he suspects that the most significant damage—fissures and cracks—were brought about first by the transfer itself (he found drill holes, surely made to keep it on the platform, and graffiti, which may relate to the

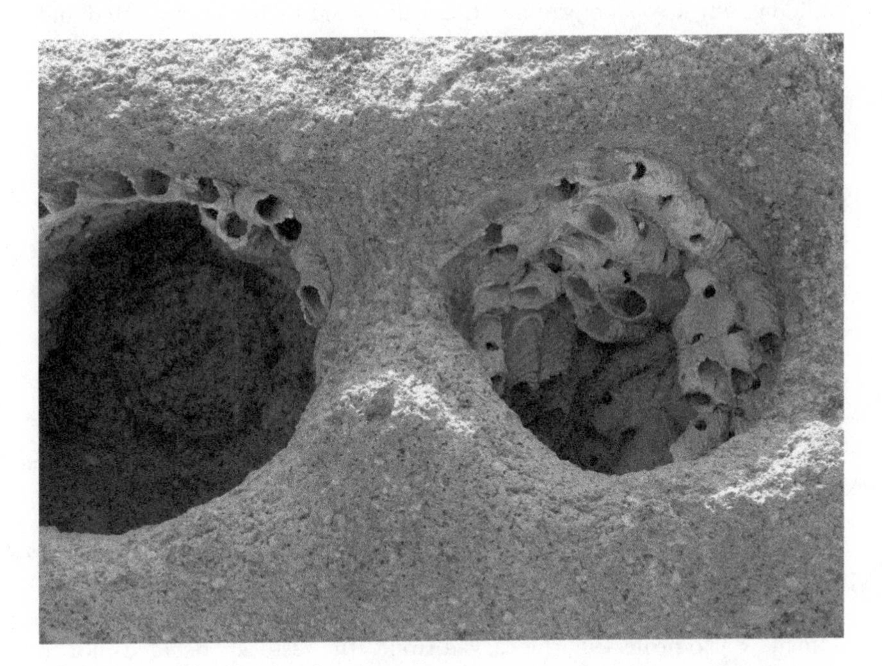

Figure 10.5 Wasp nests in the monolith. Photograph by Sergio González, 2014.

engineers' calculations), and second upon raising it into its vertical position on Paseo de la Reforma.

Although pollution and dust caused some chromatic variations, detailed studies showed that water is the element that has most corroded the object. Because it is made from basalt andesite, which has an acidic quality, the acidity of the rain does not put it in danger. The stone is porous, so the pooling of water in the "tub" on top of its headdress and in its right foot have caused water to filter in, making cracks and causing lichens, mosses, and algae to grow.[39] Describing how it took months to uproot encrusted lichens using alcohol and a steamer, and to clean wasps' nests out of the statue's "nose," Sergio González remarked that the stone is "full of life, full of microorganisms, but it also takes on a life of its own because of all the myths that surround it."[40]

The restoration project demonstrates that being so "full of life" entails risks to the statue that are directly related to its outdoor location. In fact, when the decision was made to restore the monolith, several possible ways of dealing with this were considered. One option was to move it inside the building, but it was determined that this would be too complicated and costly. The museum's restorer, Laura Filloy, recommended that a hall for the sculpture be built next to the current Teotihuacan Hall. Concerns that moving the monolith, even from outside the museum to within, could stir up a debate about its possible return to Coatlinchan, resulted in the rejection of Filloy's project.[41] Another possibility was to build a structure to protect it from the elements, but that would obstruct its viewing and would require too much upkeep. Finally, there was the possibility of creating a sort of cover that would keep water from accumulating in the headdress, but this, too, involved maintenance problems. Given these impediments, with advice from restorers from other outdoor pre-Hispanic sites, and with the help of the UNAM's Centro de Capacitación Académica de Desarrollo Tecnológico, it was decided to simply cover the stone's pores in the horizontal areas with a tetraethyl orthosilicate (a consolidant for rock); to lower the level of the fountain's parapet five centimeters, avoiding permanent contact with water; and to channel the runoff water behind the sculpture. Ultimately, the restoration project was based on the premise that, in a way, its exposure was somehow also protecting the carved stone. The restorers decided "not to eliminate the patina that has been created naturally over the course of its fifty years in its current position, since this lends it some of its value as an archaeological object and provides a naturally created protective 'layer' or 'skin.'"[42] In this way, the restoration project transformed the sculpture's outdoor location from a possible danger into a kind of patina or protection for its conservation.

In addition to slowing down the damage being done to the stone's surface, the restoration involved a deep cleaning of the sculpture's cavities, and of the fountain on which it is raised. This process revealed other aspects of the object's transformation into a being with supernatural powers, to which the city's residents appeal. For example, numerous coins were found during the cleaning. In an interview with the restoration team, the archaeologist García Mol noted that these coins had been gathered for years and used to pay the end-of-year meal for the museum staff. At one point there had even been talk of opening a bank account, since the amount of money involved was considerable. Coins were also found on top of the statue's headdress, all of which were from the sixties, seventies, and eighties, showing that people had been tossing them up there for as long as it had stood as an urban monument. The coins show that the sculpture had become an object to which the city's residents somehow entrusted their fate.

The sculpture's supernatural powers have also been invoked through the occasional offering left at its feet. During the restoration, one offering appeared in honor of the Virgin of Guadalupe, with images, flowers, and seeds. More recently, plastic flowers have also appeared. Someone must have waded through the fountain to leave these offerings there. González is not surprised that the statue has not been adulterated with graffiti since its relocation to the street because, "unlike many historical monuments, this one is experienced as a deity, and people respect it."[43]

The residents of Coatlinchan lament the sculpture's location "on the street." For many, there is an inconsistency between the patrimonial discourses that denounced the statue's fragile conservation status in Coatlinchan and that ultimately justified its removal, and its current location in the open air of the city, outside the building where national heritage is safeguarded and protected. Many describe the extraction of the monolith as an act of violence and dispossession, even though the expropriation was supported by a legal framework governing national heritage. Those who witnessed the monolith's removal in the sixties lament that its relocation was the result of a series of lies, poor management, and acts of violence on the part of local and national authorities.[44] But beyond the deed itself and how it was (or was not) negotiated, the monolith's final placement out in the open is perhaps what provokes the most consternation.

Don Felix, an older resident of Coatlinchan who passed away a few years ago, was perplexed: "I will never understand why they took our stone by force if they were just going to leave it like that, abandoned outside the museum."[45] Like don Felix, doña Luz recalled her childhood with the monolith in the Santa Clara ravine, reflecting, "It's not happy where they put it. It's sad. Only cars see it. It's not even in a nice spot, inside the halls, like the Piedra del Sol. How can it be that after such a scandal, it ended up on the street?"[46] These comments correspond to a sentiment shared by many people from Coatlinchan of different ages, genders, and ways of life, who view the monolith's final location as inappropriate and at odds with the state's purported reasons for moving it to the museum in the first place.

For the residents of Mexico City, the sculpture's location on the street is also inappropriate for a national heritage object. It often surprises city dwellers who pass alongside the sculpture in their day-to-day lives. For example, in 2009, I witnessed an elementary school teacher taking a school group to visit the museum. While he was arranging the uniformed children in front of the monolith to take a group photo, he told them: "This is a replica. Who knows where the original is, but this surely isn't authentic because it wouldn't be outside like this." He went on to emphasize, "The Piedra del Sol, the Tízoc Stone, all the authentic stones are inside the museum, very well taken care of, and we know that this one isn't pre-Hispanic because there's no way they would have left it outside like this." On another occasion in 2016, I overheard a woman explaining to her son that it was a "modern sculpture based on the Goddess of Water from Teotihuacan." Like the teacher, the woman regarded its location on the street as proof of the figure's recent manufacture. These are just two examples of a phenomenon that I recorded again and again at the monolith's current location: its placement on the street precludes it from being ancient or authentic in the eyes of the residents of one of the most crowded cities in the world.

Sergio González also noted that many people approached him as he was working on the statue to ask why he was restoring a replica. In other words, being outside the building that safeguards Mexico's heritage seems to have led to that monument's no longer being seen as an object linked to the pre-Hispanic past, having been transformed into an urban monument of another sort. Its placement on the street has fostered rumors that it is a replica and that the original is found elsewhere—whether in the museum storage areas or in Coatlinchan, both of which are more appropriate and more convincing locations for heritage than the street. The conviction, then, is that the Mexican state would never allow a treasure from its national collections to escape the traditional spaces for the display of heritage and, thus, to escape from its patrimonial grasp.

A Public Monument

In its urban location, the sculpture has been turned into a feature of the city's landscape, a key piece in the life of the great megalopolis. People use it as a meeting point, while groups of tourists and people out for a Sunday stroll gather at "the Tlaloc" before visiting one of the nearby museums or taking a walk in the park. Each day witnesses a parade of people who pose in front of the sculpture. Entire families from other parts of the country stop in front of the ruin-turned-icon-of-the-city to take a photograph with which to memorialize their visit to the capital. The statue also fulfills functions of a more utilitarian nature: street vendors use water from the fountain to wash their fruit and to keep their stalls and utensils clean. At night in particular, when there are no security guards or passersby to worry about, people have even been known to urinate in the fountain, since there are no public bathrooms in this part of the city.

Apart from these direct uses, the monolith—both a heritage object and a witness to the comings and goings of the city, simultaneously inside and outside the museum—has become a mediator and stand-in for the state. Precisely because of its ambiguous location in relation to the museum, and perhaps because of the history of its extraction and forced removal at the hands of the state's engineers, architects, and soldiers, the Coatlinchan monolith has become a key actor in the Mexican public sphere. Here it functions as a platform that enables direct dialogue with and even denunciation of the state's practices and instances of forced dispossession.

Three examples illustrate this metamorphosis. Although the statue has not been vandalized directly since its arrival and transformation into a public monument, it has been used as a vehicle for political messages. Almost immediately after it was raised as a monument in front of the museum and put on the street, the sculpture offered not only a surface on which individuals could mark dates and initials, as was the custom when it was lying prostrate in the ravine in Coatlinchan, but also a medium through which to make collective political protests and citizens' demands visible.

In 1968, just four years after its relocation, the photographer Toni Kuhn captured an image, now one of the landmarks of photography in Mexico, that shows the rough texture of the stone pasted with flyers from the student movement.[47] It is part of a series of images by the photographer about Mexican authoritarianism during the sixties, including images of broken windows and equipment destroyed by police violence. Curator and critic Alfonso Morales explains the meaning of Kuhn's image thus:

> His inventory of broken and burst out windows, which would not seem out of place in a contemporary art gallery today, included a nocturnal view of the monolith that stands as the sentry and emblem of the building that holds the most important collection of Mexican archaeological heritage. On this mass of stone representing Tlaloc, god of rain, one can clearly make out some of the flyers that students pasted on as part of their propaganda. The image of this irreverent gesture could well be a symbol of the confrontation between the student movement and other equally monolithic presences, e.g., familial tradition, the institutionalized revolution, presidentialism, or single-party rule.[48]

Thus, both the photograph and the students' gesture of pasting the flyers on the stone transformed the latter—this monument to national heritage contained in the recently inaugurated Museo Nacional de Antropología, the jewel of the state's cultural politics—into a vehicle for the voices of Mexican citizens clamoring for social and political change across the nation. Situated on the street, where it acted as a sentinel watching over the MNA rather than just another object in its collections, the pre-Hispanic monument became a substitute for that other monolith, the post-revolutionary state—a recurring metaphor for the PRI regime and its authoritarian practices—that could be intervened, profaned, and resignified by clamoring voices.

In the following decades, the sculpture's power as a political platform has been utilized by countless social movements, political parties, and unions, which take it as a gathering point for meetings, protests, and marches. In 2006, for example, in the context of the World Water Forum, several environmentalist groups used the fountain and its contents—Tlaloc being a water deity, after all—as the site of a mass demonstration in support of the right to water, in response to rumors of imminent privatizing reforms. In 2014 it served as the meeting point for a march against the telecommunications reforms of then-president Enrique Peña Nieto, who was proposing to strengthen the media conglomerate Televisa's monopoly. In both cases, it would seem that the monolith's relocation not only situated its imposing presence in public space, but also made it—albeit unintentionally—an important ally in social protests and political mobilizations aimed at protecting substances and outlets considered to be national patrimony.

Aside from its strategic location on one of Mexico City's busiest avenues, the monolith's power has been used in other fields of politics and civic struggle. Following the 2006 presidential election and the demand for a recount of the votes by the PRD's then-candidate Andrés Manuel López Obrador, who coined the slogan "ballot by ballot, booth by booth," Paseo de la Reforma was blocked just a few meters away from the monolith (figure 10.6). On this occasion, too, the sculpture was enlisted in the nearby political event. It was adorned with a large muslin, reading, "Tlaloc is clamoring, drop by drop, ballot by ballot." This slogan recalled the state's campaigns from the eighties, which had declared "Drop by drop, water will run dry" as a way of generating responsible citizens through the moderate use of another patrimonial resource: water. The muslin, thus, appealed to the substance over which this statue exerts supernatural power—water—to expand its field of influence

Figure 10.6 Gota por gota (Drop by drop). Photograph by the author, 2006.

into politics, especially the civic duty to demand due process, democracy, and transparency. This highly calibrated action granted supernatural credentials to the recount demanded by the opposition, simultaneously transforming the monolith into an actor in debates over electoral politics.

This metamorphosis into a platform for doing politics—into a means through which citizens can interpolate the state—was invoked more recently by the movement demanding justice for the disappearance of forty-three students from the Raúl Isidro Burgos Rural Teachers' College in Ayotzinapa. One December morning in 2014, months after the event, the city awoke to the monolith wearing a large red cloth with the number 43, and another banner covering the letters engraved on its pedestal (figure 10.7). This banner read: "Take me back to Coatlinchan" next to a version of the logo for the INAH, painted in black. Written in chalk on the sidewalk in front of the fountain were the words "It was the state," a phrase that, together with "They were taken alive, we want them back alive," had become the most distinctive slogan of the protests denouncing the state's responsibility for the students' disappearance at the hands of local police. With these banners and phrases, two moments in time were collapsed—the state violence of the sixties and that of today—underscoring how the monolith from Coatlinchan could actually be understood as a precursor for the contemporary Mexican state's policies of forcible disappearance. The museum ordered the banners to be removed and the chalking to be erased, yet they have reappeared through

Figure 10.7 Regrésame a Coatlinchan (Take me back to Coatlinchan). Author unknown, photo from *24 Horas el diario sin límites*, 2014.

various iterations. For example, during the marches convened in November 2014, a stencil was stuck on the marble fountain, reading, "Ayotzinapa, cradle of the rebellion," alongside a poster featuring the faces of the disappeared student teachers. In February 2015, the monolith greeted the city bearing a strip of scrap paper, reading, "43 is everyone's wound." In all these instances, because of both its membership in the pantheon of pre-Hispanic deities and its relatively recent historical transformation into heritage upon being forcibly relocated to Mexico City in the sixties, the statue was used as a platform from which to question the authoritarian, antidemocratic regime's construction of Mexican identity.

Conclusions

Even though we will never know for certain whether the monolith's current location was caused by Coatlinchan residents' rebellion or whether it was a merely last-minute aesthetic decision made by the architects and museographers in charge of the museum, or perhaps determined by a multiplicity of factors, it is clear that its position "on the street" has transformed this object into much more than a symbol of the museum. Although its location out in the open is criticized by many, especially by the people of Coatlinchan, and causes others who see it to question its authenticity, its positioning in public space has transformed it in a radical way. Having previously been imagined as the museum building's center of gravity, and as an icon of Mexico's pre-Hispanic heritage, the statue now blurs the boundaries between the inside and outside of the museum. It has been placed between a space clearly linked to the state and a space that continually escapes the official domain, to be appropriated and adapted by dissident voices and actions. The monolith's streetside location generates a new topology: it is a fold, one face of which points outward to the public space of the street, the other face of which points inward, toward the official space of the museum. The statue's location and its transformation into an agent of the Mexican public sphere can therefore be understood as the result of an equilibrium between two opposed forces, the desire on the part of the people of Coatlinchan for the monolith to remain in their territory, and the Mexican state's drive to produce a nation of homogeneous citizens, all linked by an ancestral past and a shared tangible heritage. The monolith on the street points toward the cracks, fissures, slippages, and fragility of the many objects in the museum's collections, and of the museum itself as a project of national representation. Although the 1964 Museo Nacional de Antropología was conceived by an authoritarian and centralizing state, it was built irremediably on calculation errors, contradictions, and accidents that, like the monolith from Coatlinchan, produce and enable innovative uses and new interpretive possibilities. There are indeed spaces for the objects of its collections and for the building itself to change—to continue to change—with the passage of time.

Notes

This research was completed with support from the Wenner Gren Foundation, the Center for Latin American and Caribbean Studies at New York University, and the American Council of Learned Societies.

1. For more on the sculpture's date and identification, see Sandra Rozental, "In the Wake of Mexican Patrimonio: Material Ecologies in San Miguel Coatlinchan," *Anthropological Quarterly* 89, no. 1 (2016): 181–219.
2. See Mauricio Tenorio-Trillo, "1910 Mexico City: Space and Nation in the City of the Centenario," *Journal of Latin American Studies* 28, no. 1 (1996): 75–104; Claudia Agostoni, *Monuments of Progress: Modernization and Public Health in Mexico City, 1876–1910* (Calgary: University of Calgary Press, 2003); Carlos Martínez Assad, *La patria en el Paseo de la Reforma* (Mexico City: Fondo de Cultura Económica, 2005).
3. The Piedra del Sol had a similar status for decades when it was included in the Museo Nacional's collection catalogs but remained buttressed outside the Mexico City Cathedral. See Miruna Achim and Bertina Olmedo Vera, eds., *Eduard Seler: Inventario de las colecciones arqueológicas del Museo Nacional, 1907* (Mexico City: INAH, 2018), 30.
4. See Christina Bueno, *The Pursuit of Ruins: Archaeology, History, and the Making of Modern Mexico* (Albuquerque: University of New Mexico Press, 2016); and Bueno, "*Forjando Patrimonio*: The Making of Archaeological Patrimony in Porfirian Mexico," *Hispanic American Historical Review* 90, no. 2 (2010): 215–45.
5. Many pre-Hispanic objects traveled first on paper given their weight or budgetary constraints. See Irina Podgorny, "Antigüedades portátiles: Transportes, ruinas y comunicaciones en la arqueología del siglo XIX," *Historia, Ciencias, Saude: Manguinhos* 15, no. 3 (2008): 577–95; and Miruna Achim, *From Idols to Antiquity: Forging the National Museum of Mexico* (Lincoln: University of Nebraska Press, 2017).
6. See Deborah Poole, *Vision, Race, and Modernity: A Visual Economy of the Andean Image World* (Princeton, N.J.: Princeton University Press, 1997).

7. Leopoldo Batres, *¿Tlaloc?* (Mexico City: Secretaría de Instrucción Pública y Bellas Artes, 1903).
8. Robert F. Heizer and Howel Williams, "Geologic Notes on the Idolo de Coatlinchan," *American Antiquity* 29, no. 1 (July 1963): 95–98; Eduardo Noguera, "El Monolito de Coatlichan [*sic*]," *Anales de antropología* 1, no. 1 (1964): 131–43.
9. Alfredo Chavero, *El Monolito de Coatlinchán: Disquisición arqueológica, presentada al XIV Congreso de Americanistas* (Mexico City: Imprenta del Museo Nacional, 1904).
10. Chavero, *El Monolito de Coatlinchán*; Manuel Orozco y Berra, *México a través de los siglos*, vol. 1, *Historia antigua y de la conquista* (Mexico City: Cumbre, 1884), 663–64.
11. Jesús Sánchez, "Estatua Colosal de la Diosa del Agua," *Anales del Museo Nacional de México* 2 (1886): 27–30.
12. Leopoldo Batres, "Archéologie mexicaine: Le monument de la 'Déesse de l'Eau,'" *La Nature* 18, no. 2 (1890): 263–337.
13. See Bueno, *Pursuit of Ruins*; and Bueno, "*Forjando Patrimonio*."
14. Manuel Gamio, *Forjando patria (pro nacionalismo)* (Mexico City: Porrúa Hermanos, 1916).
15. Batres, *¿Tlaloc?*, 3.
16. Luis Becerril, "La Piedra de Nezahualcoyotl o de los tecomates," *Memorias de la Sociedad Científica "Antonio Alzate"* 20 (1903): 71.
17. Instrucción Pública y Bellas Artes, 167, exp. 70, f4, n.d., AGN.
18. Pedro Ramírez Vázquez, interview with the author, June 2010.
19. Ramírez Vázquez interview.
20. E.g., Pedro Ramírez Vázquez, *Museo Nacional de Antropología: Gestación, proyecto y construcción* (Mexico City: INAH, 2008).
21. Ramírez Vázquez interview. See also Ramírez Vázquez, *Museo Nacional de Antropología*, 66.
22. On the twentieth anniversary of the move, Armando Ponce claimed that the Coatlinchan monolith was chosen only after the previously selected stele from Edzná was stolen. Armando Ponce, "Veintiún años después," *Proceso*, September 14, 1985.
23. Floorplan, AAPRV, n.d.
24. Museo Nacional de Antropología consulting board minutes, 1961, AAPRV.
25. Ricardo de la Robina, dir., *El buen restaurador ama lo antiguo: Testimonio del arquitecto Ricardo de Robina* (Mexico City: Instituto Mora, 1997), DVD.
26. Mario Vázquez, Interview with the author, July 2007.
27. Since the museum's opening, Iker Larrauri's conch shell sculpture stands on this platform.
28. Ramírez Vázquez, *Museo Nacional de Antropología*.
29. Néstor García Canclini, *Hybrid Cultures: Strategies for Entering and Leaving Modernity*, trans. Christopher L. Chiappari and Sylvia L. López (Minneapolis: University of Minnesota Press, 1995).

30. For more on the rebellion, see Sandra Rozental, "Kit to Detonate a Monolith," in *Total Destruction of the National Anthropology Museum*, ed. Eduardo Abaroa (Mexico City: Athénée Press, 2017), 76–94.
31. Enrique del Valle Prieto, interview with the author, August 2010.
32. Pedro Ramírez Vázquez, interview with the author, July 2009.
33. Alfonso Soto Soria, interview with the author, June 2009.
34. Soto Soria interview.
35. Soto Soria interview.
36. Personal communication, Dr. Dolores Tenorio Castilleros, head of the ININ project, October 2011; Instituto de Investigaciones Nucleares, *Informe Anual* (Mexico City: UNAM, 1997), 26–27.
37. *Informe del proyecto de restauración y conservación del "Tláloc" de Coatlinchan*, Museo Nacional de Antropología, 2015.
38. *Informe del proyecto de restauración*, 7.
39. According to the report, "damage related to the growth of microflora and insects' nests is reflected in the stone as a loss in the weatherproof quality of its surface, since this activity implies a process of anchorage in which the stone's composition gets disaggregated, as well as visually modified, generating stains and obscuring the visibility of those areas"; *Informe del proyecto de restauración*, 10.
40. Sergio González, interview with the author, March 2014.
41. Laura Filloy, personal communication, February 2019. Although Ramírez Vázquez had passed away, his firm, now run by his son, was also commissioned to propose a project for the statue's relocation (*Proyecto de reubicación y protección de Tlaloc*, 2013, AAPRV).
42. The restorer decided not to carry out a more aggressive cleaning via laser or bicarbonate abrasion, or even a more delicate version using peanut shells, so as not to remove this protective surface, González, interview with the author, March 2014.
43. Sergio González, interview with the author, November 2019.
44. See Rozental, *Material Ecologies.*
45. Don Felix, interview with the author, September 2008.
46. Doña Luz, interview with the author, August 2011.
47. The image, titled *Durante las manifestaciones del 68*, was published in *Imaginarios y fotografía en México 1839–1970*, ed. Emma Cecilia García Krinsky (Mexico City, Lunwerg Editores/ CONACULTA, 2005, 264), and more recently in Eduardo Abaroa, *Total Destruction of the Museo Nacional de Antropología* (Mexico City: Athénée Press, 2016), 138.
48. See Alfonso Morales, "La Venus se fue de juerga: Ámbitos de la fotografía mexicana, 1940–1970," in *Imaginarios y fotografía en México 1839–1970* (Mexico City: Lunwerg, 2005), 206.

Contributors

Miruna Achim is an associate professor in the humanities at the Universidad Autónoma Metropolitana–Cuajimalpa, in Mexico City. Her research centers on the material cultures of science and technology, the history of medicine, and the history of antiquarianism and collection building in nineteenth-century Mexico. Her more recent publications include *From Idols to Antiquity: Forging the National Museum of Mexico* (2017), *Museos al detalle: colecciones, antigüedades e historia natural* (edited with Irina Podgorny, 2014), and *Piedra, papel y tijera: Instrumentos en las ciencias en México* (edited with Laura Cházaro and Nuria Valverde, 2018). Presently, she is writing a global history of jade in the sixteenth through nineteenth centuries, which brings together studies on Mesoamerican cosmogonies and material cultures, European pharmacopeias, curiosity cabinets, and commercial routes between the New World, China, and New Zealand.

Christina Bueno is professor of history and Latino/Latin American studies at Northeastern Illinois University in Chicago. Her research has won numerous awards and fellowships. As a specialist in the history of Mexico, she is the author of *The Pursuit of Ruins: Archaeology, History, and the Making of Modern Mexico* (2016).

Laura Cházaro is associate professor at the Centro de Investigación y de Estudios Avanzados del Instituto Nacional Politécnico. Her research focuses on the material culture of the sciences, particularly on the uses, practices, and circulation of scientific and medical instruments. On this subject, she has published, among other titles, *La fisiología y sus instrumentos: Estudio y catálogo de la Colección de Fisiología del Museo de Historia de la Medicina Mexicana* (2016), and *Piedra, papel y tijera: Instrumentos en las ciencias en México* (edited with Miruna Achim and Nuria Valverde, 2018).

Susan Deans-Smith received her PhD from Cambridge University. She is associate professor of history at the University of Texas at Austin. Her research interests focus on the visual and material culture of colonial Latin America, on artisans and artists, and on the history of collections and art markets. Her recent publications include *Race and Classification: The Case of Mexican America* (co-edited with Ilona Katzew, 2009). She is currently completing a book, *Matters of Taste: Cultural Reform in Bourbon Mexico and the Royal Academy of San Carlos (1781–1821).* Her research has been supported by fellowships from the National Endowment for the Humanities, the Social Science Research Council, and the Andrew Mellon Foundation.

Frida Gorbach is associate professor at the Universidad Autónoma Metropolitana, Xochimilco, where she teaches psychology to undergraduates as well as in the Humanities PhD Program. She earned her PhD in art history at the Universidad Nacional Autónoma de México and is a member of the National Researchers System. Her current research topics arise from her book *El monstruo, objeto imposible: Un estudio sobre teratología mexicana (1860–1900)* (2008). Starting from a query about the monster's mother, she became interested in the history of hysteria in Mexico, focusing on the theoretical basis of historical discourse. Gorbach has published several articles on the linkages between monster collections, natural history, archaeology, and anthropology, and on museums, identity, and national culture within the framework of cultural studies and postcolonial critique. Her most recent monograph *Histeria e Historia: Un relato sobre el siglo XIX mexicano,* was published in 2020. With Carlos López Beltrán, she edited *Saberes locales: Ensayos sobre historia de la ciencia* (2008), and with Mario Rufer *(In)Disciplinar la investigación: Archivo, trabajo de campo y escritura* (2016).

Haydeé López Hernández holds a degree in archaeology from the Escuela Nacional de Antropología e Historia and a PhD in philosophy of science from the Universidad Nacional Autónoma de México (UNAM). Presently, she is a researcher at the Dirección de Estudios Históricos–Instituto Nacional de Antropología e Historia and professor of the Desarrollo y Gestión Interculturales-UNAM. Her most recent books, on the history of archaeology, include *Los estudios histórico-arqueológicos de Enrique Juan Palacios* (2016) and *En busca del alma nacional* (2018).

Carlos Mondragón is associate professor at the Centro de Estudios de Asia y África, at El Colegio de México, where he teaches on the anthropology and history of Oceania and Island Southeast Asia. His ethnographic research has long been centered on indigenous knowledge and environment in the Vanuatu archipelago, and more recently in Timor-Leste. He has published on culture contact in the early modern Pacific and curated two major exhibitions on Pacific collections in Mexico, besides collaborating with museums in Europe, the USA, Australia, and New Zealand.

Bertina Olmedo Vera holds a degree in archaeology from the Escuela Nacional de Antropología e Historia. She worked on the Proyecto Templo Mayor between 1980 and 2000, both on excavations and as a researcher and curator at the Museo del Templo Mayor. As a member of the Dirección de Etnohistoria del Instituo Nacional de Antropología e Historia, she has worked on sources and codices in the Nahua tradition in central Mexico. Since 2010, she has been the curator of the Mexica collection at the Museo Nacional de Antropología, in Mexico City.

Sandra Rozental is an anthropologist whose research explores national patrimony, cultural property, and claims generated by the extraction of artifacts from local contexts and other state-making enterprises. She is currently an associate professor in the Humanities and Social Sciences Division of the Universidad Autónoma Metropolitana–Cuajimalpa. Her recent publications include "Stone Replicas: The Iteration and Itinerancy of Mexican Patrimonio," *Journal of Latin American and Caribbean Anthropology* 19, no. 2 (2014); "In the Wake of Mexican Patrimonio: Material Ecologies in San Miguel Coatlinchan," *Anthropological Quarterly* (2016); and "On the Nature of Patrimonio: 'Cultural Property' in Mexican Contexts," in *The Routledge Companion to Cultural Property* (2017). She also co-directed the documentary feature film *The Absent Stone* (2013) with Jesse Lerner.

Mario Rufer studied history at the National University of Córdoba, Argentina, and earned a PhD at El Colegio de México. He is associate professor of postcolonial studies, cultural studies, and history at the Universidad Autónoma Metropolitana–Xochimilco, in Mexico City. His writing focuses on postcolonial critique, the archive, heritage, museums, and public memory. His recent publications include *La nación en escenas: Memoria pública y usos del pasado en contextos poscoloniales* (2010); *Entangled Heritages: Postcolonial Perspectives on the Uses of the Past in Latin America* (edited with Olaf Kaltmeier, 2017); *(In)Disciplinar la investigación: Archivo, trabajo de campo y escritura* (edited with Frida Gorbach, 2017); and *Nación y estudios culturales: Debates desde la poscolonialidad* (edited with María del Carmen de la Peza, 2016).

Index